# Treasures of the Taylorian: Reformation Pamphlets Volume 7

Hans Sachs

'Canon and Shoemaker'
A Reformation Dialogue in German, Dutch, and English

Edited by Philip Flacke,
Henrike Lähnemann, Jacob Ridley,
and Thomas Wood

Taylor Institution Library, Oxford, 2024

TAYLOR INSTITUTION LIBRARY
St Giles, Oxford, OX1 3NA

http://editions.mml.ox.ac.uk

© Philip Flacke, Henrike Lähnemann, Jacob Ridley, Thomas Wood

Some rights are reserved. This book is made available under the Creative Commons Attribution-ShareAlike 4.0 International (CC BY-SA 4.0 DEED). This licence allows for copying any part of the work for personal and non-commercial use, providing author attribution is clearly stated.

Digital downloads for this edition are available at https://editions.mml.ox.ac.uk/reformation.shtml.
They include audio recording, facsimiles, and a pdf eBook of the text.

The facsimile is of: *Disputacion zwischen ainem Chorherrenn vnnd Schüchmacher dariñ das wort gottes vnd ein recht Cristlich wesen verfochtten wirtt.* [Augsburg: Melchior Ramminger,] 1524
Taylor Institution Library, ARCH.8°.G.1524(26).

The cover image is a detail from the titlepage.

Typesetting by Henrike Lähnemann
Cover design by Emma Huber

ISBN 978-1-0686058-0-2

Printed in the United Kingdom and United States by Lightning Source for Taylor Institution Library

iii

# Table of Contents

Preface: Hans Sachs in Oxford     iv

Introduction     vii

    1. The Historical Context (Thomas Wood)     ix

    2. English Reformation Dialogues (Jacob Ridley)     xxix

    3. The Pamphlets in Oxford (Philip Flacke)     xxxviii

    4. The Edition (Henrike Lähnemann)     lxiii

    5. Bibliography     lxviii

Edition, Translation, Commentary of the
    Dialogue Between a Canon & a Cobbler     1
    a) German ('Chorherr & Schuhmacher')     3
    b) Dutch ('Schoenmaker & Coorhere')     88
    c) English ('Shomaker & Parson')     89

Facsimiles of the Taylorian Copy of 'Chorherr & Schuhmacher' 174

# Preface: Hans Sachs in Oxford

2024 marks the 500th anniversary of Hans Sachs publishing in quick succession four prose dialogues which became bestsellers, particularly the first one where he has his alter ego, Hans the cobbler, debate a pompous priest – and win the day, of course. That the Taylorian was aware of the significance of this publication is clear from the date of its purchasing the 'Dialogue' copy which stands at the centre of the edition: 1924. It is a fitting continuation of the series which started as project to prepare for the quincentenary of the publication of the 95 Theses in 1517. In 2017, we opened the Taylor Editions series with the 'Sendbrief vom Dolmetschen', Martin Luther's spirited (and not always accurate) defence of the way he had translated the Bible, a text which had been on the syllabus for German students in Oxford since 1917.

This has been a collective editing process over many years. Kezia Fender encoded the first version of the first dialogue in 2016 as a special option for her German and English combined BA course which was then continued by MSt. student Charlotte Hartmann as History of the Book project 'Hans Sachs in Oxford'. The second-year students of 'Paper VII', a course on early modern German literature and culture, translated among them the first half of the first dialogue in February 2024, rising to the challenge of finding idiomatic equivalents to German proverbs and insults: Alexander Archer, Harrison Cartwright, Hannah Cowley, Lucy Gibbons, Elizabeth Gur, Ivan Halpenny, Leena Kharabanda, William Marriage, Olivia Rose, Oliver Schenke, Aaron Ung, and Eleanor Willcox. They were supported by David Hirsch, a translation studies student from Heidelberg on an internship during spring 2024.

Another intern, Philip Flacke from Göttingen, continued the work in the summer term and has since stepped up to be one of the editors of this volume, responsible for the book historical side. The project even led to him starting his doctoral project on concepts of truth in

*Preface* v

Hans Sachs's texts. The bulk of the transcription work then was done by him and a number of other students, in the first place Timothy Powell who is also starting his doctorate on Hans Sachs, in this case on the reception history from Johann Wolfgang von Goethe to the GDR. Their work on the second and third dialogue, plus the transcription of the fourth dialogue by German BA finalist Nicholas Champness, have contributed to the commentary and book historical chapter in this volume and will be published as another book in the Reformation Pamphlets Series in January 2026, for the 450th anniversary of Sachs's death. Two MSt. students, Montgomery Powell and Lucian Shepherd, jointly translated the second dialogue, and, together with MSt. students Viviane Arnold and Nina Unland provided the bulk of the biblical references (which, unsurprisingly given that Hans Sachs just had spent three years mainly studying the Bible and Luther's writings based on it, make up a very high proportion of the dialogues, up to half of the actual text). Christina Ostermann, a History of the Book student of the first cohort, currently working on the history of the acquisition policy for Reformation pamphlets in the Taylorian, provided the transcription of the Dutch text and proofreading. Jacob Ridley not only annotated the early modern English but also provided the chapter on the English dialogues. We were fortunate to be able to win specialists and critical readers for different aspects, among them Andreas Wenzel and Daniel Lloyd for ecclesiastical terminology, Ulrich Bubenheimer for marginalia, and Howard Jones for linguistic advice. Numerous colleagues around Oxford joined in the discussion of translation conundrums such as how to translate the derogatory exclamation 'py pu pa' by the canon (see p. 23 for the solution we settled on, suggested by Wes Williams).

Johanneke Sytsema helped locate a copy of the elusive Dutch edition which served as a relay station between the German and the English versions of the first dialogue. Margreet Vos and the curator of early printed works, Esther van Gelder, at the Royal Library in The Hague provided a microfilm copy and bibliographic information which then allowed Asmus Ivo, curator at the University Library in Greifswald, to find the missing pamphlet bound in a Sammelband. Alexandra Franklin, Richard Lawrence, and a group of colleagues at the Weston Library helped with the book historical chapter, and the Bodleian Library gave us access to the extensive run of Lutheran pamphlets and the unique copies of the English translation and granted permission for the liberal inclusion of images in this volume, with expert help from Alexandra Franklin and the other colleagues in the early modern department. As for the previous volumes, Emma Huber as the German subject librarian at the Taylor Institution and digital lead for the library provided expert help on the digital editions aspect and designed the cover.

Oxford, October 2024<br>
Henrike Lähnemann for the editorial team

Ill. 1: The first cohort of students working on the Reformation pamphlets in the Taylorian. From left to right: Lucas Eigel, Kezia Fender, Klaus Meyer, Jennifer Bunselmeier, Charlotte Hartmann

# Introduction

Hans Sachs (1494–1576), the Nuremberg shoemaker, prolific playwright, poet, and Meistersinger, has never completely vanished from the history of German literature. But more often than not, he has been first and foremost seen as a figure of cultural history, known beyond the German-speaking area as the main character in Richard Wagner's opera 'Die Meistersinger'. His poetry suffered from being considered a mechanical product, produced *en masse*, with near-comic effects of the rhyming couplets that count syllables rather than following natural speech. This was epitomised in the Baroque mock couplet

> Hans Sachs war ein Schuh-/
> macher und Poet dazu
> (Hans Sachs was a shoe-/maker and poet, too).

The identification of his profession with his mode of writing was reenforced by Sachs's practice to write himself into his texts; he signed his poems normally in the penultimate line, finding multiple rhymes for 'Sachs'. In his first prose dialogue, he chose a different way of putting himself into the text: the main character is the cobbler Hans who has an inexhaustible stock of biblical quotations in German at hand – a reflection of the fact that the real Hans Sachs had spent the years 1520 to 1523 intensely studying the works of Martin Luther and his 1522 translation of the New Testament, not publishing anything himself in that period. But in 1523, he came back with a vengeance, and the result was the opposite of bland, monotonous, and mechanical. First, he wrote an allegorical praise of Luther as 'the Wittenberg nightingale' which became proverbial, and then a group of four sharp and witty prose dialogues, full of idiomatic phrases, proverbs, interjections, one-line put-downers, and asides, which must have been particularly entertaining for a local audience.

viii  *Introduction*

The form Hans Sachs used was one beloved by Humanists and their readers, the prose dialogue. A model which Sachs certainly knew was the early instalments of Erasmus's 'Colloquia familiaria' (started in the late 1490s, first printed edition 1518), humorous and ironic encounters between characters taking opposing positions used as Latin exercises in schools. They allow a more informal tone and the integration of everyday characters, putting forward arguments more pointedly by dividing them up between the opponents.

Hans Sachs uses a number of different expressions for this form, The first dialogue uses the Latin academic term of 'disputatio' and describes it as a 'fight': *Disputacion zwischen ainem Chorherrenn vnnd Schüchmacher darin das wort gottes vnd ein recht Cristlich wesen verfochtten wirtt.* ('Disputation between a canon and a shoemaker, in which there is a battle for the word of God and a truly Christian existence). The second and third are less confrontational between the protagonist, instead in a discursive style exchanging points of view and called a 'conversatio' (*Gesprech eines evangelischen Christen mit einem Lutherischen*) and (*Gesprech von den Scheinwercken der Gaystlichen*). The final one has two terms: 'dialogus' and 'argumentum' (*Dialogus vnd Argument der Romanisten / wider das Christlich heüflein / den Geytz vnd ander offentlich laster betreffend*).

This short, accessible format of live demonstrations of current religious topics were an immediate success, well beyond Nuremberg. Our introduction places this unique group of texts first in the historical context of Nuremberg, the first Imperial city which, only one year later, openly declared its alliance to Martin Luther – not least because of propagandists such as Hans Sachs. A comparative study of the Reformation publishing market in England in the 1540s, when the first dialogue was translated via Dutch into English forms the second part. The third part looks at the publishing history and then follows the way of the pamphlets into Oxford. A short practical guide on how to read the Early New High German texts closes the chapter.

# 1. The Historical Context
## Thomas Wood

Situated on the river Pegnitz in the heart of the Holy Roman Empire, the Nuremberg of Hans Sachs was a thriving Free City that acted in 1524 as a site of both Imperial power and religious conflict. In the late Middle Ages and into the sixteenth century, Nuremberg had been a prosperous city sitting upon a trade route between the Italian City States and the ports of the Hanseatic League with many flourishing trades and a vibrant intellectual culture. Thus goods and ideas from across the world passed through the city which itself would become a major exporter of commodities and culture. From arms and armour to sophisticated scientific instruments, all manner of wares flowed from the workshops of Nuremberg whilst great luminaries of the German renaissance such as Albrecht Dürer, Adam Kraft, and Veit Stoß called the city their home. Over the centuries Nuremberg had become a nexus at the heart of the European continent, an ideal melting pot for new ideas and dissent against the existing religious order to brew, and when the Reformation swept through the German-speaking lands over the course of the 1520s, Nuremberg was ripe for reforming.

Indeed, Nuremberg had a thriving community of humanists who were not only initially receptive to Martin Luther's ideas, especially the adoption of vernacular Bibles, but also served on the city council. The council served as *de facto* rulers of Nuremberg, overseeing the prosperity of this trading city and investing heavily in its future. They scrutinised every aspect of life in the free city and their religious convictions would dramatically alter the course of Nuremberg's future in the sixteenth century. Council members and leading figures in the city governance sympathetic to Luther in the early 1520's would include Christoph Scheurl, Wenceslaus Link, Lazarus

x  *Introduction*

Spengler,[1] Willibald Pirckheimer, Hieronymus Ebner, Kaspar Nützel, Clemens Volckamer, and Christoph Kress. Some of these men were particularly close to Luther, Link being a close personal friend while Spengler and Pirckheimer were even threatened alongside Luther with excommunication in the papal bulls of 1520 and 1521. Though the former would serve as secretary to the council and be influential in the events of 1524 and 1525, Pirckheimer meanwhile, alongside Scheurl, would ultimately side with the Catholic establishment. Those Nuremberg humanists that stuck with Luther would develop strong Protestant convictions that saw the city formally adopt Protestantism in 1525, aided in their endeavours by the theologians of the city.

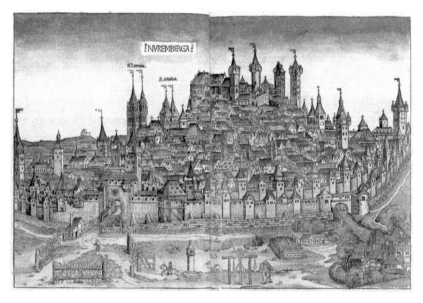

Ill. 2: Nuremberg Chronicle, Nuremberg: Anton Koberger, 1493, fol. 100.

---

[1] See Bubenheimer's discussion of Lazarus Spengler in the 'Sendbrief vom Dolmetschen', Jones / Lähnemann (2022), p. xviii. Secondary literature is cited with the short titles in the bibliography, with the exception of specialist literature for the 'English Reformation Dialogues'.'

*Historical Context* xi

As well as humanists within Nuremberg's governance who were receptive to Luther's ideas, many of the religious authorities within the city were also of a Reformation spirit. The sixteenth-century skyline of Nuremberg was characterized by the double spires and 'Buckelchor' (high Gothic choir) of its two parish churches, St Lorenz, and St Sebald, the latter named after the patron saint of the city. Within these institutions the Protestant spirit had taken hold in the years leading up to 1524. In 1522, Andreas Osiander would be appointed to St Lorenz after having worked for the previous two years as a Hebrew tutor at an Augustinian convent. A proud and defiant Lutheran preacher, Osiander was involved in multiple high-profile cases of religious controversy and conversion over the course of his life. By 1524 he had notably converted Albert of Prussia, Grand Master of the Teutonic Knights, to Lutheranism who would go on to found the Duchy of Prussia and make it the first land to officially adopt Protestantism as the state religion, and in 1525 he would be the Protestant leader of the debates which led to Nuremberg formally adopting the Reformation as first Imperial Town. Meanwhile, at St Sebald, Dominicus Schleupner had taken up residence at the recommendation of Luther from which he became a leading voice of reform in the city, giving the opening speech at the 1525 debates. These eminent preachers at the city's two major churches were supporters of the Reformation and persisted in their Protestant teachings despite pressure from Imperial authorities.

Indeed, the pro-Reformation slant of the city's authorities can be seen in their lax approach to enforcing the Edict of Worms, posting a copy of it at the town hall in 1521 while continuing to appoint men like Osiander and Schleupner to office. The council of Nuremberg had long preferred to manage religious affairs within their territory, existing in constant fractious struggle with the nearby Bishop of Bamberg who was ultimately ineffective at asserting his authority over the free city in his diocese. The zeal for reform did however find itself tempered somewhat in the early 1520s by the presence of the Imperial Diet in Nuremberg, its first session 1522 and its second in

xii *Introduction*

1524, which saw the Imperial Governing Council, Imperial Chamber Court, and papal delegation stay in the city. This mass gathering of Catholic authorities in the city saw the council of Nuremberg forced to balance the demands of those who opposed Luther's ideas with their own pre-Reformation tendencies. Indeed, Francesco Chieregati, the papal nuncio, demanded that the council only allow the printing of anti-Lutheran pamphlets. The council reluctantly censored the presses, but refused Chieregati's request to arrest preachers, instead merely advising them to avoid controversial topics in their sermons while the Diet was in the city.

When the Diet left the city in April 1524, the spirit of the Reformation began to be expressed more freely, not only from the pulpits of St Lorenz and St Sebald, but also from the presses and on the streets. This emboldened the Lutherans in the city, and it also attracted more radical religious reformers with whom they would dome to be at odds. Many religious radicals either lived in or passed through Nuremberg in 1524, carrying their ideas throughout the Empire across the trade routes that ran through the free city. In the prior century Jan Hus had stayed there on his fateful journey to the Council of Constance, and many others would pass between the city gates in 1524 who had similarly violent ends. Notably, Thomas Müntzer briefly visited the city in the latter half of 1524, maintaining a low profile and spending just enough time in the city to print a defence of his position aimed at Luther and his Wittenberg disciples before heading southwest where the first murmurings of the German Peasants Revolt could be heard. Müntzer's pamphlet, *A Highly Provoked Vindication and Refutation of the Unspiritual Soft-Living Flesh in Wittenberg Whose Robbery and Distortion of Scripture Has So Grievously Polluted Our Wretched Christian Church* served as on open letter to Luther that accused him of betraying his original vision of reform in favour of the nobility and at the expense of the peasantry.[2]

---

[2] For more on Müntzer, his radical ideologies, and differences with Luther see Drummond (2024).

*Historical Context*  xiii

This incendiary pamphlet never made its way to distribution however. Müntzer had left Heinrich Pfeiffer in the city to disseminate this work while he moved further afield, but Pfeiffer was quickly expelled from Nuremberg and the council suppressed Müntzer's pamphlet following the advice of Osiander, who would regularly offer his opinion on religious pamphlets when asked by the council while he preached at St Lorenz.

Similarly, the council would suppress the work of Andreas Bodenstein von Karlstadt. A former leader of the Reformation in Wittenberg and a friend of Luther as well as many Nuremberg humanists, Luther would eventually denounce him as a radical in 1524 and he would be expelled from Saxony in September. Though Karlstadt would not join Müntzer, his unfavorability with Luther would colour Nuremberg council's response to his associate Martin Reinhart, who attempted to have the exiled reformers's work published in the city. The publisher, Hieronymus Höltzel, would be arrested by the authorities and Reinhart was expelled from the city. Once more, the works of those disowned by Luther himself were censored by the council who cleaved more closely to the ideas espoused at Wittenberg.

Other religious radicals included the preacher Diepold Peringer who operated in the suburb of Wöhrd in the city c.1523-4. The Baptist Hans Hut regularly visited the city as a bookbinder in the 1520's and was in contact with Müntzer whilst he visited Nuremberg. Similarly, Anabaptist leader Hans Denck arrived in Nuremberg in 1523, acting as headmaster of the St Sebald church school but was banished from the city after coming into contact with Müntzer and adopting many points of his radical theology. While the council was keen to break from Catholicism, they did not wish to be seen to allow radicals, who might discredit the new faith, to thrive. Eventually however, the Protestants of Nuremberg would get their wish when the city formally adopted the Reformation in 1525. While councillors and theologians like Christoph Scheurl and Andreas Osiander were pivotal voices in the religious debates that engulfed the city,

xiv *Introduction*

Nuremberg was also a centre of pamphleteering undertaken by the artisan strata of society. These pro-Lutheran artisans would proliferate the ideas of the Reformation in their own ways and counted amongst their number men such as Hans Sachs.

Hans Sachs was born in Nuremberg in 1494 the son of Jörg Sachs, a tailor, and would go on to become a celebrated *Meistersinger*, poet, and playwright who was deeply involved in the Reformation in Nuremberg. Sachs attended Latin school in the city as well as apprenticing as a shoemaker there before undertaking the customary years of training in other places at the age of 17, leaving Nuremberg in 1511. During this period of his life Sachs would travel across the length and breadth of modern-day Germany and Austria practising his trade before a chance encounter with the retinue of Emperor Maximilian I in Wels, where Sachs had settled in 1513 to study the fine arts, saw the young shoemaker join the Imperial court. He would then for a time be situated in Innsbruck, before quitting the court in 1515 and beginning an apprenticeship under Lienhard Nunnenbeck as a *Meistersinger* in Munich. After five long years travelling as shoemaker and *Meistersinger*, Sachs would move back to his home city of Nuremberg in 1516 where he would remain for the rest of his life, practising both his crafts and enthusiastically engaging with the Reformation. He was married twice, first to Kunigunde Creutzer in 1519 with whom he had seven children that Sachs would sadly outlive, then later to the widowed Barbara Harscher with whom he had no children, marrying her the year after Kunigunde's death in 1560. Sachs himself would die in 1576 and be buried at the Nuremberg Johannisfriedhof.

In his lifetime Sachs produced a vast quantity of works, many in Knittelversen, including more than 4000 mastersongs, over 2000 poems, and a great multitude of tragedies, comedies, carnival plays, dialogues, fables, and various kinds of religious tracts. He was immensely popular in his own time, and after being largely forgotten some time after his death, Sachs's memory was revived by artists and scholars in the eighteenth century. His extensive works continue to

Historical Context xv

be performed and analysed to this day, especially those works which pertained to Sachs's support of Martin Luther.

Foremost of these religious works was his 1523 poem written in Luther's honour 'The Wittenberg nightingale, now audible everywhere' (*Die Wittenbergisch Nachtigall, die man jetzt höret überall*).

Ill. 3: Titlepage of Hans Sachs 'Die Wittenbergisch Nachtigall', [Bamberg: Georg Erlinger, 1523], copy HAB Wolfenbüttel A: 115.2 Quod. (16).

xvi *Introduction*

This new poetic voice for Lutheranism is perhaps the most famous artisan pamphlet of the German Reformation, both in terms of its contemporary reception and its historical legacy. In this piece Sachs encouraged his audience to 'wake up' and listen to the 'joyous nightingale' of Wittenberg who preached the truth to the German People. Indeed, Sachs accused the pope and his servants of using their powers to exploit and oppress simple Germans, depriving the laity of the gospel, and enacting a tyranny over both the conscience and pocketbooks of common folk. This blistering attack on the upper echelons of the Church was placed alongside a dramatic vision of Luther as a liberating figure who was not only in the right, but also simply could not be stopped. The work was as resonant as it was inflammatory, published as it was in the atmosphere of religious turbulence in Nuremberg.

A year later, Sachs published the four prose dialogues. Written and published as Nuremberg was escaping the yoke of the Imperial Diet, as the council clamped down on religious radicals, and in the time immediately preceding the religious debates of 1525, these dialogues are not only an expression of Sachs's own religious views but also of the Reforming zeal that had gripped the free city. They concern themselves with many of the most important topics of religious debate in the 1520s such as the abuses of the Church's power, monastic vows, the nature of salvation, Christian liberty, and lay access to and interpretation of scripture.

The first of these dialogues depicted a discussion between a shoemaker and a canon that ranges across many aspects of Luther's theology. The character of the shoemaker, sharing his profession with Sachs, is able to deftly and consistently counter the arguments of the canon with his scriptural knowledge whilst praising the work of Luther. The customary format of the early modern dialogue is used to great effect here as the usual authoritative roles are inverted and the canon takes on the asking role of the student whilst the shoemaker takes on the answering role of the teacher. It is on this final point that Sachs perhaps speaks in these dialogues to a prevailing

*Historical Context* xvii

school of thought amongst the people of Nuremberg. Unsurprisingly, the first dialogue's focus on scripture in many ways foreshadows the nature of the debates of 1525.

These debates were held in the Great Hall of Nuremberg's city hall between the 3rd and 15th March 1525. The talks were led by Christoph Scheurl, and were inspired by the 1523 Zurich Disputations which had ultimately seen the council of Zurich adopt the Reformation. The Nuremberg council allowed only the Bible as evidence in these discussions, disallowing appeals to canon law or references to Church tradition, not unlike the shoemaker of Sachs's fictional disputation published the year prior. This approach heavily favoured the *sola scriptura* approach of the Protestant faction who were foremostly represented by Andreas Osiander and Dominicus Sleupner. These leading figures of Nuremberg's premier religious institutions took centre stage as advocates for the Lutherans alongside Wolfgang Volprecht, the last prior of Nuremberg's Augustinian monastery, which had been an early adopter of Reformation ideas. Opposing them were a number of Catholic preachers, many with monastic backgrounds, notably the Franciscans Lienhard Ebner and Michael Fries. A victory for the Protestants in these debates was eventually proclaimed and on the 21st April Catholic Mass was banned in the city of Nuremberg. The council proceeded to institute Protestant preaching in all churches in the city and undertook a policy of closing all monasteries in and around the city. Some, like Volprecht's Augustinians, dissolved themselves, others who, like the Poor Clares led by Caritas Pirckheimer as abbess, vigorously resisted the movement, were banned from accepting new members and were eventually dissolved once the last members of the community left or died.[3] So came the end of Catholicism in Nuremberg, public opinion in the city having been swayed not just by the preaching of men like Osiander, but also by the popular publications of artisans like Hans

---

[3] See Lähnemann / Schlotheuber (2024) and Gieseler / Lähnemann / Powell (2023) for the debate surrounding the forced dissolution of convents.

xviii  *Introduction*

Sachs whose works would go on to be exported across the rest of Christian Europe.

As far as we know, Sachs's first dialogue is the only one that was translated, first into Dutch and published by one Magnus vanden Merberghe, a pseudonym that has come to be associated with Frans Freat (d. 1558).[4] Our edition has no date, owing to one of Fraet's practices of reprinting earlier works as well as the habit of Protestant Dutch printers to obscure the true authorship of their works (including printing false dates) in order to escape the censors.[5] Though unclear as to who did the original Dutch translation that Merberghe printed, the Dutch version of Sachs's dialogue follows the German closely (see footnotes in the edition on Germanisms). A few differences do arise such as the Dutch version being laid out differently with the speakers given their own clearly demarcated lines – a change that the English version would carry forward. The Dutch text then made its way into England at some point before 1546, owing to a thriving trade of printed materials between print centres like Antwerp and London.

In any case, this Dutch edition was in turn translated into English; our edition is based on one of the editions from 1548 (see below) but it must have been in circulation earlier, since the same title was put on the index during the reign of Henry VIII: 'A Godly disputation betwene a Chrysten Shomaker and a popish persone' in 1546.[6] The actual proclamation specifically bans neither by 'Frith, Tindall, Wicliff, Joy, Roie, Basile, Bale, Barnes, Couerdale, Turner, Tracy, or any book contrary to the King's 'A necessary doctrine and erudition for any christen man', or any book prohibited in that Parliament.'[7] The 1548 English version, a new edition or reworking of this pre-

---

[4] Valkema Blouw (1992), pp. 165-181; and pp. 245-272.

[5] On the Dutch Reformation print trade see: Heijting (1994), pp.143-161.

[6] John Foxe's 1563 *Actes and Monuments* mentions it amongst a list of works that had been banned, p. 573 no.40. On the date of the ban see Beare (1958).

[7] Steele (1910), pp. 30-31. See entry No. 294 8 July 1546.

## Historical Context  xix

1546 edition, is published twice, the first in Ipswich, the second later that same year in London, to which the two copies of the Bodleian belong. As usual for Dutch and English pamphlets, the size is octavo, while German pamphlets are usually printed as quartos. The other difference is that there are no woodcuts, only printer's ornaments; the English editions clearly modelled on the Dutch choice of a floral leaf opening the title, with the Dutch adding in some punctuation types arranged as an ornamental line and a flower.

Ill. 4: left: The Dutch edition, copy: UB Greifswald

Ill. 5: The Ipswich edition of the English translation by Anthony Scoloker 1548, copy: John Rylands Library

Ill. 6: The first edition Bamberg: Georg Erlinger, copy: Bodleian Tr. Luth. 34 (57) The London edition of the English translation by Anthony Scoloker 1548, copy: Bodleian Library, Vet. A1 f. 237.

xx *Introduction*

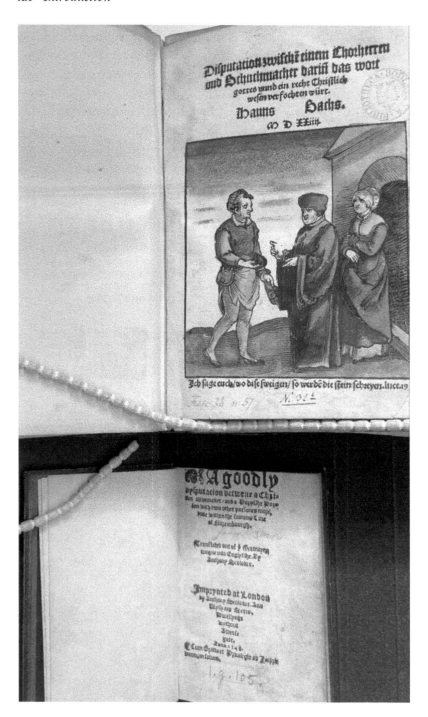

*Historical Context*  xxi

Both of these editions contain the same textual content and layout, though the type has been reset between the Ipswich and London printings, visible already in the title layout. They leave out the author's name, only stating that it was written in Nuremberg. The Dutch claims at the end that this is an incident that happened in 1522 (D8r). While the German edition typesets the dialogue as running text, probably because in the quarto format it would waste too much space, the speakers get their own, indented lines in the Dutch and English.

The man responsible for bringing Sachs to England, Anthony Scoloker (d. 1593), was a printer who established Ipswich's first printshop c.1547 and was active there and in London during 1548 before seemingly leaving the print trade. Not much is known of Scoloker's life as scant bibliographic details about him have survived; he is therefore known to us only through the materials he published in this short period. Indeed, what he chose to publish were religiously pro-Reformist works, many by continental reformers like Martin Luther and Zwingli, suggesting a Protestant faith and understanding of continental print culture.[8] Scoloker printed a number of these works at Ipswich, some in collaboration with Richard Argentine, before moving to London halfway through the year, after which John Oswen (fl. 1548) took over (it is unclear if Oswen worked at the same time as Scoloker or only came to Ipswich after Scoloker had left) before leaving Ipswich himself for Worcester the next January, leaving Ipswich without a printer until 1720. Ipswich had easy access to the continent as a thriving port town and it has been suggested Scoloker himself had strong ties to continental Europe, with signed translations from German, Dutch, and French.

---

[8] Freeman (1990), pp. 476-496.

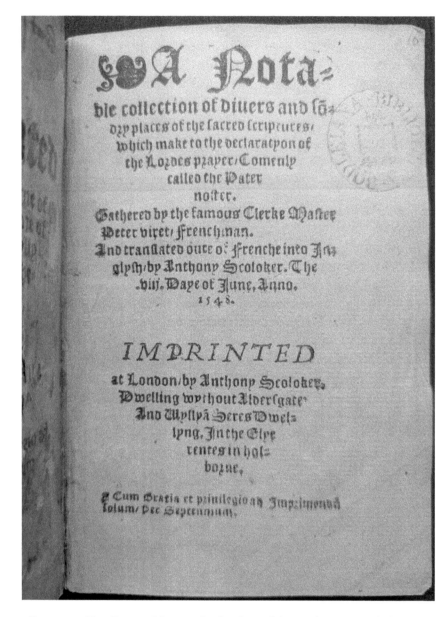

Ill. 7: *A notable collection of divers and sōdry places of the sacred scriptures, which make to the declaratyon of the Lordes prayer, gathered by P. Viret, and tr. by A. Scoloker,* London 1548. Copy: Bodleian Library Tanner 39 (10).

*Historical Context*  xxiii

A 1549 Middlesex Subsidy Roll counts him as an 'Englysmen' rather than a foreign visitor to the country, suggesting that his language expertise may have been a result of him having spent time on the continent, perhaps in religious exile under Henry VIII, or at least that he had significant ties to continental trade that passed through Ipswich and London. Scholars have suggested that, whether any such travels on the continent prior to his appearance in Ipswich were a religious exile, for mercantile purposes, or any other form of travel, he was possibly associated with the Ghent printer and typefounder Joos Lambrecht who may have given Scoloker his type and pictorial woodblocks.

All the books that mention Scoloker by name place him as active in Ipswich and London c.1547-48, or are otherwise undated (possibly being printed in 1549), making his life before this flurry of printing activity unclear and his life after his appearance in the Subsidy Roll of 1549 equally vague. References to his various addresses in London in his publications see him move across the city before his publications suddenly cease.[9] Whatever his reasons, Scoloker does not seem to have printed again, at least under his own name, and his activities during the next two decades are unknown. He may have chosen to abandon the trade after censorship laws were re-scrutinised in 1549, left England as a religious exile after the accession of Mary I in 1553 as some other Protestant printers did, or simply changed profession and never returned to printing for personal or financial reasons. Indeed, a merchant Anthony Scoloker is named in the 1567–8 London Port Book as receiving shipments of small goods including lute strings whom historians have suggested, in no small part due to the uncommon nature of the surname, to be the same individual as the Ipswich printer.[10] Given the profession of 'milliner', this Scoloker

---

[9] For a full account of Scoloker's changing addresses in London see: Blayney (2013), pp. 646-649.

[10] Page (2015), p. 68. Page provides a breakdown of everything Scoloker imported this year on p. 67. Full details of his imports can be found in the London Port Book (online).

xxiv  *Introduction*

was importing goods from Antwerp suggesting that despite no longer operating as a printer he still maintained Dutch connections on the continent.

Scoloker seems to have died in 1593, an 'Anthony Skolykers' being mentioned in the burial registers of St Mary-le-Strand as being buried on 13th May 1593. The same register mentions several others who were likely part of Scoloker's household though not all of their relations to him are perfectly clear. He was predeceased by individuals who could have been his children: one Judith Scoloker (possibly a daughter) buried 5th September 1563, and an 'Anthony Scollinger sonne of Anthonie' buried 12th May 1674. A servant of a 'Jone Scollenger' was buried only a few weeks later on 31st May 1574, perhaps giving a name to another member of the household though it is unclear as to whom. A 'Mistres Scoliker' survived Anthony and was buried 21st August 1599. Following his death, Scoloker has previously been identified by scholars as the author of the burlesque *Daiphantus, or the Passions of Love* (1604).[11] However, two references to Shakespeare's *Hamlet* (composed between 1599 and 1601) which was written after Scoloker's death, suggest a different author with Albert Pollard in his entry for Scoloker in the Dictionary of National Biography putting forward the idea of a relative of the same name as the printer being the true author of *Daiphantus*.[12] Alternatively, given that the author's name is simply written as 'An. Sc.' there may be no connection to Scoloker at all and modern attributions of *Daiphantus* to him in recent publications are simply repeating a scholarly mistake from 1807.

The London imprint of Scoloker's translation of Sachs has an additional publisher, one William Seres (died c.1579) who was a Protestant printer known to have collaborated with several famous partners including John Day (c.1522-1584) who was most famous

---

[11] The first to put this forward, and source of all later errors, was Francis Douce in his *Illustrations of Shakespeare and Ancient Manners*, Douce (1817), 2.265.

[12] Pollard in DNB Vol. 51, pp. 4-5.

for publishing John Foxe's *Book of Martyrs* (1563). Seres specialised in the printing of religious works making him the ideal partner for Scoloker to print Sachs's dialogue in London and they would collaborate on several works in 1548. Though Scoloker moved within a circle of notable Protestant printers that worked during the short rule of Edward VI (reigned 1547-1553), he seems to have operated only briefly and on the periphery of this group which sought to flood England with pro-Reformation materials.

Indeed, the Henrician restrictions on printing had been relaxed in November 1547 and those in favour of a more radical Reformation of the English Church took advantage of that fact to print swathes of both continental and domestically produced Protestant tracts. The generally pro-Reformation nature of Edward VI's government meant that these materials could be officially produced and distributed alongside the changes to English religious practices that were rolled out in the Church of England. 1548 in particular saw a wave of Lutheran works translated into English including works such as Luther's *The chief and principal articles of the Christian Faith*, Melanchthon's *The Confessions of Faith*, and Osiander's *Conjectures of the end of the world*. Zwingli, Bullinger, and Calvin also saw an array of their works published in English as, of course, did Hans Sachs.

These works proved popular, and men like William Seres were keen to get them into general circulation. Indeed, Scoloker's Ipswich printing of the first disputation must have been popular enough to warrant him reprinting it in London later that same year. However, Sachs did not enjoy the great popularity in England that the meistersinger had experienced in his home city, despite many figures of the English Reformation such as Thomas Cranmer having spent time in Nuremberg. Scoloker's extant translation of Sachs's work therefore remains as one of the few dialogues by the meistersinger to gain some level of traction in England, despite Scoloker not necessarily having worked with the original.

xxvi *Introduction*

Scoloker's translation of Sachs's dialogue was seemingly based on the Dutch edition rather than the original German. The similarities between the English and Dutch texts certainly suggest that Scoloker translated his English version solely from the Dutch copy he had access to. He even imitated the layout of the Dutch translation by indicating speakers on separate lines, though went somewhat further in his dramatization of the text by adding a cue for the opening speech. Like his Dutch predecessor, Scoloker seems to have translated Bible passages out of the work he was translating from, rather than copying them from any vernacular English version of the Bible. He also begins in a formal form of address but, in contrast to the original German and Dutch, later switches to the informal creating a more disrespectful tone. Scoloker also diverges from previous versions by creating additional domestic servants for the lead characters of his dialogue to interact instead of the female cook and servant boy of the original. These comprise a male servant whom the shoemaker initially interacts with instead of the cook, a maidservant named Katheryn who takes over the cook's role in the rest of the dialogue, and finally a male cook named John who appears near the end of the dialogue in place of the servant boy.

Scoloker makes further minor changes to the text, sometimes to appeal to his English audience, other times due to misunderstandings during translation. However, the fact that Scoloker took the time to translate Sachs' work and localise it for England, does speak volumes on the Protestant appeal of this dialogue. The themes of the abuses of the Church's power, the nature of salvation, Christian liberty, and lay access to and interpretation of scripture, so artfully rendered by Sachs, resonated with the supporters of the Reformation whether they were in Nuremberg, Antwerp, Ipswich, London, or beyond.

Historical Context xxvii

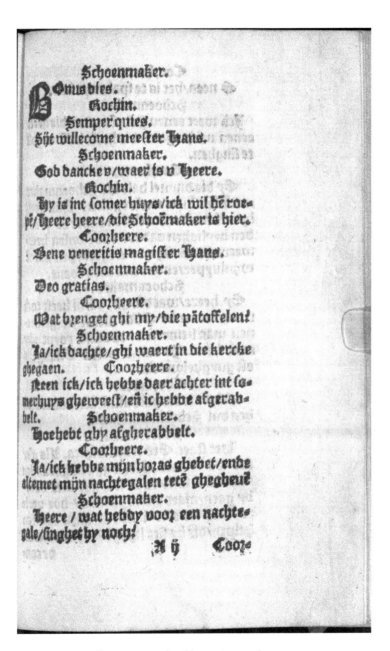

Ill. 8: UB Greifswald 542/Fv 28 adn9, a2r

xxviii  *Introduction*

⸿The Shomaker cōminge
to the parſones houſe, ſpeaketh to the
parſons ſeruaunt.

Shomaker.
Good moꝛrow good felloꝛ
Seruaunt.
Pe are welcō maſter Ioħ
Shomaker
I thanke pou ꝛ all my
hert, Where is pour maſter⸵
Seruaunt.
He is in the galleꝛy, O tary a lytle I
wyll go and call hym, maſter maſter pour
thomaker is here.
Parſon.
Bene benericis magiſter Hans.
Shomaker.
Deo gratias.      Parſon
What bꝛinge pou there⸝ do pou bꝛynge
my ſlyppers⸵
Shomaker.
Pea foꝛſoth Syꝛ, I thoughte pou had
bene in the Church.      Paꝛſon.
No mary. I was ponder behynde in ꝑ
galleꝛy and there haue I mumbled.
Shomaker.
What ſaye pou maſter Parſon⸵ haue
      a ij      pe mumꝰ

Ill. 9: Bodleian Library, Vet. A1 f. 237, a2r

# 2. English Reformation Dialogues
## Jacob Ridley

When the nine-year-old Edward VI came to the throne of England in January 1547, the floodgates of English Protestant print opened. His father Henry VIII had declared an independent Church of England in 1534, rejecting the authority of the Pope, but Henry remained theologically conservative and enforced heresy laws against the more advanced Protestants as well as Roman Catholics. When Henry died, Edward's uncle, Edward Seymour, Earl of Somerset, served as regent for the new boy king. Seymour oversaw a relaxation of Henry's censorship laws, giving the freest rein to reformist writers that they would have until the English Revolution a century later, though Catholics, and any other opponents of the royal Reformation, were of course excluded from this new liberty. The result was a release of pent-up activity, like a pressure canister being opened. The annual output of editions under Edward was almost double that in Henry's last decade.[1] Though censorship was partially reimposed in the wake of Seymour's fall from power in 1549, Edward's six-year reign would be a light in the darkness for outspoken reformers like John Bale, who had left Henry's England for European exile in the 1540s and would leave again to escape Edward's Catholic half-sister Mary, who succeeded him after his death in 1553. The peak year for the print trade was 1548, when almost 270 editions were printed in London, an English record not surpassed until 1579. By no coincidence, 1548 was the year when Anthony Scoloker printed the surviving editions of his translation of Hans Sachs.

---

[1] Literature for this part of the introduction is not part of the bibliography and cited in full. Print figures are from John N. King, 'The book-trade under Edward VI and Mary I', in Lotte Hellinga and J. B. Trapp (eds.), *The Cambridge History of the Book in Britain vol. III: 1400–1557* (Cambridge: 1999), 164–78 (pp. 165–66).

xxx   *Introduction*

Plays and dialogues (what I am going to call 'conversational' texts) were part of the Edwardine print boom.[2] Vernacular dialogues had been printed in England since the fifteenth century, and plays since at least the 1510s, but Edward's reign saw an unprecedented concentration of both. This is unsurprising given that conversational fiction was a key propaganda genre in persuading laypeople to the Protestant cause, and there were still lots of scarcely reformed English laypeople to persuade. Even though the genres differ in their function – plays are written primarily for performance, dialogues for reading – the texts printed under Edward share a didactic and controversial style. They teach the truths of the Reformation and attack Catholic errors (the Mass; saint-worship; purgatory; the sacraments; clerical celibacy; and so on), often with merciless mockery. Almost every conversational text written and/or printed in Edward's reign has a polemical or instructional focus of this kind. Scoloker himself was responsible for at least two: the translation of Sachs, and his own original composition *A goodly dialogue between Knowledge and Simplicity*, which he printed with William Seres around 1548, in which Knowledge converts Simplicity to the Protestant faith.[3]

Only three English plays are known to have been printed in the last decade of King Henry's life – two reprints of old plays by John Heywood, and the quite conservative morality play *The four cardinal virtues and the vices contrary to them* – but six survive from 1547–53, and a further four printed abroad.[4] Some were original, such as R.

---

[2] The standard work on Edwardine literature is John N. King, *English Reformation Literature: The Tudor Origins of the Protestant Tradition* (Princeton: 1982).

[3] *A goodly dyalogue betwene Knowledge and Simplicitie* (Anthony Scoloker and William Seres, [1548]; STC 6806).

[4] The three Henrician plays were all printed by William Middleton: the second editions of John Heywood, *The play of the wether* ([1544?], STC 13305.5) and *The playe called the foure PP* ([1544?], STC 13300); and the first of *The enterlude of the .iiii. cardynal vertues, [and] the vyces contrarye to them* ([c.1545]; STC 14109.7). The six printed in London under Edward were: the second edition of Heywood, [*A play of love*] ([William Copland for] John Walley, [1548?]; STC 13304); the third of *Hycke*

*English Reformation Dialogues*  xxxi

Wever's Protestant morality play *Lusty Juventus*, in which the central protagonist is converted from his immature Catholicism to a proper Reformed faith.[5] Others were translated, like the French Huguenot play *La verité cachée*, printed in anonymous English translation around 1551.[6] The four printed abroad were all by the arch-reformer John Bale, and published in Wesel in c.1547–48 for sale in England.[7] Like Scoloker, Bale had strong connections in Ipswich, where he had been head of the Carmelite friary there before his spectacular Protestant conversion. The most notable of his printed plays was *Three Laws*, in which Infidelity is personified as the Catholic arch-villain who perverts the laws of Nature, Moses, and Christ, with help from his cronies. These include Ambition the bishop; Hypocrisy the friar; and even Sodomy the monk. Bale is known to have revived this play in the marketplace of his parish in Bishopstoke, Hampshire, in 1551. Sachs's dialogue between a shoemaker and a parson is quite mild-mannered by Bale's sclerotic standards. In this context, we can understand why Scoloker's translation often amplifies the

---

*Scorner* ([printer of Smyth's *Envoy* for] John Walley, [1549?]; STC 14040); and the first of *The enterlude of Iohan the Euangelyst* ([printer of Smyth's *Envoy* for] John Walley, [c.1550]; STC 14643); ['The interlude of Detraction, Light Judgement, Verity, and Justice'] ([c.1550]; STC 14109.2), fragmentary; ['Somebody, Avarice, and Minister'] ([William Copland, 1551?]; STC 14109.3), fragmentary; and R. Wever, *An enterlude called Lusty Iuuentus* (John Wyer for Abraham Veale, [1551?]; STC 25148). This bibliographic information is from the online *Database of Early English Playbooks* (*DEEP*).

[5] STC 25148, above.

[6] STC 14109.3, above.

[7] All printed in Wesel by Derick van der Straten under the name 'Nicolaus Bamburgensis': *A tragedye or enterlude manyfestyng the chefe promyses of God vnto man* ([1547?]; STC 1305); *A brefe Comedy or enterlude concernynge the temptacyon of our lorde and sauer Iesus Christ* ([1547?]; STC 1279); *A comedy concernynge thre lawes, nof nature Moses, [and] Christ, corrupted by the Sodomytes, Pharysees and Papystes* ([1548?]; STC 1287). A fourth play on Christ's baptism, preserved now only in an 18th century manuscript transcript, was originally printed in the first eleven leaves of STC 1279, which are now missing.

xxxii  *Introduction*

shoemaker's informal and disrespectful tone and makes the parson more petulant and undignified.

*A goodly disputation between a Christian shoemaker and a popish parson* is in many ways a typical Tudor Protestant dialogue. It pits a well-educated and conscientious layman against a worldly, ignorant priest. This is the format of later argumentative dialogues like *A dialogue or familiar talk between two neighbours* (c.1554) – in which Oliver, 'a professour of the Gospell', squares off with the Catholic Sir Nicholas Noseled – or the Elizabethan *Dialogue between a soldier of Berwick and an English chaplain* (c.1566), whose honest Protestant soldier is appalled and exasperated by the one-eyed priest Sir Bernard Blinkered.[8] The fact that Sachs's speaker is a shoemaker, and therefore less formally educated than his opponent, puts him in the godly soldier's company. The upending of normal hierarchies – youth and age, laity and clergy, university and unlearned – by the Reformation was something of a trope, as was the Protestant zeal and Bible-reading of young tradesmen. This is typified by a lost play performed at King Edward's court in c.1547, which featured a priest called Old Blind Custom and a London apprentice named Hunger of Knowledge.[9] A parson is put in his place by a sincere and irreverent labourer in Luke Shepherd's boisterous verse dialogue *John Bon and Mast[er] Parson*, which is possible context for Scoloker's change from Sachs's Canon to the Parson – a less specific job title, but more culturally relevant.[10] The most famous icon of this social reversal was the semi-legendary character Piers Plowman, who had

---

[8] *A dialogue or familiar talke betwene two neighbours* (Rouen [i.e. London?]: Michael Wood [i.e. John Day?], 1554; STC 10383); [Anthony Gilby], *A pleasant dialogue, betweene a souldior of Barwicke, and an English chaplain* ([Middelburg: R. Schilders?], 1581; STC 11888); no earlier edition of the latter survives. For more on Elizabethan dialogues, see Antoinina Bevan Zlatar, *Reformation Fictions: Polemical Protestant Dialogues in Elizabethan England* (Oxford: 2011).

[9] For details of this lost play, see record #156 in Martin Wiggins, *British Drama: A Catalogue*, 11 vols (Oxford: 2012- ), vol. 1.

[10] Luke Shepherd, *Ion Bon and Mast Person* (John Day and William Seres [1548?]; STC 3258.5).

his origin in the fourteenth-century dream-poem *Piers Plowman* by William Langland. Thanks to Langland's wide-ranging criticism of clerical abuses, *Piers Plowman* was printed in 1550 as a proto-Reformation tract, and the figure of a humble but impassioned Protestant ploughman became one of the major recurring spokesmen in Reformation fiction.[11] In one early outing, for instance, we find Piers proving transubstantiation to be a romish myth in *A godly dialogue and disputation between Piers Plowman and a popish priest*, printed twice in Edward's reign.[12]

Sachs's dialogue brings in other speakers too, and some embodied action (as when the cook fetches the Bible), and has a semi-dramatic liveliness similar to a play. This quality of animation, and the speeches' colloquial prose, separates it from the very formal subset of dialogues modelled on the catechism, a set of questions and answers to teach the uneducated. Imitating the power dynamic of a classroom, these were very top-down and hierarchical – the opposite of Sachs's shoemaker – with a master instructing a pupil, a husband his wife, and so on. John Bale wrote one of these for his two sons, printed for him in 1549, in which the elder brother answers the younger's questions.[13] Scoloker's own *Knowledge and Simplicity* is in this heavily stylised form, written in rhyming stanzas most of which end with the phrase 'God's holy name'.[14] Another feature of this

---

[11] Robert Crowley printed three editions of *The vision of Pierce Plowman* in 1550 (STC 19906-7a). On Crowley's *Piers*, see John N. King, 'Robert Crowley's editions of *Piers Plowman*: A Tudor Apocalypse', *Modern Philology* 73 (1976), 342-52; and on Piers as a Protestant spokesman, see Sarah A. Kelen, 'Plowing the past: "Piers Protestant" and the authority of medieval literary history', *Yearbook of Langland Studies* 13 (1999), 101-36, and Lawrence Warner, 'Plowman traditions in late medieval and early modern writing', in Andrew Cole and Andrew Galloway (eds.), *The Cambridge Companion to Piers Plowman* (Cambridge, 2014), 198-213.

[12] Printed twice around 1550, probably by William Copland (STC 19903-3.5).

[13] John Bale, *A dialoge or communycacyon to be had at a table betwene two children* ([Stephen Mierdman] for Richard Foster, 1549; STC 1290). Mierdman might have been the printer of the Dutch translation of Sachs's dialogue which Scoloker used.

[14] STC 6806, above.

xxxiv *Introduction*

formulaic Protestant genre was heavy use of scriptural quotation to mark reliable, godly speech. In an English anti-Catholic catechism printed in Antwerp in 1545, in which Truth instructs an Unlearned Man, Truth speaks exclusively in biblical paraphrase and quotation, with chapter citations provided in the margin.[15]

The most 'theatrical' of the Edwardine dialogues are the two in which the Mass, personified as a woman of loose morals, is put on trial in a courtroom for setting herself up as an idol to be worshipped in God's place.[16] These bestselling pieces were printed in multiple editions in 1548-49 by Scoloker's London collaborator, William Seres. William Turner's *The examination of the Mass* sees Mistress Missa (her name the Latin for Mass) cross-examined by Master Knowledge and Master Freemouth, while Porphyry and Sir Philip Philargery (meaning lover-of-silver) attempt to defend her. She is finally sentenced to banishment, because, as Knowledge cautions, if they do not escort her from England 'the priestes wil kepe her stil in theyr chambres, *and* wil abuse her as they haue don before.'[17] The dark reference to sexual immorality, typical of religious polemic in this period, alludes to the English Protestant fear that priests would secretly continue to say private masses for clandestine Catholics. William Punt developed the symbolism of the idea in his *Inditement against Mother Mass*, in which Mother Mass is cross-examined by Knowledge and Verity and defended by Masters Stiffneck and Covetous; the judge is God's Word and the jury are the twelve Apostles. In the end she is sent packing back to Rome with her two brothers, Superstition and Idolatry.

---

[15] Printed after *A briefe catechisme and dialogue betwene the husbande and his wife*, trans. Robert Legate (Wesel [i.e. Antwerp: Stephen Mierdman], 1545; STC 4797.3).

[16] William Turner's *Examination of the Mass* was printed by John Day and William Seres in four octavo editions in c.1548-49 (STC 24361.5, 24362-3, 24634a); *The Inditement against Mother Mass*, attributed to William Punt, in three octavos by the same men in 1548 (STC 20499) and 1549 (20500-0.5).

[17] STC 24361.5, [G8]v.

*English Reformation Dialogues*  xxxv

The issue of the Mass is the most obvious theological difference between Scoloker's translation and other contemporary polemical dialogues. No controversy provoked so many tracts in the 1540s and 1550s as the debate whether the eucharistic bread and wine in the Mass – the Lord's Supper in the reformed English Prayer Book – were literally Christ's flesh and blood. As well as Punt and Turner, Shepherd's John Bon pours scorn on Mast Parson's belief in the Real Presence, as does Piers Plowman on the popish priest's, and so would Oliver in his dialogue with Sir Nicholas Noseled in 1554, giving their reactions to the recent reestablishment of the Mass in England by Mary I.[18] However, the default lines in German debates of the real presence of Christ were different. Sachs in this ealy stage of adopting Luther's teaching did not debate the eucharist or transsubstantiation. In contrast to the many Edwardine dialogues, which made the Mass their principle target in their assault on the Roman faith, the Shoemaker and the Parson do not mention it once.

Very few conversational texts are known to have been translated from Dutch before Scoloker, unless we include the Latin *Colloquia* of the Low Countries' most celebrated humanist, Erasmus, three of which had been published in English by 1548.[19] The really notable exception, however, is the most famous English play before Shakespeare: *Everyman*.

---

[18] STC 3258.5 and 10383, above. See also Randall Hurlestone, *Newes from Rome concerning the blasphemous sacrifice of the papisticall Masse* (Canterbury: John Mitchell for E. Campion, [1548-50?]; STC 14006), which contains four dialogues, respectively on the Mass, true worship, honouring saints, and Christian freedom.

[19] *Funus* [1526] was published in English in 1534 (Robert Copland for John Byddell; STC 10453.5); *Peregrinatio religionis ergo* [1526] in around 1540 (STC 10454); and Philip Gerrard's translation of *Epicurus* [1533] in 1545 (Richard Grafton; STC 10460); followed by Edmond Becke's translations of *Cyclops* [1529] and *De rebus ac vocabulis* [1523] in *Two dyaloges* (Canterbury: John Mitchell [c.1549-53]; STC 10459).

xxxvi  *Introduction*

Ill. 10: Titlepage of the third edition of *Everyman*, John Skot, [c.1529]; STC 10606

This is an anonymous translation of *Elckerlijc*, a play written probably in the 1480s or 1490s, perhaps in Antwerp, for a drama competition between *rederijkers*, the 'rhetoricians' whose humanistic chambers were centres of polite learning in Dutch cities.[20]

The play tells the story of a man, representing all of mankind, who is told by Death that he is about to die and face judgement. Abandoned by his family, friends, wealth, and health, he is guided by Knowledge through a sequence of sacraments, from confession to extreme unction, to make his soul ready for Heaven. The English version was printed four times in c.1518-35, making it apparently the most popular play before the English Reformation.[21] Interestingly, the translator was attempting the religious opposite to Scoloker. *Everyman* is written in explicit support of the authority of the Catholic priesthood and seven sacraments, especially the necessity of penance for sin. The translator, who was apparently working around the time of Luther's first protest, actually goes further than the original Dutch. He renames the personified character Virtue as 'Good Deeds' to make a more explicit defence of the traditional doctrine of justification by works, which was coming under pressure from theological reformers. As C. J. Wortham puts it, '*Elckerlijc* is *ante*-Reformation; *Everyman* is *anti*-Reformation.'[22] The fact that this popular piece was never reprinted after the mid-1530s shows the changing direction of the wind blowing into England from the continent.

---

[20] Both texts are printed in *Everyman and its Dutch Original, Elckerlijc*, ed. Clifford Davidson, Martin W. Walsh, and Ton J. Broos (Kalamazoo: 2007).
[21] Printed by Richard Pynson ([c.1518-19], STC 10604; [1526-28?], STC 10604.5) and John Skot ([c.1529], STC 10606); [1534?], STC 10606.5).
[22] C. J. Wortham, '*Everyman* and the Reformation', *Parergon* 29 (1981), 23-31 (p. 23).

# 3. The Pamphlets in Oxford
## Philip Flacke

The Reformation in sixteenth-century Germany was a matter of public debate to a scale that had never been seen before. It was carried by a generation, born between 1470 and 1500, whom Thomas Kaufmann has recently characterised as 'printing natives' in analogy to the digital natives of today.[1] These women and men had grown up with the new technology of printing with movable type and the resulting emergence of a media landscape fit for the fast and cheap circulation of ideas. Hans Sachs was one of them. His Reformation dialogues from 1524 reflect on what it meant to partake in a heated public debate. The pamphlets in which these texts reached an audience all over the German-speaking world provide an insight into media use not just by Sachs but by printers, booksellers, readers, collectors, politicians, and the 'gmaine mann' (edition, a2r: common man and woman!) addressed in his pamphlets.

## Printing Reformation pamphlets

Four of Sachs's prose dialogues have an 1524 imprint date. No autograph of any of these exists. This despite the fact that Sachs copied out more or less all of his literary output by hand into what eventually grew to be 34 volumes. Two indices, compiled by Sachs himself later in life, contain the folio numbers of where the four dialogues were to be found in the very first of these volumes.[2] But this volume, compiled in 1526/27, has not survived. In the second of these two indices, written half a lifetime after their publication, Sachs lists the four texts under the following short titles: 'Disputation zwischen dem Corhern', 'Von den scheinwercken', 'Das gesprech

---

[1] Kaufmann 2022, pp. 7–11.
[2] Otten1993, pp. 102–108.

mit den parfuser munichen', 'Das gesprech vom wuecher'. Even if the exact order in which they were written and published, has been a matter of academic debate,[3] it is clear, that the 'Chorherr und Schuhmacher' comes first.

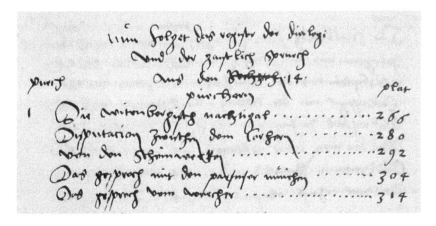

Ill. 11: Sachs's index of all of his works, second fol. 78ᵛ of the two folia numbered (reproduced after the facsimile, Sachs/Hahn 1986)

On its publication, the *Disputation zwischen einem Chorherren vnd Schuchmacher* was an immediate success. Printers in seven cities published no less than 13 editions, all dated to the year 1524: three in Bamberg, four in Augsburg, one in Speyer, one in Erfurt, one in Eilenburg near Leipzig, one in Straßburg and two in Vienna.[4] While the *Wittenbergisch Nachtigall* had first been published anonymously, the name Hans Sachs now appeared on all these editions. – All except one: The printer Matthes Maler in Erfurt got it wrong and typeset on the title page: 'Hanns Bachs'.

---

[3] Rettelbach 2019, pp. 94–96; Schuster 2019, pp. 93–94.
[4] According to the VD 16. Bamberg (Georg Erlinger): VD 16 S 219 (not listed in KG, vol. 22), S 220 (=KG, vol. 22, 7b), S 221 (=7a); Augsburg (Melchior Ramminger): S 215 (=7e), S 216 (=7c), S 217 (=7f), S 218 (=7h); Speyer (Jakob Schmidt): ZV 31754 (not listed in KG); Erfurt (Matthes Maler): ZV 13538 (not listed in KG); Eilenburg (Nikolaus Widemar): S 222 (=7d); Straßburg (Wolfgang Köpfel): S 223 (=7i); Vienna (Johann Singriener): S 213 (=7j), S 214 (not listed in KG).

xl  *Introduction*

Nuremberg is noticeably missing. As had been the case with the *Wittenbergisch Nachtigall* (Ill. 3) in the previous year,[5] Sachs did not publish his text in his home town but turned to the printer Georg Erlinger in Bamberg instead – probably because of the difficult situation for printing and selling pamphlets in Nuremberg at this point (see above Thomas Wood, *The Historical Context*). We know of the case of an old woman who was living in the Tuchscherergasse ('[d]as alte Fräulein im Tuchscheerergäßchen').[6] After she had offered copies of a newly printed pamphlet by the reformer Heinrich von Kettenbach for sale, she had to spend four days and nights chained to the pillory. This was in January or February 1524 – precisely when Sachs might have worked on his first dialogue.

Only one further German edition from the sixteenth century is known, published around 1580.[7] All of Sachs's 1524 dialogues were bestsellers but not longsellers. When later in his life Sachs compiled an edition of his own collected works, which was published in five large volumes in folio from 1558 to 1579, he did not include the four Reformation dialogues. The Dutch and English translations included in this volume were almost certainly printed without Sachs's involvement. More than two decades after the original publication, they testify to an interest in the text by new audiences and to their potential for new markets.

## Strong emotions: sixteenth-century readers

Two Franciscans dressed in religious habit enter from the right while Hans and Peter sit at a wooden table with food, drink and knives. The gestures of all four attest a lively discussion, the starting point of which is made visible by what the right monk is carrying in a large

---

[5] VD 16, see also Schottenloher 1913, p. 236. In other older publications on Sachs, Nuremberg is sometimes named as one of the towns in which the poem was printed.
[6] Cit. von Soden 1855, p. 162.
[7] VD 16 S 224 (not listed in KG, vol. 22). The printer is unknown.

basket on his arm: They are collecting candles in order to perform their monastic duties of singing, chanting and reading.

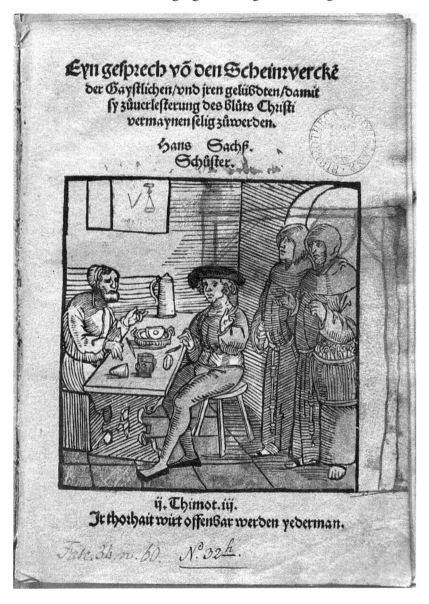

Ill. 12: The title page of *Tr. Luth. 34 (60)* with the ink additions

xlii *Introduction*

In the Oxford copy *Tr. Luth. 34 (60)* of the pamphlet showing this woodcut, presumably by Erhard Schön,[8] somebody has coloured in various parts using seven shades: yellow for the table, the monk's basket and Hans's or Peter's hair, a reddish brown for his clothes, black for his hat, a sandy brown for the chair and bench, a dark green for the floor tiles and the beaker on the table, a dark brown for the monks' tunics, and even a light beige wash shading in the flesh tones and the walls. Later, somebody, surely a different person, added drawings in brown ink: two shapes in the window (just doodles or a lamp?) and a large gallows standing outside the picture in the margin and reaching over the two monks, who have crudely been hung from it with two nooses round their necks.

This single page shows two distinct ways in which contemporaries of the Reformation engaged with the printed medium of the pamphlet. The colours are meant to increase the visual impact and the aesthetic value of the woodcut, which had proved an important selling point of prints and ideas alike. Especially illiterate audiences relied on pictures and the reading out aloud of published texts in public and private contexts. The reader who drew in ink on the page on the other hand treated the pamphlet as a cheap medium which did not have to remain pristine. His drastic imagery of having the Franciscans hung from the gallows shows an emotional response to Sachs's critique of mendicant monastic life and the climate of the Reformation. Comparable examples from the time show how on the other side Catholic readers drew on reformers' printed portraits delegitimising their sometimes saintlike appeal while also making fun of them by giving them ink moustaches.[9]

Who were the people whose engagement with Sachs's dialogues, going as far as a symbolic execution, can still be observed today? The pamphlets in the Bodleian reveal more about them. Another of these pamphlets, *Eyn gesprech eynes Euangelischen Christen mit einem*

---

[8] For this attribution see Schreyl 1976, no. 15.
[9] Rößler 2018; Warnke 1984, pp. 67–68.

*Lutherischen* shelved under *Tr. Luth. 34 (58)*, shows glosses and drawings in ink on the first and last page as well as in the margins. These include doodles of a face in profile and, on the last page, first 'Der', then, after what looks like a reference marker, 'lieb vber ale lieb hat bie | mir ein eren dieb'.[10] ('He who loves love above all has in me a thief of (his) honour'?)

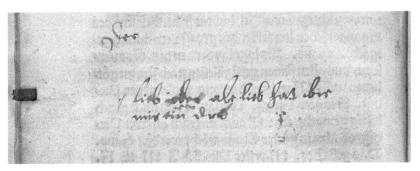

Ill. 13: Gloss on the last page of *Tr. Luth. 34 (58)*, c4ᵛ

These rhyming words read like a rebuke of the dialogue's conciliatory ending, where Sachs cites the Epistle to the Philippians: 'If there be therefore any consolation in Christ, if any comfort of love, if any fellowship of the Spirit, if any bowels and mercies, Fulfil ye my joy, that ye be likeminded, having the same love, being of one accord, of one mind' (Phil 2:1–2) and so forth. Such a sentiment would not have resonated well with a radical anti-Catholic. For it seems the scribe was no other than the person who symbolically hanged the Franciscans and of whom a more and more coherent picture unfolds.

The writing is smudged, and the reason for that can be seen on the page with the drawn-in gallows. Just above the woodcut, beneath the name of the author 'Hans Sachß. Schůster.' ('Hans Sachs. Shoemaker.'), there is the matching inkblot that resulted from the pages being pressed together when the ink was still wet. Judging by

---

[10] The words are smudged. Reading suggested by Ulrich Bubenheimer.

xliv  *Introduction*

the script, the two pamphlets now numbered 60 and 58 must have been part of the same collection in the sixteenth century already, being bound together in a volume where 58 preceded 60.

Examining the Bodleian copies, one can add at least one more pamphlet to those two. It is the *Disputation zwischen einem Chorherren vnd Schuchmacher*, numbered 57 (Ill. 6). To facilitate finding the beginning of each item in a combined volume, leather tabs were permanently fixed to the last folio of the pamphlets, each about one centimetre lower down the page than the preceding one. Over time these left a slight indent on the opposing next page, which can still be seen even if the pamphlets are bound in a different order today. All three pamphlets show matching leather tabs on the last folio and indents on the first, so that they must have been bound together following each other – in an order that exactly fits the most likely chronology of publication:[11] 57 – 58 – 60. They come from a similar region and may have been bought there. Two were printed in Nuremberg, one in Bamberg, probably all first editions. The frontispiece of 57 is coloured in, and especially the dark green of the ground and the slippers seems similar to the tone used in 60. But the shading is more intricate, differentiating between darker and lighter areas in two different colours, which shows even more care in making the pamphlet a visually appealing object. Again, the reader who drew the gallows might not have been the first owner.

In all three pamphlets, single words and short phrases have been underlined in ink, and 57 and 58 further contain some glosses that comment on these words and phrases. They all seem to have been written by the same scribe, probably identical with the artist of the gallows. At the beginning of the first dialogue, the canon wants to send Sachs and Luther to hell (the shoemaker Sachs had written about Luther using the image of a nightingale): 'Ey / <u>der teüffel holl den schûster</u> / mitsampt seiner Nachtigall' ('<u>the devil take the cobbler</u> together with his nightingale', 57, fol. A2ʳ). The reader of the

---

[11] Proposed by Otten 1993, pp. 102–108; see also Otten 1994.

pamphlet reacted by underlining the words they disagreed with and addressing the fictional canon in his gloss: 'gmach o Herle das wirt ain seltzame nachtigal sain' ('Calmly, little man, that is going to be a special nightingale'). A little later, the canon insists that the pope cannot be punished for any crime: 'Ey lieber / vnnd wenn der bapst so böß wer / das er vnzelich menschenn mit grossem hawffen zum teüffel füret / dörft in doch nyemant straffen' ('My good man, even if the pope were so evil as to lead numerous people in large crowds to the devil, still nobody would be allowed to punish him', fol. A2$^v$–A3$^r$). Again, the reader turns directly to the canon, now evidently angry and in versified form: 'so far mit jm hin / sieh das deine gwin / In der Helen din /' ('So go with him! See how your reward shall serve in hell').

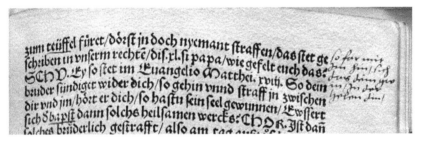

Ill. 14: Gloss in *Tr. Luth. 34 (57)*, fol. A3$^r$

At the end of 57 (fol. C3$^r$), the reader comments on the closing biblical verse in a way that seems very similar to the note on the last page of 58. The edition ends with Paul's words 'Ir Bauch jr got' ('Their belly, their God') of Paul (Phil 3.19). As in 58, the reader makes use of a mark in the form of a virgule which might in both cases serve to connect the printed word with the handwritten note and continues with a rhyme: 'die warheit schlecht sy zu tott | dan sy nur gottes spott' ('truth kills them as they are only a mockery to God'). The glosses of 57 and 58 show a reader who engages enthusiastically with the text, taking a strong anti-Catholic stance. In 57 they defend Sachs while in 58 they apparently disagree with his plea for patience and consolation.

Apart from 57, 58 and 60, there are five further German editions of Sachs's Reformation dialogues in the Bodleian collection. They, too, preserve signs of their usage and history: the different sizes to which they were cut down earlier, painted edges, leather tabs and the impressions of leather tabs, finger prints, one more gloss, folio numbers as well as numbers and letters to count items. All of these show how typesetters, earlier readers and owners interacted with the pamphlets making them individual objects that tell personal stories about the usage of these printed materials from the Reformation in their time and after.

Ill. 15: Fingerprints in *Tr. Luth. 34 (59)*, fol. B2ᵛ, probably of one of the people operating the press

For example, in the pamphlet numbered 55 somebody wrote the name 'Raichenburger' in the inner margin. This reverses the placement of a printed or handwritten catchword which anticipates the first word of a new page at the foot of the preceding one to assist binding and reading: the gloss here repeats the end of the last line of the previous page ('Reychenbur.') at the beginning of the next one. The desired effect must have been to facilitate reading, probably out loud and perhaps even in different voices or with different performers, as the page break coincides with a change of speaker.

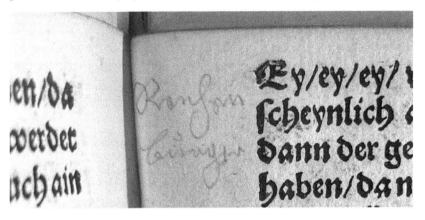

Ill. 16: Gloss in *Tr. Luth. 34 (55)*, fol. B1ʳ

Different features speak of various collections in which many of the pamphlets were apparently combined and bound together at some point between their publication in 1524 and their integration into their current order at the beginning of the nineteenth century. Among these is the foliation, written in large, round numbers in the upper corners of print number 56. Their easily recognisable forms appear quite often in the pamphlets shelved under *Tr. Luth.* in the Bodleian Library, though in none of the other seven Sachs dialogues.[12] The same is true for the green fore edge of 55. It can be seen on a number of pamphlets in the collection, which have all been trimmed to about 14.1 to 14.6cm width.[13] On one of these, *Tr. Luth.*

---

[12] In the neighbouring volumes, the following pamphlets show this foliation: *Tr. Luth. 36 (102)* with the folio numbers 9–36, *Tr. Luth. 35 (67)* with numbers 95–102, *Tr. Luth. 35 (80)* with numbers 119–126, *Tr. Luth. 36 (103)* with numbers 127–159, *Tr. Luth. 33 (56)* with numbers 246–257 and *Tr. Luth. 35 (85)* with numbers 344–351. Perhaps, if one were to search more volumes, a complete reconstruction of this former collection could be achieved.

[13] In the neighbouring volumes, the following pamphlets have this size and edges in the same shade of green: *Tr. Luth. 31 (167)*, *Tr. Luth. 31 (169)*, *Tr. Luth. 31 (190)*, *Tr. Luth 36 (90)*, *Tr. Luth. 50 (9)* and *Tr. Luth. 50 (16)*.

*31 (190)*, it is apparent that the trimming and colouring of the edges are later than some handwritten entries, which could be from the sixteenth century. So it might well be that the green fore edges and maybe some of the other signs of former collections tell us less about how the pamphlets were used by contemporaries of the Reformation and instead attest to their later history when they had already become objects of the past. At this time, they had become a matter of interest for collectors, historians and libraries.

Ill. 17: Green-coloured edges in the *Tr. Luth.*

## Collectors, auctioneers and librarians

At the core of the Bodleian special collection called *Tractatus Lutherani*, which includes eight copies of Sachs's Reformation dialogues, are 84 volumes with c. 1,670 Latin and German tracts from the context of the German Reformation, all of them published between 1518 and 1550, and many of them pamphlets.[14] They were collected by Johann Gottlob May (1754–1821), a schoolmaster and librarian from Augsburg.[15] An advertisement from 1818, when May's collection was sold at Sotheby's in London, mentions that it was by this point already 'chronologically arranged',[16] another that it was 'carefully arranged in chronological order'.[17] The *Annals of the Bodleian Library* record the acquisition of a 'very valuable and curious series of original editions of Latin and German tracts, issued by the German reformers between 1518 and 1550', already bound 'in eighty-four volumes'.[18] So it seems that May himself put them in the order they appear in today and had them bound in brown leather. He did not trim them but left them in their different shapes and sizes.

---

[14] Cf. Bodleian Library 2024; Attar 2016, p. 329; Jefcoate/Kelly/Kloth 2000, p. 297; Bloomfield/Potts 1997, p. 515.

[15] The name variant 'Johannes', which most often appears in English publications, seems to be a misunderstanding of May's Latinisation of his name as 'Joannes Gottlob May' on the two Latin title pages of his catalogue (May 1818, s. p., cf. also the same Latinisation under the Latin preface in May 1798, p. IV). I cannot find the name 'Johannes' anywhere in historical sources from May's lifetime.

[16] 'Intelligence, Literary, Scientific, &c.' 1818, p. 123.

[17] 'Literary Notice of Dr. *May*'s Collection' 1818, p. 210. Both advertisements largely follow the wording of Samuel Sotheby, as can be seen in his preface to May's catalogue of the collection. There it says: 'The Collection is carefully arranged in chronological order' (Sotheby? 1818, fol. 6ᵛ).

[18] Macray 1890, p. 303.

1  *Introduction*

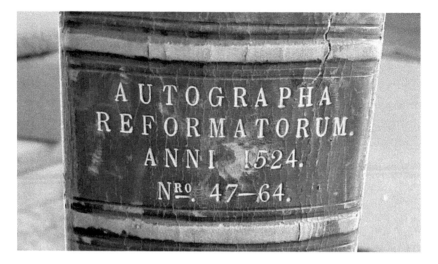

Ill. 18: *Tr. Luth. 34*, the volume that contains, amongst other publications from 1524, the eight Sachs editions

May had accumulated the pamphlets over a period of thirty years, incorporating in turn collections of the theologian Matthias Jacob Adam Steiner (1740–1796) and the historian Georg Wilhelm Zapf (1747–1810), both of them contemporaries of May in Augsburg.[19] More is known about the work and collecting habits of these two than about those of May. Zapf published various studies on the Reformation and the history of book printing.[20] Steiner collected everything from natural curiosities to engravings, coins, bibles and stained glass.[21]

It is not clear if any of the eight editions in question were part of Steiner's or Zapf's collections or where else they came from. The sales

---

[19] 'Having besides an opportunity of enriching his own Collection with a great part of those of Steiner and Zapf of Augsburg, he succeeded in getting together a more numerous and perfect assemblage of Tracts, illustrative to the early history of the Reformation than had ever been before made.' (Sotheby(?) 1818, fol. 5ᵛ, cf. Jefcoate / Kelly / Kloth 2000, p. 297).

[20] Cf. Schön 1898; Gradmann 1802, pp. 801–809.

[21] Baader 1795, pp. 93–100, contains a detailed footnote on Steiner's collections that comprises no less than eight pages, despite the book being written as a travel report.

The Pamphlets in Oxford li

catalogues for their libraries, both probably co-written by May, do not list the pamphlets under their titles, but include entries like '[Ein Fascikel mit] 18 seltnen Originalschriften, die durch die Reformation Luthers zu Augsburg u. Nürnberg veranlaßt worden' ('a fascicle of 18 rare original publications prompted by the Lutheran Reformation in Augsburg and Nuremberg'),[22] '12. Tractatus divers argument. et auctor. Deutsch', published '1523–25', 'Gebunden' ('12 pamphlets of various subjects and authors in German, published 1523–25, bound'), and '50.' plus another '48. Tractatus divers. argument. et auctor. in lingua lat. et. germ.', published '1524', 'Ausgeschnitten' ('[98 (?)] pamphlets of various subjects and authors in German, published 1523–25, loose (?)').[23] It may well be that some of the eight Sachs pamphlets were among those but it is uncertain.[24] In his handwritten catalogue of his own collection, which is kept in the Bodleian, May lists all eight pamphlets but does not indicate where or when he bought them.[25]

May's catalogue of the *Tractatus Lutherani* mainly fulfils the function of an inventory. It designates two numbers to each item – apparently an older and a newer sorting system. Both numbers appear on the pamphlets as well. Apart from that, the focus of the catalogue lies on bibliographical information suitable for identifying the prints. May lists titles, author, the number of printed pages ('S.' for 'Seiten').

---

[22] May / Wilhelm 1797, p. 139. For Steiner's library cf. also May 1798.

[23] Beyschlag / May / Bürgle 1812, pp. 416 f. For Zapf's library cf. also Zapf 1787 (in which I could not find mention of Reformation pamphlets).

[24] It could also be that May did not want to put items on public sale which he preferred to buy for himself and hence did not list them in the sales catalogues.

[25] May 1818, fol. 75ʳ–75ᵛ. Warm thanks go to Alan Coates and Oliver House for their help locating the manuscript, which is now shelved under *Library Records c. 1819* (formerly under R.6.212).

lii  *Introduction*

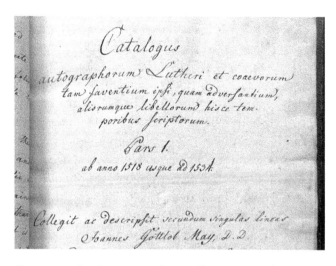

Ill. 19: May's handwritten catalogue of his collection (May 1818)

To this he adds the date and place of publication (for the eight pamphlets mostly 's. l.' for *sine loco* or 's. l. et a.' for *sine loco et anno*), the publisher ('s. n. t.' for *sine nomine typographorum*), the book format ('4.' for *quarto*). He gives exact information on the printed elements of the title pages including line breaks, mottos and woodcuts. What May's catalogue widely ignores, are signs of usage and provenance – aspects regarding the prints as individual copies with a specific history different from other copies of the same print.

Ill. 20: May's handwritten catalogue of his collection, fol. 75ʳ with the entry for *Tr. Luth. 34 (56)*

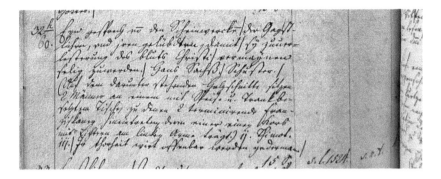

Ill. 21: May's handwritten catalogue of his collection, fol. 75ᵛ with the entry for
*Tr. Luth. 34 (60)*

For example, following an exact transcription of the title on *Tr. Luth. 34 (60)* (Ill. 12), he describes its frontispiece in the following words: 'Auf dem darunter stehenden Holzschnitte sitzen 2 Männer an einem mit Speise u. Trank besetzten Tische, zu denen 2 terminirende Franziskaner hineintreten deren einer einen Korb mit Lichtern im linken Arme trägt.' ('In the woodcut beneath there are two men sitting at a table set with food and drink. Two Franciscan monks enter collecting alms, one of whom is holding a basket with candles on his left arm.') May does not make note of the fact that the woodcut has been coloured in, nor of the ink drawings and the ink blot on the title page or the leather tab secured to the last folio. In the case of *Tr. Luth. 34 (57)* he does note the coloured frontispiece but only to distinguish the print from the previous one: 'Der nämliche Holzschnitt wie beym vorigen, aber illuminirt.' ('The same woodcut as in the previous one but illuminated.')

In 1818, the Bodleian purchased May's collection at Sotheby's in London for 95 Pounds and 15 Shillings.[26] The acquisition fell under the direction of Bulkeley Bandinel, who had been named Bodley's Librarian in 1813 and remained in that position until 1860. Bandinel had more money at hand than his predecessors thanks to new library statutes approved in 1813 and to an increased deposit of new British

---

[26] Cf. Macray 1890, p. 303.

liv *Introduction*

publications following the Copyright Act of 1814.[27] He used part of this money to buy libraries of private collectors all over Europe, acquiring amongst others printed books and manuscripts in Greek, Latin, Hebrew, Sanskrit, Italian and German. 'It was the scale of the acquisitions made when Bandinel was Bodley's Librarian that marked his time in office as one of the greatest periods of expansion of the collections.'[28]

According to the *Annals*, the *Tractatus Lutherani* 'probably comprise [...] as complete a gathering of these controversial publications, so easily lost or destroyed from their small extent and often ephemeral character, as can anywhere be found.'[29] In this evaluation the account takes its cue from a preface to May's handwritten catalogue of the collection – a text which advertises its value and which, it has been presumed, might have been written by Samuel Sotheby himself.[30] Sotheby, who, though a bibliophile, of course had a financial interest in the pamphlets, is known to have routinely hyped interest in his holdings.[31] In the case of the *Tractatus Lutherani* this includes his repeated claim that among them are numerous autographs by Luther and other reformers.[32] Sotheby also gives a reason why the pamphlets might be of academic value in a library in Britain:

> It would be superfluous after these details, to say more of the interest and high value of this Collection for any public and private Library; – for every one, acquainted with literature, must be convinced, that without the aid of similar Collections, it is impossible to investigate the History of the Reformation on the Continent, which is so

[27] Cf., also for his purchases, Clapinson 2020, pp. 138–142.
[28] Ibid, p. 139.
[29] Macray 1890, p. 303.
[30] Jefcoate/Kelly/Kloth 2000, p. 297.
[31] Cf. Micklich 2024 about a purchase for the Bodleian in 1835 of a manuscript falsely advertised to have probably been written by Melanchthon and Sotheby's marketing strategy of 'fabricating a Bibliotheca Melanchthonia' (Georg Kloss).
[32] Apart from Sotheby(?) 1818 cf. also the advertisements 'Intelligence, Literary, Scientific, &c.' 1818 and 'Literary Notice of Dr. May's Collection' 1818.

intimately connected with the History of the Reformation of this Country.[33]

Ill. 22: The preface to May's handwritten catalogue of his collection, possibly written by Samuel Sotheby, 1818

In addition to the eight German editions of Sachs's Reformation dialogues, all published in 1524 and part of the *Tractatus Lutherani*, the Bodleian holds two copies of the English translation published by

---

[33] Sotheby(?) 1818, fol. 6ᵛ.

lvi *Introduction*

Anthony Scoloker in 1548. One of these, too, entered the collection in the time of Bandinel. It was part of the immense collection of prints, books, manuscripts and other items that was bequeathed to the library in 1834 by Francis Douce (1757–1834).[34] Douce's copy of *A goodly dysputacion betwene a Christen Shomaker and a Popysshe Parson*, however, preserves only the second part of the octavo volume, quires C & D.

For this reason, a complete second copy, printed in London like Douce's, was purchased in 1885. It had belonged to Richard Heber (1773–1833), a bibliomaniac, who had a special interest in early English drama and whose immense collection of books and pamphlets, according to the *Encyclopædia Britannica*, 'over-ran eight houses'.[35] This collection was sold at Sotheby's from 1834 to 1837. The London edition of *A goodly dysputacion* appears in the fifth volume of the 13-volume sales catalogue.[36] Despite the rarity of the title, Heber owned two copies. A second one, an earlier edition printed in Ipswich, is listed in the second volume of the catalogue.[37] The London copy was bought (or given to) the theologian and art collector John Fuller Russell (1814–1884), whose library was again sold at Sotheby's. The 1885 sales catalogue mentions the rarity of the title: 'Very scarce. The Author was probably the facetious Hans Sachs. This copy sold for £2. 3s. in Heber's sale.'[38] In the Bodleian copy of this catalogue can still be seen the annotations regarding the purchase.[39] The first entry, 'com. 53', must mean that the library commissioned its agent to spend a maximum of 53 shillings (or £2.

---

[34] For Douce's bequest cf. Clapinson 2020, pp. 143–148.
[35] *Encyclopædia Britannica* 1911, vol. 13, p. 167.
[36] *Bibliotheca Heberiana* 1834, p. 65.
[37] *Bibliotheca Heberiana* 1835, p. 94.
[38] Catalogue Russell 1885, p. 34.
[39] Shelved under *2591 d.1 Sotheby 1885 Jan–June*. Many thanks go to Simon Phillips for his kind help in locating and making sense of the Bodleian copy of the sales catalogue.

13s.), the second, 'got at 32', that the winning bid was only 32 shillings (or £1. 12s.).

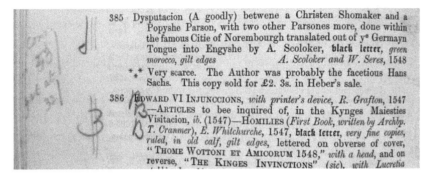

Ill. 23: Entry for *A goodly dysputacion* in the Bodleian copy of the sales catalogue for John Fuller Russell's library (*Catalogue Russell* 1885, p. 34)

Ill. 24: Front flyleaf of *Vet. A1 f. 237*, where someone has noted 'Fuller Russel sale, 1885'

lviii  *Introduction*

Besides the ten copies of Sachs's Reformation dialogues in the Bodleian, an additional German copy from 1524 is kept by the Taylor Institution Library for Modern European languages which is the basis for our edition.[40] Bound in a simple brown cardboard cover with marbled paper on the outside, it is an edition of the *Disputacion zwischen ainem Chorherrenn vnnd Schüchmache*. According to an inscription on the front flyleaf, it was once given as a birthday present: 'Dem lieben Bruder Adolf zu seinem 65sten Geburtstage, den 7. Juli 1879.' ('To dear brother Adolf for his 65th birthday, July 7, 1879'). The copy was bought by the Taylorian in December 1924 for £5 – by far the most expensive purchase listed on that page in the register of additions – from the bookseller Gustav Fock in Leipzig.[41] With this acquisition being the last, a total of eleven original copies of Sachs's Reformation dialogues had been added to Oxford collections in the period from 1818 to 1925.[42]

The five-hundred-year history of the eleven copies involves diverse parties with varying interests, yet all (or almost all) strongly invested in Reformation pamphlets. The rapid succession of the four publications, quickly reprinted in a number of towns all within a single year, speaks of a fast-paced media landscape, which could swiftly react to current debates. Sachs made use of this as he wrote his four dialogues, focusing on different aspects, altering his stance and trying out literary strategies in a newly reinvented genre. The printing history is also a history of censorship and the difficulties and dangers of publishing in the time of the Reformation. How heated the debate was, can be seen most prominently in the emotional responses of one reader arguing with the text and its characters in the

---

[40] The provenance research has been done by Christina Ostermann, who is currently working on the acquisition of Reformation holdings for the Taylorian. Thanks also go to Gareth Evans for his help looking into the collection.

[41] Cf. Taylor Institution Library: *Register of additions to the Library* 1922–34, as well as Taylor Institution Library: *Cashbook of the Finch Fund*, s. p. According to the cashbook, £5 2s. were paid to Fock in January 1926 (£5 for Sachs, 2s. for an edition of Goethe's *Faust* by Heinrich Düntzer).

[42] For an overview of the eleven copies cf. also Hartmann 2015.

*The Pamphlets in Oxford* lix

margins and symbolically hanging the two Franciscans in one of the frontispieces. Overall, the engagement of early readers shows how a pamphlet in the sixteenth century could be very different things: a valued object embellished with intricately coloured woodcuts, a functional text medium to be worked with, annotated and bound in miscellany volumes or even possibly a short-lived product of what must have seemed a mass production of affordable up-to-date prints that could be used for doodles. The copies that have survived still bear witness to their original multimedia contexts between text, image and performance, public and private, single pamphlet, miscellany volume and library.

Later, the collectors, bibliophiles, historians and auctioneers of the eighteenth and nineteenth centuries looked at them from different perspectives. The pamphlets had become historical objects, whose value could lie in their rarity and collectability, their use as historical sources or their alleged connection to famous men from the past. The acquisition for libraries, in Oxford from 1818 to 1925, marked them as matters of public research. This continues to this day, but the questions we ask them have changed, first with a growing interest in literary and sociological aspects of the texts and in recent years increasingly in material aspects of the individual copies. These can tell us more about the time of their publication, the people who interacted with them, the changing perspectives over the centuries and about the texts themselves.

lx  *Introduction*

# List of the Sachs dialogues in Oxford

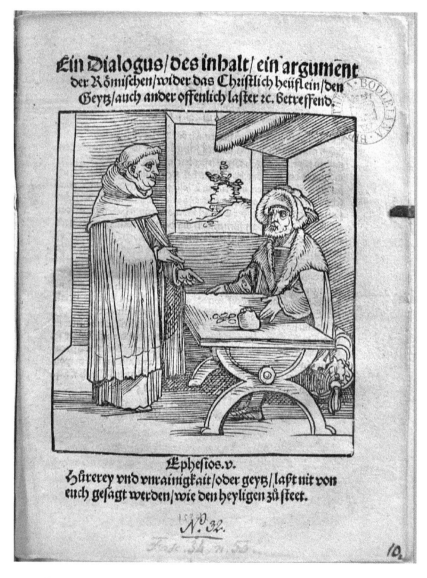

Ill. 25: Titlepage of *Tr. Luth. 34 (53)*, the first pamphlet in the collection

*The Pamphlets in Oxford* lxi

Tr. Luth. 34 (53)
*Ein Dialogus / des inhalt / ein argumēt | der Rômischen / wider das Christlich heüflein / den | Geytz / auch ander offenlich laster 2c. betreffend.* [Nuremberg: Jobst Gutknecht,][43] 1524.
(Weller 1868: 18(a); KG, vol. 22: 9a; Pegg 1973: 3550; Köhler 1996: 3989; VD 16 S 211.)

Tr. Luth. 34 (54)
*Ain Dialogus vnd Argument | der Romanisten / wider das Christlich heüflein / | den Geytz vnd ander offentlich laster betreffend 2c.* [Augsburg: Philipp Ulhart, 1524.]
(Weller 1868: 18(d); KG, vol. 22: 9d; Pegg 1973: 3552; Köhler 1996: 3991; VD 16 S 210.)

Tr. Luth. 34 (55)
*Ain Dialogus vnd Argument | der Romanisten / wider das Christlich heüflein / | den Geytz vnd ander offentlich laster betreffend 2c.* [Augsburg: Philipp Ulhart, 1524.]
(Weller 1868: 18(c); KG, vol. 22: 9c; Pegg 1973: 3551; Köhler 1996: 3990; VD 16 S 209.)

Tr. Luth. 34 (56)
*Disputacion zwyschen ainem Chorherre | vnd Schůmacher / Darinn das wort | gottes ain recht Christlich wesenn | verfochten wirt.* [Augsburg: Melchior Ramminger,] 1524.
(Weller 1868: 17(e); KG, vol. 22: 7e; Pegg 1973: 3553; Köhler 1996: 3994; VD 16 S 215.)

Tr. Luth. 34 (57)
*Disputation zwischē einem Chorherren | vnd Schuchmacher dariñ das wort | gottes vnnd ein recht Christlich | wesen verfochten würt.* [Bamberg: Georg Erlinger,] 1524.
(Weller 1868: 17(a); KG, vol. 22: 7b; Pegg 1973: 3554; Köhler 1996: 3995; VD 16 S 220.)

Tr. Luth. 34 (58)

---

[43] According to VD 16 online. Otherwise the printer is usually identified as Hieronymus Höltzel.

lxii *Introduction*

*Eyn gesprech eynes Euangelischen | Christen / mit einem Lutherischen /
darin | der Ergerlich wandel etlicher / die | sich Lutherisch nennen /
angelzaigt / vñ brüderlich gelstrafft wirt.* [Nuremberg: Hieronymus
Höltzel,] 1524.
(Weller 1868: 20(b); KG, vol. 22: 10c; Pegg 1973: 3558; Köhler
1996: 4001; VD 16 S 302.)

Tr. Luth. 34 (59)
*Ain Gesprech aines Euangeli-lschen Christen / mit ainem Lutherischen |
darinn der Ergerlich wandel etli-lcher / die sich Lutherisch nennē |
angezaigt / vnd brüderlich | gestrafft wirdt.* [Augsburg: Philipp
Ulhart,] 1524.
(Weller 1868: 20(e); KG, vol. 22: 10g; Pegg 1973: 3560; Köhler
1996: 3999; VD 16 S 297.)

Tr. Luth. 34 (60)
*Eyn gesprech vō den Scheinʒverckē | der Gaystlichen / vnd jren
gelübdten / damit | sy zůuerlesterung des blůts Christi | vermaynen selig
zůwerden.* [Nuremberg: Hieronymus Höltzel, 1524.]
(Weller 1868: 19(b); KG, vol. 22: 8c; Pegg 1973: 3562; Köhler 1996:
4006; VD 16 S 321.)

# 4. The Edition
## Henrike Lähnemann

Early modern German was written to be performed. This is true for all Reformation pamphlets but particularly important to remember for Hans Sachs's dialogues. Even though they were not written to be staged like his 'Fastnachtspiele' (bawdy Shrovetide plays), they use the same stylistic devices of frequent interjections, question and answer ping-pong, and insults. The audience would have had exposure to German verse and prose largely as listeners, whether through mystery plays, sermons, or public performance of the works of the 'Meistersinger'. The best approach to these dialogues is therefore to read them aloud, in line also with the argument that Martin Luther put forward e.g. in the 'Sendbrief vom Dolmetschen' for the importance of idiomatic expression and the 'street value' of language.

This short introductory guide has been part of the whole series of the Reformation pamphlets but this is the first run of editions from Southern Germany with a distinctly different dialect by the author and - perhaps more importantly - the typesetters and printers, distinct from the East Central German of Leipzig / Erfurt / Wittenberg. All Sachs pamphlets discussed come from a cluster of towns within today's Bavaria: The Imperial Free City of Nuremberg, the home of Hans Sachs where he lived all his life; Bamberg, the episcopal seat 60km north of Nuremberg, a Catholic stronghold; however, it was less strict in enforcing publishing censorship than the ever-suspecting Nuremberg town council. Both cities belonged to the East Franconian area. Finally the flourishing trade centre Augsburg, 150km south of Nuremberg, where the reprint of the first edition of the first dialogue was produced which opens our edition, with an active print scene which picked up all new publications from

lxiv  *Introduction*

best-selling authors such as Hans Sachs, which used mainly Swabian dialect conventions.

1. Dialect
   The edition shows a mix of East Franconian and Swabian features. Typical of East Franconian are the swapped plosives, voiced b, d, g used for unvoiced p, t, k, and vice versa, particularly at the beginning of words: 'poden' for NHG 'Boden'; 'driegerei' for 'Trügerei'. The other characteristic is a wide use of e-elision (apo- and syncope), resulting in many truncated forms such as 'Cristn' or 'bericht' for 'berichtet', while Central German tends to preserve the full forms with the final schwa-e. Typical of Nuremberg is the use of 'e' for 'ö' as in 'Kechin' for 'Köchin'.

2. Punctuation
   Early modern editions use full stops, brackets, question marks, and virgules as punctuation marks. The '/' Virgel (virgule or forward slash) is the main means of structuring sentences, and can stand for both a comma and a semicolon. It is best to treat a virgule like a musical caesura, to pause for breath. Often the full stop at the end of a sentence is omitted, particularly if a capital letter follows.

3. Abbreviations
   Typesetters took over from manuscripts some handy ways to save space. The main abbreviation mark is a bar (macron) over characters '-'. As a nasal bar above any letter, it replaces a following n such as 'warē' = waren or (mainly for Latin case endings) an m such as 'Jtē' = Item. The macron is also habitually used for 'vn̄' = und. Confusingly, the rounded z-form 'ʒ' stands both for z and for a number of established abbreviations, particularly in 'dʒ' / 'wʒ'= das / was. In the transcription, ʒ has been rendered as z where it stands for the affricate sound /ts/ and has been resolved where it is used as

*Edition* lxv

abbreviation. Occasionally a hook is used for the -er ending, e.g. 'd' = der; this has also been resolved in the transcription.

4. u/v/w – v/f – i/j/y, and different s– and r–forms
The Roman alphabet had only one symbol for u and v and one for i and j. u/v/w are interchangeable, as are i/j/y, and v/f are both used for f, e.g. 'vnd' = und; 'zuuor' = zuvor; 'new' = neu; 'vleissig' = fleißig; 'jch' = ich. In most cases, letters are pronounced as in the equivalent modern German word.
The two typographically different forms for s (long ſ versus round s) and for r (the round form of r = 2 being mainly used after characters with a rounded right-hand border such as o or – in some fonts – h) in the type set have not been distinguished in the transcription because they are simply graphic variations. Confusingly, the round r can also be used to stand for the more 7-shaped Tironian note 'et', used exclusively for 'etc.'. This has been replaced with the ampersand '&' which also started life as representing 'et' (the form is a ligature of an uncial 'e' and a lower-case 't').

5. Umlauts
The umlaut sound would have been in the same position as in modern German, but there is no strict rule for writing it. In most cases, an umlaut should be used wherever one occurs in modern German. The Augsburg print workshop used superscript 'e' for 'ö' and long 'ä' as in 'hören' and 'vnzälich' (= 'unzählich'), 'ü' for umlaut-u (probably to avoid confusion with 'o' above 'u' in words with old diphthong 'uo' such as 'brüder'), 'e' for short 'ä'.

6. Double versus single consonants and s/ß, k/ck, z/tz, r/rh, t/th
There is no consistency in writing single and double consonants such as f/ff or n/nn, nor is there a difference in pronunciation, i.e. 'gottlich' and 'gotlich' are pronounced the same. This also applies to s and ß (the latter started out as a ligature of long ſ and z to indicate a double consonant), to k

lxvi    *Introduction*

and ck (the spelling for double k), and to z and tz. Note that z always sounds like modern German z, i.e. /ts/, not like English z. Again, almost all consonants can be pronounced like their modern German equivalents.

7. Use of h and e after vowels; long and short vowels
While in medieval German each letter would have been sounded, e.g. 'lieb' would have had a diphthong in the middle, 'e' after other vowels had become silent in the sixteenth century. This is evident from the use of e after i where there never was a diphthong, e.g. the word 'diesen'. The same applies to h. In most instances a following e or h indicates a long preceding vowel, but this is not consistent, e.g. 'jhm' can stand both for modern *im* and *ihm*. Do not therefore pronounce h and e after vowels, but use long vowels as in modern German.

8. Word division and 'Zusammenschreibung'
Hyphens in the form of '=' are used frequently but not consistently to indicate the continuation of words across line-breaks; if typesetters ran out of space in a line, they would assume that the reader would be able to link words without this visual prompt. Clear single words have been joined in the transcription but the irregular use of spaces between compounds has not been normalized.

9. Capital letters
Capital letters are used as in English to indicate the beginning of new sentences and for proper names but also for emphasis in words; these have not been normalized since they can be used for highlighting key terms.

10. Syncope, apocope, and contraction
Unstressed vowels are often absent where we should expect them in NHG; this is particularly pronounced in Upper German dialects, see above, either mid-word (syncope), e.g.

*Edition* lxvii

'gsagt', 'gnug', or at word-end (apocope). Such vowel loss can cause confusion, e.g. 'gelob(e)t', which looks like a present, may stand for the preterite 'gelob(e)te'. Sometimes a consonant is lost along with a vowel, especially a repeated consonant, e.g. 'laut' for 'lautet', 'veracht' for 'verachtet', 'verstorben' for 'verstorbenen'. Vowel loss also occurs by contraction between words, e.g. 'ers' for 'er es', 'nympts' for 'nimmt es', 'zun' for 'zu den'.

11. Zero inflections and absence of ge- prefixes
Some neuter plurals have a zero-inflection in ENHG and look like singulars, e.g. 'das/die werk', 'das/die wort'. Strong adjectives in the nominative and accusative singular could also be zero-inflected, e.g. 'solch vnleidlich tyranney'.

12. Omission of auxiliaries and personal subject pronouns
The auxiliaries haben and sein are sometimes omitted, especially in subordinate clauses. Personal pronouns are also sometimes left out where they would appear in NHG.

# 4. Bibliography

The bibliography is a combination of full references for short titles used in the footnotes of the introduction and some general introductory books. This is obviously not exhaustive and is designed mainly for anglophone students of historical linguistics. Further resources are available at the Reformation editions website of the Taylorian https://editions.mml.ox.ac.uk/topics/reformation.shtml

## 1. Abbreviations

DEEP – *Database of Early English Playbooks*. Open Access.

DWb. – *Deutsches Wörterbuch*. https://woerterbuchnetz.de/?sigle=DWB. References 's.v.' (sub voce) reference the lemma which is explained.

Fnhd. Wb. – *Frühneuhochdeutsches Wörterbuch*. https://fwb-online.de/.

KJV – *The Holy Bible, Conteyning the Old Testament, and the New: Newly Translated out of the Originall tongues: & with the former Translations diligently compared and reuised, by his Maiesties speciall Comandement.* London: Robert Barker 1611. Open Access Version on biblija.net.

KG – Adalbert von Keller and Edmund Goetze: *Hans Sachs*. 26 vols., Tübingen: 1870–1908. Repr. Hildesheim: Olms 1964.

L45 – Martin Luther: *Biblia: das ist: Die gantze Heilige Schrifft: Deudsch Auffs new zugericht. D.Mart.Luth.* Wittemberg: Hans Lufft 1545. Open Access Version on biblija.net.

STC – A. W. Pollard and G. R. Redgrave (eds.) (1976–1991): *A Short-Title Catalogue of Books Printed in England, Scotland and Ireland, and of English Books Printed Abroad 1475–1640*. Second edition, revised and enlarged, begun by W. A. Jackson and F. S. Ferguson, completed by K. F. Pantzer. London: The Bibliographical Society.

VD 16 – *Verzeichnis der im deutschen Sprachbereich erschienenen Drucke des 16. Jahrhunderts.* Open Access (Full bibliographic reference for all Reformation pamphlets with linked-in digitized copies, continually updated; links: http://gateway-bayern.de/VD16+[letter]+[number]).

WA – *Martin Luther: Werke. Kritische Gesamtausgabe [Weimarer Ausgabe].* Weimar 1883 ff.

VLC – *Vulgata Clementina, 1592. Biblia Sacra juxta Vulgatam Clementinam.* M. Tweedale (ed.). http://vulsearch.sourceforge.net/html, accessed via biblija.net – the Bible on the Internet. Biblical books are given with the abbreviations used for the Vulgate.

## 2. Editions

Davidson, Clifford, Martin W. Walsh and Ton J. Broos (eds.) (2007): *Everyman and its Dutch Original, Elckerlijc.* Kalamazoo: Medieval Institute Publications.

Hahn, Reinhard (ed.) (1986): *Das handschriftliche Generalregister des Hans Sachs: Reprintausgabe nach dem Autograph 1560 des Stadtarchivs Zwickau von Hans Sachs.* Köln et al.: Böhlau.

Köhler, Reinhold (ed.) (1858): *Vier Dialoge von Hans Sachs.* Weimar: Böhlau. Open Access.

Seufert, Gerald H. (ed.) (1974): *Hans Sachs: Die Wittenbergisch Nachtigall: Spruchgedicht, vier Reformationsdialoge und das Meisterlied Das Walt got.* Stuttgart: Reclam.

Spriewald, Ingeborg (ed.) (1970): *Die Prosadialoge von Hans Sachs.* Leipzig: VEB Bibliographisches Institut.

## 3. Manuscripts

[May, Johann Gottlob] (1818): [Catalogue of Tract. Luth.] (*Catalogus autographorum Lutheri et coaevorum tam faventium ipsi, quam adversantium, aliorumque libellorum hisce temporibus scriptorum.* [Partes 1 et 2.] *Collegit ac descripsit secundum singulas lineas Joannes Gottlob May, D. D. Philosophiae ac archaeologiae Professor in Gymn. Annaeo. Aug. Vindel. 1810.*). Oxford, Bodleian Library, Library Records c. 1819 (formerly under R.6.212).

[Sotheby, Samuel (?)] (1818): 'Some Account of Dr. May's of Augsburg Collection of Tracts on the Reformation'. Bound together with May 1818. Oxford, Bodleian Library, Library Records c. 1819, fol. 3–6.

Taylor Institution Library: *Cashbook of the Finch Fund.* Oxford, Taylor Institution Library, TL 2/5/2.

Taylor Institution Library: *Register of additions to the Library (accession registers)* 1922–34. Oxford, Taylor Institution Library, TL 3/2/8.

lxx  *Bibliography*

# 4. Printed Sources

Baader, Klement Alois (1795): *Reisen durch verschiedene Gegenden Deutschlandes in Briefen*, vol. 1. Augsburg: Johann Melchior Lotter. Open Access.

[Beyschlag, Eberhard, Johann Gottlob May and Commerzienrath Bürgle] (ed.) (1812): *Verzeichnis der ansehnlichen und auserlesenen Büchersammlung des verstorbenen Herrn Geheimen Rathes Georg Wilhelm Zapf, welche 1812 am 6. des Heumonats und folgende Tage in Augsburg Lit. F. Nro. 151 in dem Lorbe'schen Gute nächst dem Katzenstadel an die Meistbiethenden verkauft werden soll*, Augsburg. Open Access.

*Bibliotheca Heberiana. Catalogue of the library of the late Richard Heber, Esq., part the second, removed from his houses in York-Street and at Pimlico, which will be sold by Auction by Messrs. Sotheby and son ...* (1834). London: Nicol. Open Access.

*Bibliotheca Heberiana. Catalogue of the library of the late Richard Heber, Esq., part the fifth, removed from his house at Pimlico, which will be sold by Mr Wheatley ...* (1835). London: Nicol. Open Access.

*Catalogue of the First Portion of the Extensive & Valuable Library of the Late Rev. John Fuller Russell, ... which will be sold by auction by Messrs. Sotheby, Wilkinson & Hodge ...* (1885). London, J. Davy & Sons.

Douce, Francis (1807): *Illustrations of Shakspeare, and of Ancient Manners: With Dissertations on the Clowns and Fools of Shakespeare; on the Collection of Popular Tales Entitled Gesta Romanorum; and on the English Morris Dance*, vol. 2. London: Longman, Hurst, Rees, and Orme. Open Access.

*Encyclopædia Britannica* (1911), 11th ed. Wikisource edition.

Gradmann, Johann Jacob (ed.) (1802): *Das gelehrte Schwaben: oder Lexicon der jetzt lebenden schwäbischen Schriftsteller*. Ravensburg: self-published. Open Access.

'Intelligence, Literary, Scientific, &c.', *The Repository of Arts, Literature, Fashions, Manufactures, &c.* Second series V, 26 (February 1, 1818), pp. 122–24. Open Access.

'Literary Notice of Dr. *May*'s Collection of Reformation Tracts; (Autographa Lutheri et Reformatorum.)', *The Gentleman's Magazine: and historical chronicle* (March 1818), pp. 208–11.

*Bibliography* lxxi

Macray, William Dunn (1890): *Annals of the Bodleian Library Oxford with a Notice of the Earlier Library of the University*. Oxford: Bodleian Library, 2nd ed. Open Access.

[May, Johann Gottlob] (ed.) (1798): *Catalogus Bibliorum quae collegit Matthias Jacobus Adamus Steinerus, b. m. pastor quondam eccles. evang. ad aedes St. Udalrici Augustae Vindel. et quae d. XXV. Novembr. MDCCIIC. aut omnia simul, aut singula plus licitantibus vendentur in aedibus Weilerianis*. Augustae Vindel[icum]: Brinnhausser. Open Access.

[May, Johann Gottlob and Gottlieb Thomas Wilhelm] (eds.) (1797): *Verzeichnis der ansehnlichen und auserlesenen Bücher- und Kunstsamlung Weiland Herrn Matthias Jacob Adam Steiners, Pfarrers an der evang. Kirche zu St. Ulrich in Augsburg, welche den 16ten October 1797 zu Augsburg in Weilerischen (ehemals Maschenbauerischen) Hause nächst dem Weinstadel an die Meistbietenden verkauft werden soll*. [Augsburg:] Brinhaußer. Open Access.

Schön, Theodor: 'Zapf, Georg Wilhelm'. *Allgemeine Deutsche Biographie* 44 (1898), pp. 693 f. Open Access.

Zapf, Georg Wilhelm (1787): *Merkwürdigkeiten der Zapfischen Bibliothek*. 2 vols. Augsburg: Christoph Friedrich Bürglen/self-published. Open Access here and here.

## 5. Secondary Literature

Arnold, Martin (1990): *Handwerker als theologische Schriftsteller: Studien zu Flugschriften der frühen Reformation (1523–1525)*. Göttingen: Vandenhoeck & Ruprecht.

Attar, Karen (ed.) (2016): *Directory of Rare Books and Special Collections in the United Kingdom and the Republic of Ireland*. London: Facet.

Bagchi, David (2016): 'Printing, Propaganda, and Public Opinion in the Age of Martin Luther' in *Oxford Research Encyclopedia of Religion*. Oxford: OUP. Open Access.

Barton, Anne (1990), *The Names of Comedy*, Oxford: OUP.

Beare, Mary (1958): 'The later dialogues of Hans Sachs', *Modern Languages Review* 53, pp. 197–210.

Bernstein, Eckhard (1993): *Hans Sachs: mit Selbstzeugnissen und Bilddokumenten*. Reinbek bei Hamburg: Rowohlt.

Blayney, Peter W. M. (2013): *The Stationers' Company and the Printers of London, 1501–1557*. Cambridge: CUP.

lxxii  *Bibliography*

Bloomfield, B. C. and Karen Potts (ed.) (1997): *A Directory of Rare Books and Special Collections in the United Kingdom and the Republic of Ireland.* London: Library Association, 2nd ed.

Bodleian Library (2024): *Rare Books. Named collections index.* Last Updated September 2, 2024. Open Access.

Clapinson, Mary (2020): *A Brief History of the Bodleian Library.* Oxford: Bodleian Library, rev. ed.

Creasman, Allyson F. (2012): *Censorship and Civic Order in Reformation Germany,1517–1648: 'Printed Poison & Evil Talk'.* London / New York: Routledge.

Drummond, Andrew (2024): *The Dreadful History and Judgement of God on Thomas Müntzer: The Life and Times of an Early German Revolutionary.* London/New York: Verso.

Freeman, Janet Ing (1990): 'Anthony Scoloker, the "Just Reckoning" Printer', and the Earliest Ipswich Printing' *Transactions of the Cambridge Bibliographical Society* Vol. 9 No. 5, pp. 476-496.

Füssel, Stephan (2019): *Gutenberg,* transl. by Peter Lewis London: Haus Publishing.

Hartmann, Charlotte (2015–16): *Hans Sachs in Oxford: Bodleian and Taylorian Library: Wittenberg Nightingale and Reformation Dialogues* https://hanssachsinoxford.wordpress.com/.

Heijting, Willem (1994): 'Early Reformation Literature from the Printing Shop of Mattheus Crom and Steven Mierdmans' *Nederlands archif voor kerkgeschiedenis/Dutch Review of Church History* Vol. 74, No. 2, pp.143-161.

Holzberg, Niklas (2021): *Hans Sachs.* Stuttgart: Kohlhammer.

Holzberg, Niklas and Horst Brunner (2020): *Hans Sachs: Ein Handbuch.* 2 vols. Berlin/Boston: de Gruyter.

Jefcoate, Graham, William A. Kelly and Karen Kloth with the Assistance of Holger Hanowell and Matthias Bauer (eds.) (2000): *Handbuch deutscher historischer Buchbestände in Europa,* vol. 10: *A Guide to Collections of Books Printed in German-speaking Countries before 1901 (or in German elsewhere). Held by Libraries in Great Britain and Ireland.* Hildesheim/Zürich/New York: Olms-Weidmann.

Kaufmann, Thomas (2022): *Die Druckmacher: Wie die Generation Luther die erste Medienrevolution entfesselte.* München: C. H. Beck.

# Bibliography    lxxiii

Kelen, Sarah A. (1999): 'Plowing the past: "Piers Protestant" and the authority of medieval literary history', *Yearbook of Langland Studies* 13, pp. 101–36.

King, John N. (1976): 'Robert Crowley's editions of Piers Plowman: A Tudor Apocalypse', *Modern Philology* 73, pp. 342–52.

———— (1982): *English Reformation Literature: The Tudor Origins of the Protestant Tradition*. Princeton: PUP.

———— (1999): 'The book-trade under Edward VI and Mary I' in *The Cambridge History of the Book in Britain*, ed. by Lotte Hellinga and J. B. Trapp, vol. 3: 1400–1557. Cambridge: CUP, pp. 164–78.

Köhler, Hans-Joachim (1996): *Bibliographie der Flugschriften des 16. Jahrhunderts. Teil 1: Das frühe 16. Jahrhundert (1501–1530)*, vol. 3. Tübingen: Bibliotheca Academica.

Krümpelmann, Maximilian: 'The History of the Taylorian Copies', in Jones / Lähnemann (2020), pp. xxxix–lxvi. Open access.

Lähnemann, Henrike and Eva Schlotheuber (2024): *The Life of Nuns. Love, Politics, and Religion in Medieval German Convents*, transl. by Anne Simon, Cambridge: Open Book Publishers. Open Access.

Micklich, Rahel (2024): 'Whose hand? Unearthing an Unknown Manuscript in the Bodleian' in *History of the Book. Exploring the World of Books at Oxford*, ed. by Henrike Lähnemann. Open Access.

Otten, Franz (1993): *mit hilff gottes zw tichten ... go zw lob vnd zw auspreittüng seines heilsamen wort: Untersuchungen zur Reformationsdichtung des Hans Sachs*. Göppingen: Kümmerle Verlag.

———— (1994): 'Die Reformationsdialoge des Hans Sachs. Revidierte Chronologie und ihre Auswirkungen auf das "Bild" des Nürnberger Dichters der Reformation' in Dieter Merzbacher et al.: *500 Jahre Hans Sachs: Handwerker, Dichter, Stadtbürger*. Wiesbaden: Harrassowitz, pp. 33–37.

Page, Christopher (2015): *The Guitar in Tudor England: A Social and Musical History of Musical Performance and Reception*. Cambridge: CUP.

Pegg, Michael A. (1973): *A Catalogue of German Reformation Pamphlets (1516–1546) in Libraries of Great Britain and Ireland*. Baden-Baden: Valentin Koerner.

Pollard, Albert Frederick (1897): 'Scoloker, Anthony (fl. 1548)', in *Dictionary of National Biography*, vol. 51, ed. by Sidney Lee, pp. 4 f. Open Access.

## lxxiv Bibliography

Ranisch, Salomon (1765): *Historischkritische Lebensbeschreibung Hanns Sachsens ehemals berühmten Meistersängers zu Nürnberg*. Altenburg: Richter. Open Access.

Reske, Christoph (2015): *Die Buchdrucker des 16. und 17. Jahrhunderts im deutschen Sprachgebiet. Auf der Grundlage des gleichnamigen Werkes von Josef Benzig*. Wiesbaden: Harrassowitz, 2nd ed.

Rettelbach, Johannes (2019): *Die nicht-dramatischen Dichtungen des Hans Sachs: Grundlagen, Texttypen, Interpretationen*. Wiesbaden: Reichert.

Rößler, Hole: 'Das nicht mehr schöne Bildnis. Druckgraphische Porträts als Medien der Diffamierung in der Frühen Neuzeit', *Medienphantasie und Medienreflexion in der Frühen Neuzeit. Festschrift für Jörg Jochen Berns*, ed. by Thomas Rahn and Hole Rößler. Wiesbaden 2018, pp. 79–113.

Schreyl, Karl Heinz (1976): *Die Welt des Hans Sachs: 400 Holzschnitte des 16. Jahrhunderts*, ed. by the Stadtgeschichtliche Museen. Nürnberg: Hans Carl.

Schuster, Susanne (2019): *Dialogflugschriften der frühen Reformationszeit: Literarische Fortführung der Disputation und Resonanzräume reformatorischen Denkens*. Göttingen: Vandenhoeck & Ruprecht.

Steele, Robert (1910): *A Bibliography of Royal Proclamations of the Tudor and Stuart Sovereigns and of Others Published Under Authority 1485–1714*, vol. 1. Oxford: Clarendon Press. Open Access.

Valkema Blouw, Paul (1992): 'The Van Oldenborch and Vanden Merberghe pseudonyms or Why Frans Fraet had to die', *Quaerendo 22*, pp. 165–81 and 245–72.

Warner, Lawrence (2014): 'Plowman traditions in late medieval and early modern writing' in *The Cambridge Companion to Piers Plowman*, ed. by Andrew Cole and Andrew Galloway. Cambridge: CUP, pp. 198–213.

Warnke, Martin (1984): *Cranachs Luther: Entwürfe für ein Image*. Frankfurt a. M.: Fischer.

Weller, Emil (1868): *Der Volksdichter Hans Sachs und seine Dichtungen: Eine Bibliographie*. Nürnberg: Jacob Sichling. Open Access.

Wiggins, Martin (2012): *British Drama 1533–1642: A Catalogue*, vol. 1. Oxford: OUP.

Wortham, C. J. (1981): 'Everyman and the Reformation', *Parergon 29*, pp. 23–31.

Zlatar, Antoinina Bevan (2011): *Reformation Fictions:Polemical Protestant Dialogues in Elizabethan England*. Oxford: OUP.

# Bibliography   lxxv

## 6. Taylor Editions: Reformation Pamphlets

Oxford: Taylor Institution Library
Treasures of the Taylorian, Series 1: Reformation Pamphlets

Jones, Howard (ed.) (2017): *Martin Luther: Sendbrief vom Dolmetschen. An Open Letter on Translation*. (First edition of the text with a freer translation). Open Access.

Jones, Howard, Martin Keßler, Henrike Lähnemann and Christina Ostermann (eds.) (2018*): Martin Luther: Sermon von Ablass und Gnade, 95 Thesen. Sermon on Indulgences and Grace and the 95 Theses*. Open Access.

Jones, Howard and Henrike Lähnemann (eds.) (2020): *Martin Luther: Von der Freiheit eines Christenmenschen. On Christian Freedom*. Open Access.

Wareham, Edmund, Ulrich Bubenheimer and Henrike Lähnemann (eds.) (2021): *Martin Luther: Passional Christi und Antichristi. Passional of Christ and Antichrist*. Open Access.

Jones, Howard and Henrike Lähnemann (eds.) (2022): *Martin Luther: Ein Sendbrief vom Dolmetschen und Fürbitte der Heiligen. An Open Letter on Translation and the Intercession of Saints*. 2nd ed. Open Access.

Gieseler, Florian, Henrike Lähnemann and Timothy Powell (eds.) (2023): *Martin Luther: 'Mönchkalb' and 'Ursache und Antwort' Two Anti-Monastic Pamphlets from 1523*. Open Access here and here.

## 7. Bible Quotations

Biblical books are quoted in the abbreviations established for the Vulgate. The list gives the Latin names of the books and the titles established by Martin Luther for his Bible translation.

OT (Old Testament / Altes Testament)

Gn (Genesis / Das erste buch Mose), Ex (Exodus / Das ander buch Mose), Lv (Leviticus / Das dritte buch Mose), Nm (Numeri / Numbers / Das vierde buch Mose), Dt (Deuteronomium / Deuteronomy / Das fünffte buch Mose), Ios (Joshua / Josua),
Idc (Iudices / Judges / Der Richter), Rt (Ruth), 1–2 Sm (Samuel), 3–4 Rg (Regum / Kings / Der König), 1–2 Par (Paralipomenon /

## lxxvi  *Bibliography*

Chronicles / Chronica), 1 Esr (Esra / Ezra), 2 Esr (Ezrae secundus / Nehemiah / Nehemia), Est (Hester / Esther),

Iob (Job / Hiob), Ps (Psalmi / Psalms / Psalter), Prv (Proverbiorum / Proverbs / Sprüche Salomonis), Ecl (Ecclesiastes / Prediger Salomonis), Ct (Canticum Canticorum / Song of Songs / Hohelied Salomonis),

Is (Isaiae / Isaiah / Jesaia), Ier (Jeremiah / Jeremia), Ez (Ezekiel / Hesekiel), Dn (Daniel), Os (Osee / Hosea), Ioel (Joel), Amos (Amos), Abd (Abdias / Obadiah / ObadJa), Ion (Jonah / Jona), Mi (Micha / Micah), Na (Nahum), Hab (Habakkuk / Habacuc), So (Sofoniae / Zephaniah / Zephanja), Agg (Aggei / Haggai), Za (Zechariah / Sacharja), Mal (Malachi / Maleachi), Idt (Judith), Sap (Sapientiae Salomonis / Book of Wisdom / Das Buch der Weisheit), Tb (Tobia / Tobit), Sir (Ecclesiasticus / Book of Sirach / Jesus Syrach), Bar (Baruch), 1–2 Mcc (Maccabeorum / Maccabees)

NT (New Testament / Newes Testament)

Mt (Mattheus / Matthew), Mc (Marcus / Mark), Lc (Lucas / Luke), Io (Johannis / John), Act (Actuum Apostolorum / Acts of the Apostles / Der Aposteln Geschicht),

Rm 1–2 (ad Romanos / Romans / an die Rŏmer), 1–2 Cor (ad Corinthios / Corinthians / an die Corinther), Gal (ad Galatas / Galatians / an die Galater), Eph (ad Ephesios / Ephesians / an die Epheser), Phil (ad Philippenses / Philippians / an die Philipper), Col 1–2 (ad Colossenses / Colossians / an die Colosser), Th (ad Thessalonicenses / Thessalonians / an die Thessalonicher), 1–2 Tim (ad Timotheum / Timothy / an Timotheum), Tit (ad Titum / Titus / an Titum), Phlm (ad Philemonem / an Philemon), 1–2 Pt (Petri / of Peter / S. Peters), 1–3 Io (Iohannis / of John / S. Johannis), Hbr (ad Hebraeos / Hebrews / an die Ebreer), Iac (Iacobi / of James / Jacobi), Iud (Iudae / of Jude / Jude),

Apc (Apocalypsis / Revelation / Offenbarung Johannis)

# Edition, Translation, Commentary 'Canon and Cobbler'

The edition is a semi-diplomatic transcription of the 16th-century German, Dutch, and English version of Hans Sachs's first Reformation dialogue 'Canon and Cobbler'. Abbreviations have been resolved and marked in *italics*. r- and s-forms have been standardized but not u/v- and i/j-forms. The original punctuation has been kept but the text has been divided into paragraphs according to speaker. On the printing history of the various editions, see the introduction.

## a) German: Disputation zwischen einem Chorherrn...

Taylor Institution Library, Arch. 8° G. 1524 (26)
*Diſputacion zwiſchen ainem Chor|herʒenn vnnd Schüchmacher | dariñ das wort gottes vnd ein recht Chriſtllich weſen verfochtten wirtt.*
[Augsburg: Melchior Ramminger,] 1524.
(Weller 1868: 17(d); KG, vol. 22: 7c; Pegg 1973: 3555; Köhler 1996: 3992; VD16 S 216.)
Collation: A–C4, 4°.

Transcription: Kezia Fender & Charlotte Hartmann, translation & footnotes: Henrike Lähnemann with support by Howard Jones, Viviane Arnold, Montgomery Powell, Lucian Shepherd, & Nina Unland. Online https://editions.mml.ox.ac.uk/editions/dialogue/

The commentary consists of two sets of footnotes. Those on the edition side (left-hand pages) are not a full linguistic analysis, but are designed to help readers understand Luther's German and typographical features, comparing Early New High German (ENHG) forms with modern (NHG) usage and English parallels. The footnotes to the English translation (right-hand side) include biblical references and other background information.

## 2 *'Chorherr und Schuhmacher' (1524) German Edition*

(a1r) Disputacion zwischen ainem Chorherrenn vnnd Schüchmacher[1] darin*n* das wort gottes vnd ein recht Cristlich wesen verfochtten[2] wirtt.

Hanns Sachs M D XXiiij.

Ich sag euch / wa[3] dise schweige*n* / so werde*n* die stein schreie*n*. lu*c*e.[4] 19

---

[1] = NHG Schuhmacher, 'shoemaker', used interchangeably with 'Schuster', 'cobbler'.
[2] 'verfechten' = literally 'fencing for sth.', used metaphorically for defending.
[3] = NHG 'wo', here in the sense of 'when, if'. Hans Sachs quotes verbatim from Martin Luther's translation of the New Testament (see bibliography) but he and / or the typesetter of the dialogues frequently use dialectal or more colloquial word forms than the Wittenberg printers of the September and December Testament who come from a different region and are also aiming for a wider audience than Hans Sachs. See the footnotes on the right hand side for the version of the last Bible published during Luther's life time (L45) and, for reference, the King James Version (KJV).
[4] Biblical references which are usually shortened are expanded in parallel with other references. Names of Biblical books are given in the genitive because the full phrase would be 'the book of' or here 'the gospel according to / of', i.e. 'luce' is the medieval Latin form of the genitive, reducing the 'æ' to 'e'.

*Translation* 3

(a1r) Disputation between a canon and a shoemaker,
in which the word of God and a truly Christian existence
are championed.

Hans Sachs, 1524

I tell you: if these stayed silent, the stones would cry out.
(Luke 19)[5]

The woodcut is a faithful copy of the first edition (see Ill. 6),
although some of the lines are less elegant owing to the copying
process, particularly in the facial features. The cobbler has an
artisan's headgear, similar to that worn e.g. by Michael Wolgemut
in Dürer's 1516 portrait of his teacher, to keep the hair out of his
face and a tunic with a soft collar over a long-sleeved shirt and
presumably stockings. On his belt is a money purse which is
buttoned up. His feet which are in a walking pose, as if he is just
arriving from the left, are in low-heeled, non-pointed black shoes.
He holds one of the slippers in each hand and faces the canon who
is slightly shorter and stockier than him. The canon wears a closed
floor-length gown with long wide sleeves and a soft cap on his head
over a chubby face with a hint of a double chin. He is adopting a
disputatory stance, with index fingers extended. Behind him, in the
archway of the house facade, stands the cook who mirrors the
cobbler in that she wears a short-sleeved over-garment over a long
under-skirt; the latter is visible because, with her crossed arms, she
is lifting up the over-skirt to her belt, indicating that she is – like
the cobbler – in work gear.

---

[5] On the biblical quotations and abbreviations, see the bibliography. The quotation
here comes from Christ's answer to the Pharisees calling on him to rebuke his
disciples: Lc 19.40 *Er antwortet / vnd sprach zu jnen / Jch sage euch / Wo diese werden
schweigen / so werden die Steine schreien.* (L45). And he answered and said unto them,
I tell you that, if these should hold their peace, the stones would immediately cry
out. (KJV).

# 4 *'Chorherr und Schuhmacher' (1524) German Edition*

(a1v) \*\*\*blank\*\*\*

(a2r) *Schůster.*[6] BOnus[7] dies[8] Kŏchin.

Kŏchin. Semper quies[9] Seyt[10] wylkum*m*[11] mayster[12] Hanns.

Schůster[13]. Got danck euch / wa ist der herr?

Kŏchin. Er ist im Sum*m*erhauß / Ich wil im[14] růffen / Herr / herr der Schůchmacher ist da.

Khorherr.[15] A[16] / Beneueneritis[17] mayster Hans.

---

[6] The indication of the speaker is left out here since the first initial is reserved for the start of the dialogue proper.

[7] Capitalisation of the second letter because the first letter is a woodcut initial and not part of the line.

[8] Latin expression to indicate the learning of the cobbler, literally 'good day'. An established greeting formula in contemporary Latin phrasebooks, prompting the following rhyming answer by the cook.

[9] Literally '[may you] always [have] quiet/rest/peace'.

[10] = NHG 'Seid'; y/i are used interchangeably; 'd' is written as 't' to reflect the terminal devoicing of voiced plosives (b, d, g become p, t, k). The cook employs the polite form of 'ihrzen' (you in the plural) which is also used by the cobbler to address her. The civilized exchange sets the scene, and contrasts with the disparaging language of the canon who later resorts to swear words and curses.

[11] = NHG 'willkommen'. Hans Sachs and / or the printer reflect the spoken apocope of endings such as 'en' after nasal. Alternatively, the nasal bar could be resolved as 'n' to stand for the final consonant since the distribution of double and single consonant (whether 'wilkumen' is spelled with one or two 'l's and one or two 'm's) is irregular.

[12] ENHG 'Meister' = title for a master craftsman, artisan, cf. 'Meistersinger'.

[13] 'Schuster' and 'Schu(c)hmacher' are used interchangeably in the dialogue. DWb s.v. 'schuster': 'das wort ist eine bastardbildung aus schuh und lat. sutor, die auf das deutsche sprachgebiet (hd. nd. nl.) beschränkt ist und etwa seit dem 13. jahrh. auftaucht'. 'Schuster' nearly died out in the later ENHG period, just surviving as a frequent surname and in proverbs such as 'Schuster bleib bei deinem Leisten' which is later also referenced in this dialogue.

[14] = NHG 'ihm'. 'rufen' in ENHG + dat.

[15] c- and k-spellings are interchangeable. 'chorherr' literally: lord of the choir.

[16] Sachs uses interjections to convey the orality of the dialogue: a, ey, ja, nun, o, pi, pa, pu. For 'a' as expression of happy surprise, see DWb s.v., a nearly lyrical first entry by the brothers Grimm for their dictionary.

[17] 2 ps. pl. future perfect of Latin 'benevenire', to be welcome. The canon repeats the welcome phrase of the cook in Latin, also using the formal plural form.

*Translation* 5

(a1r) \*\*\*blank\*\*\*
(a2r) Cobbler: Good day, Cook!
Cook: Peace to you! Welcome, Master Hans![18]
Cobbler: God bless you! Where is your master?
Cook: He is in the summerhouse – I'll call him. Master, master! The shoemaker is here!
Canon[19]: Ah, welcome, Master Hans.

---

[18] Hans Sachs uses throughout the dialogues the 'Hans' characters as his alter ego. The level of literacy which the cobbler is given corresponds to Sachs's education. Sachs would have learned Latin from textbooks which had this type of phrases at the beginning. The opening exchange is listed as 'verba responsionis' (words of answer) in the grammar book 'Es tu scholaris', see also Fischart, Geschichtsklitterung, Part No. 131. 'Dann darumb grüsset man Bona dies, daß der ander antworte semper quies' (the reason for greeting somebody with 'bona dies' is to have the other respond with 'semper quies'). Sachs also uses this pair of greeting formulae to comic effect in an exchange between Till Eulenspiegel and a priest in his drama 'Der Eulenspiegel mit den blinden' (4 September 1553).

[19] Canons are higher-ranking priests who are part of the chapter of a cathedral or, as is the case in Nuremberg, a large and influential city church, following a rule of life, but not in a monastic community, a member of the so-called secular clergy. Nuremberg had two influential and well-endowed parish churches in the city: the older parish of Sebald north of the river Pegnitz, and the more affordable newer development of Lorenz south of the river. Hans Sachs's workshop was in the Sebald district, near the central market place.

## 6 'Chorherr und Schuhmacher' (1524) German Edition

Schůster. Deo gratias.[20]
Khorherr. Was bringt yr mir die pantoffel[21]?
Schůster. Ya / ich gedacht / yr wert schon in die kirchen gangen.
Chorherr. Nayn / ich bin hynden im summerhauß geweßt[22] / vnd hab abgedroschen.[23]
Schůster. Wie hond[24] ir gedroschen?
Chorherr. Ya / ich hab mein horas[25] gebeet[26] / vnnd hon[27] alemit meiner nachtigal zů essen geben /
Schůster. Herr was hond ir für eyn nachtigall / Singtt sy noch.
Chorherr. O nain / es ist zů spatt im jare.
Schůster. Ich waiß ein schůchmacher Der hat ein nachtigal / die hatt erst angefanngenn zů singen.

---

[20] The cobbler tops the canon by not only thanking him in Latin, but also using a liturgical phrase, the response to 'Benedicamus Domino' (Let us bless the Lord) at Vespers or Masses said without the 'Gloria in excelsis'.

[21] ENHG for an indoor shoe without a heel; loanword (end of the 15th cent.) from French 'pantoufle'; the etymology is unclear; Humanists of the 16th cent. tried to declare it a Greek loan word from *pantóphellos* ('made all of cork'). Here used in an ironic way for comfortable footwear to indicate the indulgent lifestyle of the canon.

[22] 'gewest' is a central and upper German variant from the 13th cent. to the older form 'gewesen' which is the only form surviving into NHG. Hans Sachs uses it alongside 'gewesen' and 'gesein', see DWb. s.v. I.u.α.

[23] 'dreschen' in the sense of 'mechanical speaking' is preserved in NHG 'abgedroschen' meaning an empty phrase or empty talk. Secular clergy, the 'chorherren', are accused of this also in other early modern texts, e.g. in the German translation of Gargantua, 22a (quoted after DWb s.v. 'chorherrisch'): 'schlappart nit auf chorherrisch die wort in euch, wie der hund die sup, sondern kauet und widerkauet sie wie die küh' (don't slobber up words in the manner of canons like the dog its soup, but rather chew and ruminate them like cows).

[24] = NHG 'habt'; regional dialect of 'o' for 'a'.

[25] Latin acc. pl. from 'hora', 'hour'. The canon as member of the clergy is obliged to keep the Divine Office with the 'Hours', the eight prayer-times of Prime, Matins, Lauds, Terce, Sext, None, Vespers, Compline, although these are frequently run together/prayed back to back.

[26] = apocopated form of 'gebetet' with double e marking the length of the vowel.

[27] = NHG 'habe', based on the MHG alternative form of 'hân' for 'haben', again with 'o' instead of 'a'.

*Translation* 7

Cobbler: Thanks be to God!

Canon: Are you bringing me my slippers?

Cobbler: Yes, I thought you had already left for church.

Canon: No, I've been at the back in the summerhouse and been threshing[28].

Cobbler: What do you mean, you have been threshing?

Canon: Indeed, I've prayed my Hours and fed my nightingale at the same time.

Cobbler: Sir, what sort of nightingale do you have? Is it still singing?

Canon: Oh no, it's too late in the year for that.

Cobbler: I know a shoemaker with a nightingale that has just begun to sing.[29]

---

[28] See the early modern Dutch ('afgerabbelt' = 'unwound') and early modern English ('mumbled') equivalents which show that the meaning is not a thorough process (as modern English 'trash out' would be), but indicating carelessness; a more idiomatic rendering might be 'reeled off' or 'rattled off'.

[29] Reference to the first Reformation publication by Hans Sachs in the same year, the 'Spruchgedicht' (epic poem) 'Wittenbergisch Nachtigall' which celebrated Martin Luther as the nightingale singing at dawn, with an allegorical framework of church affairs thinly disguised as different animals, not very complimentary to the Catholic opponents of Luther – Pope Leo (Latin for 'lion') appears as lion etc. The ironic strategy of having his alter ego protagonist, the cobbler Hans, talk about his creator, the cobbler Hans Sachs, must have amused and delighted the local readership. The publication was a huge success, see Introduction.

# 8  'Chorherr und Schuhmacher' (1524) German Edition

Chor*herr*. Ey der teuffel hol den schůster / mit sampt seiner Nachtigal / wie hat er den allerhayligisten vater den Bapst / die hailige*n* vetter[30] / vn*d* vns wirdige herren außgeholhipt[31] / wie ein holhipbůb.

Schůst*er*. Ey / herr fart schonn[32] / Er hat doch nur ewern gotzdienst / leer / gebot vn*d* eynkom*m*en / de*m* gmainen man*n* / angezaygt / vn*d* nur schlecht[33] oben vberhyn / ist dan*n* solches ewer wesen / holhüpel[34] werck.

Chor*herr*. Was get es aber solchs vnser wesen den tollen[35] schůster ane?

Schůst*er*. Es steet Exodi[36] am xxiij. So du deines feyndes Esel vnder dem last sihest ligen / nit laß in / sonder hilff im / Soll dan*n* eyn getåuffter christ / seinem brůder nit helffen / so er in sech[37] ligen inn der beschwert seiner gewyssen?

Chor*herr*. Er solt aber die gaistlichen vnnd geweychten[38] nit dareyn gemengt han (der Eselkopff) die wissen vor wol / was sünd ist.

---

[30] The list goes down the church hierarchy, the 'heilige Väter' meaning the cardinals and bishops.

[31] MHG 'hole hipe' = hollow baked roll; 'holhipen' = insult; based on the market criers selling baked good. 'holhipbub': somebody crying out at a market to sell baked goods.

[32] Imp. of 'faren' simply means 'to be, to behave'; 'schon' = NHG 'schonend', gentle, soft; idiomatic way of saying: take it easy, stay calm, move with care, see DWb s.v. 'fahren' 11.

[33] Adv. for 'schlicht' = simple.

[34] As above = publicly decried work.

[35] ENHG 'toll' = mad (as in 'Tollwut' = rabies or 'Tollhaus' = madhouse).

[36] Latin genitive of 'Exodus'. Here and in the following quotations from the Bible (except for the letters) the genitive is used since this is an elliptic construction for 'Liber Exodi' ('the book of Exodus') etc.

[37] = NHG 'sähe'.

[38] = NHG 'Geweihten', those who have received the 'Weihe' (ordination, one of the seven Catholic sacraments), here used as a double formula for clergy, incorporating both those in religious orders (monks / nuns) and secular clergy (bishops / priests / deacons / the minor orders).

*Translation* 9

Canon: Ah, the devil carry off that cobbler along with his nightingale! Oh how he decries the most holy father, the pope, the holy fathers and us worthy clergymen like a market crier!

Cobbler: Come on, Sir, calm down! He has only been explaining your church services, teachings, commandments and income to the common man, and even so only scratched the surface. Are your affairs not more than a marketing stunt?

Canon: But how do our affairs concern the mad shoemaker?

Cobbler: Exodus 23 states: If you were to see that your enemy's donkey is laid low by the weight of its burden, do not abandon it, but help it![39] Should not a baptised Christian then help his brother, if he saw him laid low, burdened with a bad conscience?

Canon: But he (this donkey-head) should not have involved the clergy and those who are ordained in this, for they already know full well what sin is.

---

[39] Ex 23.5 *Wenn du des / der dich hasset / esel sihest vnter seiner last ligen / Hüt dich vnd las jn nicht / sondern verseume gern das deine vmb seinen willen.* (L45). *If thou see the ass of him that hateth thee lying under his burden, and wouldest forbear to help him, thou shalt surely help with him.* (KJV).

## 10 *'Chorherr und Schuhmacher' (1524) German Edition*

Schůster. Seynd[40] sy aber sündigen / So spricht Ezechiel xxxiij. Syhest du deynen brůder sündigen / so straff in / oder ich wil sein blůt von deinen henden fodern / der halb soll vnd můß ein geteuffter seinen sündigen Brůder straffen er sey geweicht oder nit.
Chorherr. Seyt ir Euangelisch.[41]
Schůster. Ya /
Chorherr. Habt ir nit gelesen ym

---

[40] ENHG 'seind' = 'seit' in the sense of 'since'.

[41] The term 'evangelisch', literally 'conforming to the Gospel (Evangelium)', becomes pragmatically specified in the early 1520s to define those who followed the Reformation motto of *sola scriptura* (Scripture as the only guideline), equivalent to modern English 'Protestant', Fnhd. Wb. s.v. 4. The term 'evangelical' which, in the 16th century, was the English equivalent of 'evangelisch', later came to denote a specific form of low church or Pietist Protestantism which was back-translated into 20th cent. German as 'evangelikal'.

*Translation*  11

Cobbler: Yet if they were to sin, Ezekiel 33 states: If you see your
   brother sinning, you must punish him, or I will demand his blood
   from your hands![42] So all those who are baptised shall and must
   chastise their sinning brother, ordained or not.
Canon: Are you a Protestant?
Cobbler: Yes, I am.
Canon: Well, haven't you read in

---

[42] A loose paraphrase of the biblical passage which again emphasizes the 'brotherly'
nature of chastizing, replacing the biblical 'wicked' or 'godless' with a sinning
'brother', Ez 33.8 *Wenn ich nu zu dem Gottlosen sage / Du Gottloser must des todes
sterben / Vnd du sagst jm solchs nicht / Das sich der Gottlose warnen lasse / fur seinem
wesen / So wird wol der Gottlose vmb seines gottlosen wesens willen sterben / Aber sein
blut wil ich von deiner hand foddern.* (L45). When I say unto the wicked, O wicked
man, thou shalt surely die; if thou dost not speak to warn the wicked from his way,
that wicked man shall die in his iniquity; but his blood will I require at thine hand.
(KJV).

## 12 'Chorherr und Schuhmacher' (1524) German Edition

(a2v) Euangelio Mathei am vij. richtet nit so werdt ir nit gericht Aber ir Lutherischen[43] nempt solche sprüch nit zů hertzen[44] / sůcht in auch nit nach[45] / wenn[46] sy sein wider euch.

Schůster. straffen[47] vnd richtten ist zwayerlay / wir vndersteen[48] vnns nit zů richten (welches allayn got zůgehört / wie Paulus sagt zůn Römern am xiiij. Nyemant sol einem andern seinen knecht richten &c.) Sonder ermanen vnd straffen / wie got durch den prophetten Esaiam am lviij. spricht / Schrey / hor nitt auff / Er-höch[49] dein stymm wie ein busan[50] zů uerkünden meinem volck sein missethat &c.

Chorherr. Es steet auch Exodi. xxij. du solt den obern nit schmehen in deinem volck.

Schůster. Wer ist denn der oberst im volck / ist nit der Kayser / vnd nachmals Fürsten Grauen mit sampt der Ritterschafft[51] / vnd weltlicher oberhand[52]?

Chorherr. Nayn / der bapst ist eyn vicarius Christi[53] / darnach die cardinel bischoffe[54] / mit sampt dem gantzen gaistlichen stand /

---

[43] The canon uses 'lutherisch' (Lutheran) synonymously with 'evangelisch'. In the later dialogues, Sachs polemically plays 'evangelisch' off against 'lutherisch', see the second dialogue where the answer to 'are you *lutherisch*?' is 'no, I am *evangelisch*'.

[44] 'zu Herzen nehmen', literally 'to take to heart' in the sense of 'taking it seriously with body, mind, and soul'.

[45] ENHG 'nachsuchen' = 'to investigate, seriously consider', = NHG 'untersuchen'.

[46] 'wenn' here = MHG 'wanne' (causal, not conditional); NHG = denn.

[47] ENHG 'strafen' in older sense of 'criticize publicly' rather than 'punish'.

[48] ENHG 'sich unterstehen' = 'to undertake rashly'.

[49] ENHG 'erhöhen' = NHG 'erheben', 'to lift'.

[50] = NHG 'Posaune'. From Latin 'buccina' via Old French 'buisine' into MHG 'busûne'. Since Luther's Bible translation 'Posaune' has become the established term; see the quotation from the 1545 Bible.

[51] ENHG 'Ritterschaft', literally 'knightage', landed gentry as a social class between the higher nobility and the common people.

[52] 'oberhand' literally means those who have the upper hand = NHG Obrigkeit.

[53] Latin title for the pope, literally 'the vicar (i.e. deputy, representative) of Christ'.

[54] Not NHG 'Kardinalbischöfe', bishops with the powers of cardinals but two different ranks, counting down from the pope via the cardinals and the bishops to the 'normal' clergy. In the Dutch and English versions these are also two terms.

(a2v) Matthew's gospel, chapter 7: Do not judge, and you shall not be judged.[55] But you Lutherans clearly do not take such teachings to heart, and do not even try to fully understand them, as they go against what you stand for.

Cobbler: Chastising and judging are two different things. We do not presume to judge (which is the preserve of God himself alone, as Paul states in Romans 14: nobody should judge another's servant etc.[56]) but rather warn and chastise them, as God says through the prophet Isaiah: Shout, never stop! Raise your voice like a trombone to make known to my people their transgression etc.[57]

Canon: It also states in Exodus 22: Do not rail against the ruler of your people.[58]

Cobbler: But who is this 'ruler of the people'? Is it not the emperor, and after him the princes, the dukes, right down to the nobility and the secular authorities?

Canon: No, of course not. The pope is Christ's representative, followed by cardinals, bishops together with all the clergy

---

[55] Mt 7.1 1 *RJchtet nicht / Auff das jr nicht gerichtet werdet.* (L45). *Judge not, that ye be not judged.* (KJV).

[56] Rom 14.4 *Wer bistu / das du einen frembden Knecht richtest? Er stehet oder fellet seinem HErrn / Er mag aber wol auffgerichtet werden / Denn Gott kan jn wol auffrichten.* (L45). *Who art thou that judgest another man's servant? to his own master he standeth or falleth. Yea, he shall be holden up: for God is able to make him stand.* (KJV).

[57] Is 58.1 *RVffe getrost / schone nicht / Erhebe deine stim wie eine Posaune / vnd verkündige meinem Volck jr vbertretten / vnd dem hause Jacob jre sunde.* (L45). *Cry aloud, spare not, lift up thy voice like a trumpet, and shew my people their transgression, and the house of Jacob their sins.* (KJV).

[58] Ex 22.27 *DEn Göttern soltu nicht fluchen / Vnd den Obersten in deinem Volck soltu nicht lestern.* (L45). Ex 22.28 *Thou shalt not revile the gods, nor curse the ruler of thy people.* (KJV)

14 *'Chorherr und Schuhmacher' (1524) German Edition*

vo*n* de*n* steet in gaistlichen rechten. C. Solite. de maioritate et obedientia[59] Sy bedeutten die son*n* / vnd der weltlich gewalt bedeut de*n* mon Deßhalb ist der bapst vil mechtiger dan*n* der Kaiser / welcher im sein fûß küssen mûß.

Schûst*er*. Ist der bapst ein solcher gewelttiger herr / so ist der gewißlich kain Stathalter Christi[60] / wan*n* Christus spricht Joan*ni*. am. xviij. Mein reych ist nit von diser welt / vnd Joan*ni* .vi. Floch cristus da man in zûm künig machen wolt / Auch sprach cristus zû seinen junger / Luce. xxii. Die weltlichen küng herschen / vnd die gewaltigen haißt ma*n* gnedige herren / ir aber nit also / der grŏst vnder euch sol seyn wie der jüngst[61] / vnd der fürnemest wie der diener / Deßhalb der bapst vn*d* ir gaistlichen / seyt nur dyener der christlichen gemain / wa ir a*n*derst[62] auß got seyt / der halb mag man euch wol straffen.

Chor*h*err. Ey der bapst vnd die seinen / sein nit schuldig gottes gepotten gehorsam zû sein / wie inn gaistlichen rechten stet. C. Solite de maioritate et obedientia / auß dem schleußt sich[63] / das der bapst kain sünder ist / sonder der allerhayligist / derhalb ist er vnstraffpar.

Schûst*er*. Es spricht Joan*nis* .i. cano-

---

[59] Canon law is quoted in Latin with the established abbreviations such as 'c.' for 'capitulum'.

[60] The cobbler uses the regular German translation for the term 'vicarius Christi', meaning that he understood exactly the canonical term.

[61] 'jüngst' can mean 'youngest' or 'newest / latest' as in the phrase 'Jüngstes Gericht' (Last Judgement).

[62] The edition has a typo of 'u' instead of 'n' 'auderst'. Here ENHG 'anders(t)' in the sense of Fnhd. Wb. s.v. 7 'under the condition that'.

[63] ENHG 'sich schließen' = NHG 'sich erschließen, schlussfolgern', 'it can be concluded'.

about whom it is written in canon law, in the chapter *Solite de majoritate et obedientia*: These stand for the sun, and the secular powers for the moon.[64] Therefore, the pope is far more powerful than the emperor, who has to kiss his feet.[65]

Cobbler: If the pope is such a powerful lord, then he is surely not a representative for Christ on earth. For Christ says in John 18, My kingdom is not of this world;[66] and in John 6, Christ fled when people wanted to make him King.[67] Christ also said to his disciples, Luke 22: The earthly Kings have dominion and the mighty are called gracious Lords; but you are not to be like that; the greatest among you should be like the least, and the most noble like the servant.[68] Therefore, the pope and you clergymen are but servants of the Christian community, if you are truly of God. Because of that, you may well be chastised.

Canon: Well, the pope and his clergymen are not bound to obey God's commandments, as written in canon law in the chapter *Solite de marioritate et obedientia*. From this it follows that the pope is not a sinner, but rather the holiest of all; therefore he cannot be chastised.

Cobbler: The first letter of John as quoted in the first chapter of canon law

---

[64] In Canon Solitae. [Friedberg, Vol II, I.33.6.] *Imperium non praeest sacerdotio...* 'The government does not preside over the priesthood, but it is under it, and it is bound to obey it. Or in this way: A bishop should not be subject to princes, but should preside over them.' The practice of the canon to counter the Bible with quotations from canon law is reminiscent of the 'Passional Christi und Antichristi' (1522), where on every left hand side Christ is shown with biblical quotations and the pope (identified with the Antichrist) on the right hand side with quotations from canon law, see Taylor Editions: Reformation Series 4.

[65] The pope having his feet kissed is polemically juxtaposed with Christ washing the feet of the apostles in the 'Passional Christi und Antichristi', fol. 4r.

[66] Jo 18.36.

[67] The same combination of Bible verses is also in the 'Passional', A1v, where Christ in the wilderness is juxtaposed with the pope as a kind of warlord, leading an army.

[68] Lc 22.25–26.

## 16  'Chorherr und Schuhmacher' (1524) German Edition

(a3r)nica .j. Wer sagt / er sey on sünd / der ist ein lugner / deshalb ist
der bapst ein sünder oder lugner / vnd nicht der allerhailigest
sonder zů straffen.

Chorherr. Ey lieber / vnd wenn der Bapst so bőß wer / das er vnzålich
menschenn mit grossem hauffen zům teuffel fůret / dőrst[69] in doch
nyemant straffen / das stet geschriben in vnserm rechten / dis. xl.
si papa / wie gefelt euch das

Schůster. Ey so stett im Euangelio Mathei. xviij. So deyn brůder
sündiget wider dich / so gee hin vnd straff in zwyschen dir vnd
im / hőrt er dich / so hastu sein seel gewunnen / Eussert sich[70] der
bapst dann solchs hailsamen wercks?

Chorherr. Ist dann sollichs brůderlich gestrafft / Also am tag
außzůschreyenn?

Schůster. Ey es volgt weytter im text / wa dich dein brůder nit hőrt /
so nymm noch ein oder zwen zů dir / hőrt er dich noch nitt so
sags der gemain[71] / hőrt er die gemain auch nit / so laß in geen wie
ain hayden / wie da her domine[72]?

Chorherr. Ey liber was ists dann nutz / wenn ir vns gleich lanng auß
schreyt? wie hollüpper / wir kern vns doch nichts daran / wir
halten[73] vns des Decretals.

---

[69] ENHG '(ge-)turren' = 'to dare'.

[70] ENHG 'sich (ent-)äußern' + gen. = 'to dispense with'.

[71] ENHG 'die gemein(de)' = 'community' in general or '(religious) congregation'
more specifically. The short form survives in NHG in phrases such as 'Gemeinwohl'
= 'the common good' and 'gemeinsam' = 'together'.

[72] Latin vocative of 'dominus', lord. Emphasizes the irony of the cobbler calling out
the canon with biblical quotations.

[73] ENHG 'halten' + gen. = NHG 'sich an etwas halten', 'to adhere to something'.

(a3r) says: Whoever claims to be without sin, is a liar.[74] Therefore, the pope must be a sinner or a liar, and is not the most holy, but is to be chastised.

Canon: My friend, even if the pope were so evil that he led innumerable people altogether straight to the devil, nobody would dare to punish him. That's what is written in our decrees. Distinction 40, the *Si Papa*.[75] What do you say to that?

Cobbler: Well, the gospel of Matthew chapter 18 states: If your brother sins against you, go and chastise him directly, just you and him: if he listens to you, you have gained his soul.[76] Does the pope refuse to do beneficial work like this, then?

Canon: Is that what you call an admonition between brothers then, calling a man out so openly?

Cobbler: Well listen, the scripture goes on: If your brother will not listen to you, then take one or two more with you, and if he still does not listen, tell it to the congregation; if he does not listen to the congregation either, let go of him like of a pagan.[77] What about that, Sir Canon?

Canon: Dear man, there's no point in calling us out like a market crier; we'll ignore it and stick to canon law.

---

[74] 1 Jo 1.8 *So wir sagen / Wir haben keine sünde / So verfüren wir vns selbs* […]. (L45). *If we say that we have no sin, we deceive ourselves* […]. (KJV).

[75] Friedberg, Vol. I, Distinctio 40, c. 6. p. 146. *Si Papa suae et fraternae salutis negligens* ….: 'If the Pope, being negligent of his own and his brethren's salvation, is criticized as useless and remiss in his works, and moreover remains silent about the good, which harms him more than anything else, nevertheless he leads countless masses of people with him, destined for the first bondage of hell, to be scourged for eternity with many stripes. No mortal dares to openly condemn his faults here, because he, being the judge of all, is to be judged by no one, unless he is found to have deviated from the faith. For the sake of his perpetual well-being, the entire community of the faithful prays all the more fervently, understanding that their own salvation, after God, depends heavily on the Pope's well-being'.

[76] Mt 18.15–16.

[77] Mt 18.16–17.

## 18 'Chorherr und Schuhmacher' (1524) German Edition

Schůster. Es spricht cristus Mathei. x. Wa man euch nit hŏrt / so schütlet den staub von ewern fůssen zů eyner zeugknus / das in das reich gottes nahent ist gewesen / den[78] von Sodoma vnd Gomorra wirt es treglicher[79] sein am jungsten gericht / dann sollichem volck / wie wirt es euch dann geen so ir kain straff wolt annemen.

Chorherr. Nu gib ich das nach[80] wo es gelert / verstendige leüt thâten / aber den layen zimmpt es nicht

Schůster. straffet doch ein Esel den prophetten Balaam / Numeri. xxii. Warumb solt dann nicht eynem layen zymmen ein gaistlichen zů straffen.

Chorherr. Eynem schůster zymmptt mitt leder vnnd schwertz[81] vmbzůgeen[82] / nicht mitt der hailigen geschrifft.

schůster. Mit welcher hailiger geschrifft wolt irs beybringen[83] / einem getaufften cristen nit in der schrifft zů forschen / lesen / schreyben? dann Cristus sagt Johannes .v. durchsůcht die gschrifft / die gibt zeugknus vonn mir / so spricht der Psalmist .j. Selig ist der man der sich tag vnnd nacht yebett[84]

---

[78] = NHG 'denen', dat. pl. of the demonstrative pronoun, or an elliptic construction for 'dem lande der', see the L45 translation.

[79] ENHG 'treglicher' = NHG 'erträglicher'.

[80] ENHG 'nachgeben' + acc. = 'to concede'.

[81] = NHG (Schuh-)Schwärze, a mixture of soot and bees wax to polish shoes.

[82] Similar to the proverb 'Schuster bleib bei deinem Leisten' (cobbler, stick to your last [the wooden mold of a foot on which a shoe is shaped]) which is attributed to a story about Apelles hearing a cobbler criticize his deficient painting of a shoe which he subsequently corrected - but then when the cobbler started criticizing the painting of the leg as well, told him to stick to shoe matters.

[83] ENHG 'beibringen' = 'to bring forth an argument, prove'.

[84] = NHG 'übet'.

Cobbler: Christ says in Matthew 10: If nobody listens to you, then shake off the dust of your feet as a testimony that the kingdom of God has been near to them. Those people of Sodom and Gomorrah will fare better on the day of Judgment than these people.[85] How will you fare then if you won't accept chastisement?

Canon: Well, I would concede if it were done by learned, knowledgeable people: but it is not becoming for lay people.

Cobbler: Does the donkey not reprimand the prophet Balaam in Numbers 22?[86] So, why should it not be proper for a lay person to chastise a clergyman?

Canon: A shoemaker is fit only for working with leather and polish and not with holy scripture!

Cobbler: With what holy scripture do you want to demonstrate that a baptized Christian should not study, read and write on the Bible? For Christ says in John 5: Search scripture for it bears witness of me.[87] And also the psalmist says in Psalm 1: Blessed is the man that

---

[85] Mt 10.14 *VND wo euch jemand nicht annemen wird / noch ewer Rede hören / So gehet eraus / von dem selben Hause oder Stad / vnd schüttelt den staub von ewren Füssen.* 15 *Warlich / Jch sage euch / dem Lande der Sodomer vnd Gomorrer wird es treglicher ergehen am jüngsten Gericht / denn solcher Stad.* (L45). *And whosoever shall not receive you, nor hear your words, when ye depart out of that house or city, shake off the dust of your feet.* 15 *Verily I say unto you, It shall be more tolerable for the land of Sodom and Gomorrha in the day of judgment, than for that city.* (KJV).

[86] In Numbers 22.28, God opens the mouth of the donkey to criticize Balaam who refused to follow God's command.

[87] Jo 5.39 *SVchet in der Schrifft /* [...] *sie ists / die von mir zeuget /* [...]. *Search the scriptures* [...] *and they are they which testify of me.* (KJV).

20 *'Chorherr und Schuhmacher' (1524) German Edition*

(a3v) Im gesetz des herren / So schreybt Petrus in der ersten Epistel am iij. Seynd allezeyt vrbittig[88] zů uerantwurtung yederman der grund fodert der hoffnung die in euch ist / So leert Paulus die Ephesier am vj. Fechten wider den anlauff[89] des teuffels / mit dem wort gotes / wôlches er eyn schwert nennt / Herr wie wurd wir beston[90] / so wir nichts yn der geschrifft[91] westen[92]?

Chorherr. Wie die gens am wetter.[93]

Schůster. Ir spot wol die juden wissen ir gesetz vnd propheten frey außwendig / sollen dann wir cristen nit auch wissen das Euangelium jesu christi wôlches ist die krafft gottes / allen die selig sollen werden wye Paulus .j. Corinthios .j.

Chorherr. Ja yr solts wissen / wie aber? wye euch Cristus haißt Mathei xxiij. Auff Moses stůl hand sich gesetzt die schrifftgelertten / vnd phariseyer / alles nun was sy euch sagen / das thůt / das bedeut die tåglichen predig / handt yr layen nit genůg daran?

Schůster. Ey es steet am selbenn ort Mathei am xxiij. Sy binden schwere untrågliche purden vnd legens dem menschen auf den hals / solche purden bedeüten on zweyffel vnd gewiß ewre menschen gebot / damit ir vns Layen dringt vnd zwingt vnd macht vns bôse gewissen / Warumb solt wir euch dann volgenn?

---

[88] = NHG 'erbötig', 'ready to serve'.

[89] ENHG 'anlauf' = 'attack'.

[90] = NHG 'bestehen', based on the short MHG alternative form 'bestân' with Franconian 'o' for 'a'.

[91] ENGH '(ge-)schrift' = scripture in the sense of the Bible.

[92] = NHG 'wüssten'.

[93] ENHG 'wetter' with a wider range of meaning, covering 'weather', 'lightning', 'bad weather'; here = NHG 'Unwetter', 'storm'.

(a3v) meditates on the law of the Lord day and night.[94] And Peter writes in the first epistle in the third chapter: Be ready always to give an answer to anyone who asks you a reason for the hope that is in you.[95] And Paul teaches the Ephesians in the sixth chapter to resist the attack of the devil, with the word of God, which he calls a sword.[96] Sir, how would we survive if we knew nothing of scripture?

Canon: Like geese in bad weather.[97]

Cobbler: You must be joking! The Jews know their law and prophets off by heart, should we Christians not also know the gospel of Jesus Christ, which is the power of God for all those who should become blessed, as Paul states in 1 Corinthians 1?[98]

Canon: Indeed, you should know it. But how? As Christ bids you in Matthew 23: On Moses' seat the scribes and pharisees have sat themselves. Now everything they tell you to do, do![99] This is what the daily sermon should do. Is that not enough for you lay-people?

Cobbler: Well, in the same place Matthew chapter 23 it is written: they tie heavy, unbearable burdens and lay them on people's necks.[100] Such burdens without doubt certainly stand for your man-made commandments, with which you urge and compel us lay-people and give us a bad conscience. Why then should we follow you?

---

[94] Ps 1.1 *WOl dem der* […] 2 […] *hat lust zum Gesetz des HERRN / Vnd redet von seinem Gesetz tag vnd nacht.* (L45).

[95] 1 Pt 3.15.

[96] Eph 6.11.

[97] Proverb, implying that lacking knowledge of the Bible is not bothering the canon, he is impervious to it as waterbirds are to rain, cf. Wander, Sprichwörterlexikon, s.v. *286. 'S versauft kei' Gans im Regenwetter.

[98] Paraphrase of 1 Cor 1.23–24.

[99] Mt 23.2. Possibly an ironic comment by Hans Sachs on the misuse of Scripture by the canon since Mt 23.3 continues: *Aber nach jren wercken solt jr nicht thun / Sie sagens wol / vnd thuns nicht. / but do not ye after their works: for they say, and do not.*

[100] Mt 23.4.

## 22 'Chorherr und Schuhmacher' (1524) German Edition

Chor*herr*. Wie wolt yr das mit gschrifft beweysen.

Schůst*er*. Cristus spricht im gemelt*en* capitel / Wee euch gleyßner vnd heuchler / Die ir das himelreych zůschließt vor den mensch*en* / yr geet nit hineyn / vn*d* dye hyneyn geen wellen / laßt ir nit hynein.

Chor*herr*. Ey sollichs hat cristus zů den priestern der Juden gesagt / Vmb vnns priester ist es vil ein ander ding.

Schůst*er*. Ey herr yr hond / euch erst der phariseer angenom*men* / die auff dem stůll Mosi sitzen &c. Sam*m* sey es von euch priestern vnnd münich geredt. wie dann war ist / Also auch ist das von euch geredt / Wann ewere werck geb*en* gezeugknus / dan*n* ir freßt der witw*en* heüser wie der text weitter sagt. Herr ir habt euch verstigen.

Chor*herr*. Py pu pa[101] / wie seind ir Lutherischen so naßweiß[102] / yr hört daz graß wachssenn[103] / wenn eyner eyn spruch oder zwenn wayßt /

---

[101] An expression of contempt – an example of the colloquialisms which Sachs introduces to enliven the dialogue. In NHG 'pah' survives as an interjection (which DWb s.v. claims arose only in the 18th cent.), in a similarly way to English 'bah'. Similarly, examples of 'puh' as an interjection of disgust given DWb s.v. are also all from the late 18th cent., while an earlier form 'pfu' is given as a loan word from French 'pouah'. The most common NHG interjection of disgust is 'pfui'. The Dutch and Tudor translations both resort to 'fie' and in a similar place later to 'tush', both also used in Coverdale's Bible translation. The 1596 pamphlet 'Haue with You to Saffron-Walden' by Thomas Nashe mentions a rhyme as already old: 'Fy, Fa and fum, I smell the blood of an Englishman'. Another similar sound cluster would be 'pah, piffle'. Shakespeare's King Lear shouts, 'Fie, fie, fie! pah, pah!'

[102] ENGH 'naseweis' (literally: having a discerning nose, in MHG used for animals who can sniff out a trace) is used only as an insult for those who put their nose into everything and are sniffy about other people, opinions etc.

[103] 'das Gras wachsen hören' as idiomatic expression for overconfidence by claiming a particularly acute sense of perception in the same way as 'naseweis'.

Canon: How can you prove that with scripture?

Cobbler: Christ says in the aforementioned chapter: Woe betide you pretenders and hypocrites who close the kingdom of heaven for the people. You won't be going there, and those who want to go there, you won't let in.[104]

Canon: Well, Christ uttered such things to the priests of the Jews. It is quite a different thing for us priests!

Cobbler: Well, sir, you began by referring to the Pharisees who sit upon the seat of Moses and so forth. The same may be said about you priests and monks, which is true. It is equally said about you, since your works testify to this, for you devour the houses of widows – as the text continues. You, sir, have got yourself into a corner.[105]

Canon: Poppycock! How you Lutherans are such know-it-alls, you can hear the grass growing. If any one of you lot know one or two lines

---

[104] Mt 23.13 *WEh euch Schrifftgelerten vnd Phariseer / jr Heuchler / die jr das Himelreich zuschliesset fur den Menschen / Jr kompt nicht hinein / vnd die hinein wöllen / lasset jr nicht hin ein gehen.* (L45). *But woe unto you, scribes and Pharisees, hypocrites! for ye shut up the kingdom of heaven against men: for ye neither go in yourselves, neither suffer ye them that are entering to go in.* (KJV).

[105] Literally: 'climbed up the wrong way'.

## 24 'Chorherr und Schuhmacher' (1524) German Edition

(a4r) auß dem Euangelio / so vexiert[106] ir yederman mit.

Schůster. Ey herr zürnet nit / ich meins gůt.

Chorherr. Ich zürne nit / aber ich můß euchs ye sagen / es gehôrt den layen nit zů / mit der schrifftt vmb ze gon[107].

Schůster. Spricht doch cristus Mathei am vij. Hůt euch vor den falschen propheten / vnd Paulus[108] zůn Philipern. am iij. Secht auff die hund / so vnns dann die schrift nit zimmpt zů wissen / wie sollen wir solche erkennen.

Chorherr. Solichs gehôrt den bischoffenn zů / wie Paulus zů Thitto .j. Er soll scharpf straffen die verfůrer.

schůster. Ya sy thůns aber nit sonder das wider spil / wie am tag ist.

Chorherr. Da laß mann sy vmb sorgen.

Schůster. Nain vns nit also / wellen sy nit / so gepürt vns selb darnach schauenn / wann kainer württ des anndern purde tragen.

Chorherr. Ey lieber sagt was ir wôlt / es gehôrt den layen nit zů / mit schrifft vmb zů gon / wie Paulus sagt .j. Corinthios .vij. Eyn yedlicher wie in der herr berůffen hat / so wanndel er / hôrt irs nun ir hand vor schrifft begertt?

---

[106] ENHG loan word from Latin 'vexare' (to vex), very popular in the 16th cent.

[107] = NHG 'umzugehen'. ENHG 'gan' or in the local dialect 'gon', the MHG short form of NHG 'gehen'

[108] typo in edition: 'n' instead of 'u'.

Translation   25

(a4r) from the gospel, you use it to vex everyone.

Cobbler: Well, sir, don't be angry! I mean well.

Canon: I'm not angry, but I have to keep telling you, it is not for lay-people to deal with scripture.

Cobbler: Does Christ not say in Matthew chapter seven: Beware of false prophets,[109] and does not Paul say in Philippians chapter 3: Watch out for dogs.[110] If it is not appropriate for us to know scripture, how shall we recognise them?

Canon: Such things are the preserve of the bishops, according to Paul in his Epistle to Titus 1: He shall severely punish those who tempt.[111]

Cobbler: Yes, but they don't do that, but rather the opposite, this is plain as day.

Canon: Let them worry about that.

Cobbler: No, we won't have that! If they won't help, then it's up to us, since no one else will bear the other's burden.

Canon: Well my dear fellow, say what you will: it is not for lay-people to deal with scripture, as Paul says, 1 Corinthians 7: Every-one should live according as the Lord has called them.[112] Do you hear now? You were the one that previously wanted scripture.

---

[109] Mt 7.15 *SEhet euch fur / fur den falschen Propheten / die in Schafskleidern zu euch komen / Jnwendig aber sind sie reissende Wolffe /*(L45). *Beware of false prophets, which come to you in sheep's clothing, but inwardly they are ravening wolves.* (KJV).

[110] Phil 3.2 *Sehet auff die Hunde / sehet auff die bösen Erbeiter / sehet auff die Zur-schneitung* (L45). *Beware of dogs, beware of evil workers, beware of the concision.* (KJV).

[111] The canon does not literally quote from Luther's translation, in contrast to the cobbler. Tit 1.10: *DEnn es sind viel frechen / vnd vnnütze Schwetzer vnd Verfürer / sonderlich die aus der Beschneitung /11 welchen man mus das maul stopffen / Die da gantze Heuser verkeren / vnd leren das nicht taug / vmb schendliches Gewins willen.* (L45). *For there are many unruly and vain talkers and deceivers, specially they of the circumcision:* 11 *Whose mouths must be stopped, who subvert whole houses, teaching things which they ought not, for filthy lucre's sake.* (KJV)

[112] 1 Cor 7.20 *Ein jglicher bleibe in dem ruff / darinnen er beruffen ist.* (L45). *Let every man abide in the same calling wherein he was called.* (KJV).

# 26 'Chorherr und Schuhmacher' (1524) German Edition

Schůster. ja Paulus redt vom eusserlichen stand vnd handlung / von knechten vnd freyen / wie am selben ort vnd capittel klar stet. Aber hie ist das wort gottes noch yederman vnuerbottenn zů handeln.

Chorherr. Ey hôrt ir nit Ir můßt vor durch die hailig weich berůfft sein / vnnd darnach vonn der oberkait erwôlt werden dartzů / sunst zimmpt es euch nicht mit der hailigen schrifft vmbzůgon.

Schůster. Christus spricht Luce an dem x. Die erndt ist groß / aber der arbayter ist wenig bit den herren der erndt / das er arbaiter schick in sein ernndt Derhalb můß der berůff nit eusserlich sonder ynnerlich von gott sein / eusserlich aber sind alle prediger berůffen der falschen gleich so wol / als die gerechten.

Khorherr. Ach es ist narrenn werck mit eurem sagen.

Schůster. Euch ist wie den jungern Luce an dem ix. Die verdroß das ein ander auch teuffel außtryb in dem namen Christi / Christus aber sprach weret ynn nicht / dann wer nit wider euch ist / der ist mitt euch / Derhalb wa ir recht cristen weret / soltt ir euch vonn hertzen frewenn

*Translation* 27

Cobbler: Yes, Paul speaks of outward status and behaviour, of servants and of the free, as is clearly stated in the same place and chapter. But here acting on the word of God is not prohibited to anyone.

Canon: Look, are you even paying attention? You must first be called into holy orders and then chosen by senior officials, or else it is not appropriate for you to engage with holy scripture.

Cobbler: Christ says in Luke 10: The harvest is plentiful, but the labourers are few; pray to the Lord of the harvest, that he may send labourers for his harvest.[113] Therefore, the calling from God must not be from without, but from within. Externally, however, all preachers are called, the false as well as the righteous.

Canon: Oh, what folly, the way you talk!

Cobbler: You are like the disciples in Luke 9 who were annoyed that another was also casting out demons in the name of Christ. But Christ said to them: Do not stop them, for whoever is not against you, is with you.[114] Therefore, if you were a proper Christian, you should

---

[113] Lc10.2 *Die Erndte ist gros / der Erbeiter aber ist wenig / Bittet den Herrn der erndten / das er Erbeiter aussende in seine erndte.* (L45). *The harvest truly is great, but the labourers are few: pray ye therefore the Lord of the harvest, that he would send forth labourers into his harvest.* (KJV).

[114] Lc 9.50 *Weret jm nicht / Denn wer nicht wider vns ist / der ist fur vns.* (L45). *And Jesus said unto him, Forbid him not: for he that is not against us is for us.* (KJV).

## 28 'Chorherr und Schuhmacher' (1524) German Edition

(a4v) das man auch layen fünd so die feindtschafft diser welt auff sich
laden / vmb des wort gottes willen.

Chor*herr*. Waz geet euch aber nôt an?[115]

Schûs*ter*. Da hond wir in der tåuff dein teufel vnd seinem reich wyder
sagt / Derhalb sein wir pflichttig wider in / vnd sein reich zû
fechten / mitt dem wort Gottes vnnd auch also darob zû wagen
seinen leib / eer vnnd gût.

Chor*herr*. Schawet jr leyen darfür wie jr weib vnd kynnd neret.

Schûs*ter*. Christus verpeuts Mathey. am .vj. sprechend sorget nit was
jr essen vnnd tryncken noch annthûn wôllet / vmb solliche ding
sorgen die heyden / sûcht von erst das reych gottes vnd sein
gerechtigkeit / dyse ding werden euch alles zû fallen. Vnd Petrus
.j. cano*nicis*[116] .iiij. werfft alle eure sorg auf den herren / dan*n* er
sorgt für euch. Auch christus Mathei .iiij. Der mensch lebt nicht
allein vom brot sonder von einem yeglich*en* wortt das durch den
mund gottes geet.

Chor*herr*. Laßtt euch daran benûgen vn*d* bacht[117] nit.

Schûs*ter*. Arbeit*en* sol wir / wie Adam gepoten ist. Gene*sis* .iij. vnd
Job am v. Der mennsch ist geporn zû arbeit*en* / wie der vogel zûm
flug. Wir aber solle*n* nit sorgen / sonder got vertrauen. Derhalb
müg wir wol dem wort gotes anhangen / welchs ist der beste teil.
Luc*e* .x.

---

[115] 'mich geht Not an' = 'ich bin dazu genötigt', 16th cent. version of MHG *not* +
gen., DWb s.v. (*noth*) II.4.

[116] Here 'canon.', normally the abbreviation for canon law, simply seems to stand for
chapter. The chapter number is also wrong. The wrong chapter number 'iiij' for 'v'
might be prompted by the chapter number for the following quotation for Matthew
chapter 4 = iiij.

[117] From ENHG 'pochen', to insist, with typical Franconian swap of plosives.

(a4v) heartily rejoice that one can also find lay-people who take on the enmity of this world for the sake of God's word.

Canon: Why does this trouble you?

Cobbler: Because in baptism we have renounced your devil and his kingdom. Therefore we are obliged to fight against him and his kingdom with the word of God, and so be prepared to risk our bodies, honour, and good as well.

Canon: Look instead, you lay-people, at how to provide for your wives and children.

Cobbler: Christ forbids it in Matthew 6, saying: Do not worry about what you will eat or drink or what you will put on; such things are what pagans worry about. Seek first the Kingdom of God and His righteousness, and all these things will also be given to you.[118] Also, as the first letter by Peter, canon 4, advises: Cast all your anxieties upon the Lord, for he cares for you.[119] Moreover, in Matthew 4, Christ says, Man shall not live by bread alone, but by every word that passes through the mouth of God.[120]

Canon: Let yourselves be content with that, and do not insist on more!

Cobbler: We should work, as Adam was commanded in Genesis 3,[121] and as stated in Job 5: Man is born to labour as the bird is born to fly.[122] However, we should not worry but trust in God. Therefore, let us adhere to the word of God, which is the best part, as in Luke 10.[123]

---

[118] Mt 6.31 *DArumb solt jr nicht sorgen / vnd sagen / Was werden wir essen?* [...] (L45).

[119] 1 Pt 5.7 *Alle ewer sorge werffet auff jn / Denn er sorget fur euch.* (L45).

[120] Mt 4.4 *Vnd er* [...] *sprach / Es stehet geschrieben / Der Mensch lebet nicht vom Brot alleine / Sondern von einem jglichen wort / das durch den mund Gottes gehet.* (L45).

[121] Gn 3.19, God's prediction that Adam will have to work 'in the sweat of his face'.

[122] Sachs's translation is close to the Latin while Luther and the King James Version went for a different reading of the Hebrew text of Job 5.7 *Homo nascitur ad laborem, et avis ad volatum.* (VLC). *Der Mensch wird zu vnglück geborn / wie die Vögel schweben empor zufliegen.* (L45). *Yet man is born unto trouble, as the sparks fly upward.* (KJV).

[123] Lc 10.42 Jesus praises Mary for having 'chosen the good part', listening to him.

30  '*Chorherr und Schuhmacher*' (1524) German Edition

Chor*herr* Wa wolts jr layen gelernt haben? kan eur mancher[124] kain Bůchstaben.

Schůst*er*. Christus spricht Joannis am .vj. sy werden all von got geleert.

Chor*herr*. Es můß kunst auch da seyn / wa für weren die hohen schůl

Schůst*er*. Auff welcher hohe*n* schůl ist. Joan*nes* gestanden? der so hoch[125] geschrib*en* hat (im anfang w*as* das wort / vn*d* d*as* wort was bey got. Joan*nis* .j) war doch nu*n* ein fischer / wie Marci .j. steet.

Chor*herr*. Lieber diser hett den heiligen geist / wie Actu*um*. am .ii.

Schůst*er*. steet doch Johelis .ij. Vnd es soll geschehen in den lesten tagen / spricht got / Ich wil außgiessen von meine*n* geist / auff alles fleisch. &c. Wie wen*n* es von vns gesagt wer.

Chor*herr*. Nein / es ist von de*n* aposteln gesagtt / wie Petrus anzeucht / Actuum .ij. Darumb packt euch mit dem geist.

schůst*er*. Christus sprycht Johannis .vij.

---

[124] gen. partitivus 'euer mancher' = NHG 'mancher von euch'.

[125] 'hoch' in the sense of elevated, beyond ordinary, with spiritual meaning.

Canon: Where do you laypeople claim to have learned this? Many of you cannot even read!

Cobbler: Christ says in John 6: They will all be taught by God.[126]

Canon: There must also be formal training. What else would universities be for?

Cobbler: At which university was John, who wrote so deeply 'In the beginning was the word, and the word was with God' etc., John 1?[127] He was only a fisherman, as Mark 1 says.[128]

Canon: Dear man, he had the Holy Spirit, as in Acts 2.[129]

Cobbler: But Joel 2 states: And it shall come to pass in the last days, says God. I will pour out my Spirit upon all flesh etc.[130] What if it were said of us?

Canon: No, it is said of the apostles, as Peter explains, Acts 2.[131] So be done with your talk of the Holy Spirit!

Cobbler: Christ speaks in John 7:

---

[126] Jo 6.45 *Es stehet geschrieben in den Propheten / Sie werden alle von Gott geleret sein. Wer es nu höret vom Vater / vnd lernets / der kompt zu mir.* (L45).

[127] Jo 1.1 *JM anfang war das Wort / Vnd das wort war bey Gott / vnd Gott war das Wort.* (L45). *In the beginning was the Word, and the Word was with God, and the Word was God.* (KJV). The St John's Prologue held a special status in the Middle Ages, often used as a charm.

[128] Mk 1.19 tells of Christ calling James and John, the sons of Zebedee, as disciples directly from their fishing boats.

[129] Acts 2 tells how all the disciples were filled with the Holy Spirit at Pentecost.

[130] In the Luther-Bible, the numbering of the chapters is changed and this is Joel 3.1 *VND nach diesem / wil ich meinen Geist ausgiessen vber alles Fleisch* […]. (L45). Sachs follows the numbering of the Vulgate, but rather than translating from there, takes Luther's translation of Peter's Pentecost sermon in Acts 2.17: *Vnd es sol geschehen in den letzten tagen / spricht Gott / Jch wil ausgiessen von meinem Geist auff alles Fleisch.* (L45). Joel 2.28 *Et erit post hæc: effundam spiritum meum super omnem carnem* (VLC). *And it shall come to pass afterward, that I will pour out my spirit upon all flesh.* (KJV).

[131] Acts 2.14–17.

32 *'Chorherr und Schuhmacher' (1524) German Edition*

(b1r) wer an mich glaubt (wie die geschrifft sagt) von des leib werden fliessen flüß des lebendigen wassers / daz aber (spricht der Euangelist) redt er von dem heiligen geist / welichen entpfahen solten die an in glauben.

Chorherr. Wie ich mayn jr stynckt nach Mantuano[132] dem ketzer / mit dem hailigen geist.

Schüster. Spricht doch Paulus .j. Corinthios .iij. Wysset jr nicht das jr der tempel gottes seyt / vnd der geyst gottes in eüch wonet? vnd Gallatas .iiij. Weyl jr dann kinder seynd / hatt Gott gesanndt den geist in eure hertzen der schreyt Abba lieber vatter. Vnd Tito .iij. Nach seyner barmmhertzigkait macht er vnns selig / durch das bad der wider gepurt / vnd verneurung des hailigen gaists / welchen er außgossen hat reichlich in vns. Vnnd zůn Rŏmern .viij. So nun der geist des / der Jesum von todten auferweckt hat / in euch wonet.[133]

Chorherr. Ich empfind keins heiligen geist in mir / ich vnd jr seyn nit dartzů geadelt[134].

schüster. Warumb heißt jr dann die gaistlichen / So jr den geyst Gottes nit hond? jr solt haissen die geistlosen.

Chorherr. Es seinnd ander leut / weder ich vnd jr die den geist gotes haben.

---

[132] A mistake for Montanus, the second-century Phrygian heretic and founder of Montanism, who taught spontaneous inspiration by the Holy Spirit. The mistake is carried over into the Dutch and English version. The spelling is perhaps by confusion with the Italian Carmelite poet Mantuan (d. 1516), who was popular with Protestants.

[133] The syntax is broken, since only the first half of the verse Rom 8.11 is quoted.

[134] 'geadelt', literally 'ennobled', here in the sense of 'ordained'.

## Translation 33

(b1r) Whoever believes in me, as the scripture says, out of their body will flow rivers of living water.[135] But the Evangelist says that he speaks of the Holy Spirit, who should be received by those who believe in Him.

Canon: What? I mean, you reek of Montanus, the heretic, with your talk of the Holy Spirit.

Cobbler: But Paul says in 1 Corinthians 3: Do you not know that you are the temple of God and that the Spirit of God dwells in you?[136] And Galatians 4: Because you are children, God has sent the Spirit into your hearts, crying out: Abba, dear Father![137] And Titus 3: According to his mercy he saves us through the bath of rebirth and the renewal of the Holy Spirit, which he has poured out into us abundantly.[138] And in Romans 8: So if the Spirit of him who raised Jesus from the dead dwells in you.[139]

Canon: I feel no Holy Spirit in me, I and you are not privileged for it.

Cobbler: Why then are you called spiritual people, if you do not have the Spirit of God? You should be called the spiritless.

Canon: There are other people, neither you nor I, who have the Spirit of God.

---

[135] Jo 7.38. Jesus preaching following the miraculous feeding of the crowd.

[136] 1 Cor 3.16. Paul is arguing against factions in the congregation.

[137] Gal 4.4. Paul preaching about the fulness of time.

[138] Tit 3.4–5 *Da aber erschein die freundligkeit vnd Leutseligkeit Gottes vnsers Heilandes / Nicht vmb der werck willen der Gerechtigkeit / die wir gethan hatten / Sondern nach seiner Barmhertzigkeit / machet er vns selig / Durch das Bad der widergeburt / vnd ernewerung des heiligen Geistes /.* (L45). *But after that the kindness and love of God our Saviour toward man appeared, Not by works of righteousness which we have done, but according to his mercy he saved us, by the washing of regeneration, and renewing of the Holy Ghost.* (KJV)

[139] Rom 8.11 *So nu der Geist / des / der Jhesum von den Todten aufferwecket hat / in euch wonet / So wird auch derselbige der Christum von den Todten aufferwecket hat / ewre sterbliche Leibe lebendig machen / vmb des willen / das sein Geist in euch wonet.* (L45). *But if the Spirit of him that raised up Jesus from the dead dwell in you, he that raised up Christ from the dead shall also quicken your mortal bodies by his Spirit that dwelleth in you.* (KJV).

## 34 'Chorherr und Schuhmacher' (1524) German Edition

Schůster. Ir dürfft nit vmbsehen nach infeln[140] / oder nach roten pirreten[141] got ist kain anseher der person / Actuum. x. Es stet Esaias / lxvj. Der geist gottes wirt růen auf eim zerknischten hertzen.

Chorherr. Zeigt mir ein.

schůster. Es spricht mit runden worten Paulus zůn Rômern .viij. Wer Christus geist nitt hatt / der ist nit sein.

Chorherr. O des armen geists / den jr Lutherischen hand / ich glaub er sey kolschwartz. Lieber was thůtt doch eur heiliger geist bey euch / ich glaub er schlaff tag vnd nachtt man spirt[142] in ye nyendert.

schůster. Christus spricht Mathei vij. Ir solt eur heiltumb nit den hunden geben / noch dye perlein für die schweyn werffen / anff das die selbigen nytt mytt fůssen zertreten.

Chorherr. Lieber schempt jr euch nitt sollyche grobe wort vor mir außzůziehen.

Schůster. Ey lyeber Herr zürnt nit / es ist die heilig schrifft

Chorherr. Ja / ja / ja / jr Lutherischen / sagt vil vom wort gots / vnd werdt doch nur ye lånn

---

[140] MHG/ENHG 'infel' from medieval Latin infula = headdress of a bishop or abbot, mitre.

[141] = NHG 'Barret', a soft cap worn by clergy as is the case in the title woodcut for the pamphlet.

[142] = NHG spürt.

Cobbler: You must not look around for mitres or for soft red caps. God has no regard for personal appearance, Acts 10,[143] Isaiah 66: The Spirit of God will rest on a contrite heart.[144]

Canon: Show me one!

Cobbler: Paul sums it up in Romans 8: He who does not have the Spirit of Christ is not his.[145]

Canon: O the poor spirit you Lutherans have! I think it's black as coal! Dear man, what is your Holy Spirit doing with you? I believe it sleeps day and night, you can never feel it.

Cobbler: Christ says in Matthew 7: Do not give what you have that is holy to the dogs nor cast pearls before swine, so that they do not trample them underfoot.[146]

Canon: Dear man, are you not ashamed to utter such coarse words in front of me?

Cobbler: Oh, dear sir, don't get angry: it's Holy Scripture.

Canon: Yes, yes, yes, you Lutherans say a lot about the word of God and yet you only get worse the

---

[143] Act 10.34 talks about the expansion of the mission to the gentiles, with Peter conceding: *Nu erfare ich mit der warheit / das Gott die Person nicht ansihet* (L45). *For all those things hath mine hand made, and all those things have been, saith the LORD: I perceive that God is no respecter of persons.* (KJV).

[144] Paraphrase of Is 66.2 with God's promise to look with favour on a contrite heart: *ad quem autem respiciam, nisi ad pauperculum, et contritum spiritu, et trementem sermones meos?* (VLC). *Jch sehe aber an / den Elenden vnd der zubrochens Geists ist / vnd der sich fürchtet fur meinem wort.* (L45). *to this man will I look, even to him poor and of a contrite spirit.* (KJV).

[145] Rom 8.8 *Die aber fleischlich sind / mügen Gotte nicht gefallen. 9 Jr aber seid nicht fleischlich / sondern geistlich / So anders Gottes geist in euch wonet. Wer aber Christus geist nicht hat / Der ist nicht sein.* (L45). *So then they that are in the flesh cannot please God. 9 But ye are not in the flesh, but in the Spirit, if so be that the Spirit of God dwell in you. Now if any man have not the Spirit of Christ, he is none of his.* (KJV).

[146] Mt 7.6 *JR solt das Heiligthum nicht den Hunden geben / vnd ewre Perlen solt jr nicht fur die Sew werffen / Auff das sie die selbigen nicht zutretten mit jren Füssen / Vnd sich wenden / vnd euch zureissen.* (L45). *Give not that which is holy unto the dogs, neither cast ye your pearls before swine, lest they trample them under their feet, and turn again and rend you.* (KJV).

36 *'Chorherr und Schuhmacher' (1524) German Edition*

(b1v)ger ye erger / ich spür an kainem kein besserung.

schůster. christus spricht Luce. xvii. Das reich gottes kumpt nit eusserlich oder mitt auff mercken / das man môcht sprechen / sich hye / oder da / sonder es ist inwendig in euch / das ist so uill / es stet nit in eusserlichen wercken.

Khorherr. Das spürt man an dem gotzdienst wol / jr betet nichts / vnd sůcht weder die kirchen noch tagzeyt[147] / oder gar nichtz mer / Ist dann ein solchs reych gottes in euch Lutherischen? Ich glaub es sey des teuffels reich

schůster. Ey cristus sagt Johannes .iiij. Es kumpt die zeyt vnd ist schon yetzund / das man weder auff disem berg / noch zů Hierusalem / den vatter wirt anbeten / sonder die warhafttigen anbetter werden den vatter anbetten im gayst vnd in der warhait / dann der vater wil auch haben / die in also anbeten wann gott ist ein gayst / vnd die in anbetten / die müssen in im gayst der warhait anbetten / Hyemit ligt darnyder alles kirchen geen vnd ewer tagzeyt / vnd auch alles gebet nach der zal / welchs on allen gaist vnd warhait sonder vil mer / nach stat vnd zal / eusserlich verdrossen / vnd schlefferig gemurmelt wirt / dauon cristus klagt / sprechent / Mathei .xv. Diß volck eert mich mitt den leftzen / vnd ir hertz ist weytt von mir.

---

[147] Tagzeiten = Hours of the Divine Office (Matins, Vespers etc.)

*Translation*  37

(b1v) longer you go on; I don't notice any improvement in anyone.

Cobbler: Christ says in Luke 17: The kingdom of God does not come outwardly or with notice, so that one might say: Look here, look there, but it is within you, that is, it does not consist in outward works.[148]

Canon: That is something one can clearly sense in your worship: you do not pray and you neither seek out churches nor observe the Hours nor anything else. Is there then such a kingdom of God in you Lutherans? I believe it is the devil's kingdom.

Cobbler: Christ says in John 4: The time is coming and is already now, that neither on this mountain nor in Jerusalem will the Father be worshipped, but the true worshippers will worship the Father in spirit and in truth, since the Father also wants those who worship him in this way; because God is a spirit, and those who worship him, must worship him in the spirit of truth.[149] With this all church-going and your Hours of Divine Office are brought to nought, as well as all praying by numbers, which, without any spirit and truth, but rather according to occasion and number, is mumbled, an outward show, jaded and half-asleep; this is what Christ complains about, saying in Matthew 15: This people honours me with their lips, and their heart is far from me.[150]

---

[148] Lc 17.20 *DA er aber gefraget ward von den Phariseern / Wenn kompt das reich Gottes? Antwortet er jnen / vnd sprach / Das reich Gottes kompt nicht mit eusserlichen Geberden / 21 Man wird auch nicht sagen / Sihe hie / oder da ist es. Denn sehet / Das reich Gottes ist inwendig in euch.* (L45). *And when he was demanded of the Pharisees, when the kingdom of God should come, he answered them and said, The kingdom of God cometh not with observation: 21 Neither shall they say, Lo here! or, lo there! for, behold, the kingdom of God is within you.* (KJV).

[149] Jo 4.21 & 23. Part of Christ's conversation with the Samaritan woman at the well, explaining that the salvation is to be brought to everybody.

[150] Mt 15.8 *Dis Volck nahet sich zu mir mit seinem Munde / vnd ehret mich mit seinen Lippen / Aber jr Hertz ist ferne von mir /* (L45). *This people draweth nigh unto me with their mouth, and honoureth me with their lips; but their heart is far from me.* (KJV).

38 *'Chorherr und Schuhmacher' (1524) German Edition*

Khor*herr*. Spricht doch cristus Luce. xviij. Yr solt on vnderlaß betten.

Schů*ster*. Ya das betten im gaist mag on vnderlaß geschehen / Aber eur vil beten verwürfft cristus Math*ei* vi. Spricht ir sollt nit vil plappern.

Kor*herr*. Lieber was ist das für eyn gebeett oder Gotzdienst im gaist vnd in der warhait / leert michs / so darf ich nimmer gen metin / vnd mein horas nim*m*er betten.

schů*ster*. Leßt das biechlin Martin Luthers / von der cristenlichenn freyhait / wŏlchs er dem bapst Leo x. zůgschickt hat / da find jrs kurtz beschriben.

Kor*herr*. Ich wolt das der Luther mit sampt sein bůchern verpren*n*t wurd / ich hab ir[151] nye kains[152] gelesen / vn*d* wil ir noch kains lesen

schů*ster* Ey w*as* vrtaylt ir dann

Khor*herr*. Wie das ir den lieben hailigen auch nim*m*er dyenet?

Schů*ster*. cristus spricht Mathei .iiij Du solt gott dey

---

[151] = NHG 'ihrer'; genitivus partitivus; the NHG construction would be 'keines von ihnen'.

[152] Double negation ('nie kains' and 'noch kains') in ENHG is used for emphasis.

Canon: But Christ says Luke 18: You should pray without ceasing.[153]

Cobbler: Yes, praying in the Spirit may be done without ceasing. But Christ rejects your constant praying in Matthew 6, and says: You should not babble too much.[154]

Canon: My dear man, what kind of prayer or worship is this 'in spirit and in truth'? Teach me, and I may no longer need to go to Matins and pray my Hours.

Cobbler: Read Martin Luther's booklet on Christian freedom, which he sent to Pope Leo X, where you will find a brief description.[155]

Canon: I would like Luther to be burnt along with his books! I've never read any of them, nor will I ever read any of them.

Cobbler: Well, how can you judge them then?

Canon: How is it that you also no longer serve the dear saints?

Cobbler: Christ says Matthew 4: Worship your

---

[153] Lc 18.1 *ER saget jnen aber ein Gleichnis dauon / Das man alle zeit beten vnd nicht lass werden solt /.* (L45). *And he spake a parable unto them to this end, that men ought always to pray, and not to faint;.* (KJV).

[154] Mt 6.7 *Vnd wenn jr betet / solt jr nicht viel plappern / wie die Heiden / Denn sie meinen / sie werden erhöret / wenn sie viel wort machen.* (L45). *But when ye pray, use not vain repetitions, as the heathen do: for they think that they shall be heard for their much speaking.* (KJV).

[155] Martin Luther, 'De libertate christiana' (1520). On the publication history and the theological background see Taylor Editions 3, ed. Jones / Lähnemann (2020).

40 'Chorherr und Schuhmacher' (1524) German Edition

(b2r)nen herren anbeten / vnd dem allayn dienen.

Khorherr. Ja wyr müssen aber fürsprechen[156] haben bey got.

schůster. Es sprichtt Joannes .j. canonicis .j.[157] vnd ob yemandt sündiget / so haben wyr einen fürsprechen Bey got jesum christum
der gerechtt ist / vnd derselb ist die versünung für eur sünnd.

Korherr. Ja lyeber ja / not bricht eysen / so euch ein hand entzwey
wer / jr wurdt bald sant wolffgang annrůffen.

schůster Nein / Chrystus sprycht Mathei xj. kumptt her zů mir alle
die jr můselig vnnd Beladen seyt / ich wil euch erquicken / wa
wölt wir dann besser hilff sůchen? Ir hond abgötter auß den
hayligen gemacht / vnnd vns dardurch von cristo abgefürt.

Khorherr. Ja jr habts wol vergloßt[158] / Wie das jr lutherischen nimmer
fast / lert euchs der lutherische geyst?

schůster.Fasten ist vnns von Gott nit gepoten / sonder frey gelassen /
christus spricht Mathei vj. wann jr Fasten welt / so lond[159] eurm
haupt der salben nit geprechen / spricht nit / jr solt oder mûßt
fasten / wie vnßere stieffvätter[160] zů Rom thůn.

Khorherr. Ja ir fastet aber gar nymmer.

schůster. Ich glaub rechtes fastens fasten die handtwerckßleut mer /
ob sy gleych im tag viermal essen / dann all münich / nunnen
vnnd pfaffen die inn dem gantzen Teuttschen land seyn / es ist am
tag ich mag nichs mer dauon sagen.

---

[156] acc. pl. of ENHG 'fürspreche' = NHG 'Fürsprecher' (advocate).

[157] As on a4v in the quotation from 1 Peter, 'canon.', normally the abbreviation for
canon law, simply seems to stand for chapter. The chapter number is also again
wrong. The wrong chapter number 'j' for 'ij' might be prompted by the number for
the letter.

[158] ENHG (ver)glos(s)en = 'to gloss' (NHG 'glossieren', i.e. to explain a text by
expanding, paraphrasing or commenting. This can be neutral or, esp. with the prefix
'ver-', negative. Here the canon implies that the cobbler provides a tendentious
reading of the Bible for his own interpretation.

[159] imperative pl. of ENHG 'lan' or in the local dialect 'lon', the MHG short form of
NHG 'lassen'.

[160] ENHG constructions of relationship with 'stief-' (step-) can be neutral
descriptions of family relationship, but more often describe a negative treatment,
worse than could be expected of family members.

*Translation* 41

(b2r) Lord God and serve him alone![161]
Canon: Yes, but we have to have intercessors with God.
Cobbler: John says in the first letter: And if anyone sins, we have an advocate with God, Jesus Christ, who is righteous, and he is the propitiation for your sins.[162]
Canon: Yes, dear man, yes, necessity breaks iron.[163] If one of your hands were broken, you would soon call upon St Wolfgang.[164]
Cobbler: No, Christ says in Matthew 11: Come to me, all you who are burdened and laden, and I will refresh you.[165] Where better then shall we seek help? You have made idols of the saints and thereby led us away from Christ.
Canon: Yes, yes, you have glossed it very well. How is it that you Lutherans never fast? Does the Lutheran spirit teach you this?
Cobbler: Fasting is not commanded by God but left as a free choice. Christ says in Matthew 6: If you want to fast, do not let your head go without its ointments;[166] do not say that you should or must fast, as our stepfathers in Rome do.
Canon: Yes, but you never fast at all!
Cobbler: I believe that in terms of proper fasting, craftsmen fast more, even if they eat four times a day, than all the monks, nuns and priests in all the German lands. It's blatantly obvious, I don't want to say any more about it.

---

[161] Mt 4.10. Jesus answers the devil who wants to tempt him to worship him.

[162] 1 Jo 1.1-2 *Vnd ob jemand sündiget / So haben wir einen Fursprecher bey dem Vater / Jhesum Christ / der gerecht ist / Vnd derselbige ist die versönung fur vnser sünde.* (L45). *And if any man sin, we have an advocate with the Father, Jesus Christ the righteous: And he is the propitiation for our sins.* (KJV).

[163] Proverb, Wander s.v. Noth 144. Luther also uses it in 'Ursache und Antwort', Gieseler / Lähnemann / Powell (2023), p. 110.

[164] Wolfgang, the 10th cent. bishop of Regensburg, is the patron saint of Regensburg, the diocese south of Nuremberg, and of several crafts such as sculptors; he is called upon for different bodily ailments.

[165] Mt 11.28. After having been proclaimed Messiah, Jesus promises salvation.

[166] Mt 6.16–18. The meaning of the verse is that fasting should not be done as a demonstrative act of religious observance; by keeping to a routine of body care, the fasting can be kept secret.

## 42 'Chorherr und Schuhmacher' (1524) German Edition

Kor*herr*. So schweygt ich will aber reden / es leg am fasten d*as*
wenigst / jr lutherische*n* freßt aber flaisch dartzů am freytag / das
euchs[167] der teüffel gesegne.

schů*ster*. Flaisch essen ist von got auch nit verpotten / derhalben ist es
nit sünd / dann so weyt man die vnwissenden schwachen nitt
erger / christus spricht Math*ei* xv. Was zům mund eingeet / verun-
reint den menschen nyt / sonder w*as* zům mund außgeet verun-
reindt den menschen / als arg gedenck / mordt / eebruch /
hůrerey / diebstal / falsch zeugknus / lesteru*ng* / vn*d* Paulus .j. cho-
rin*thios* .x. Alles was auff dem fleischmarck feilst[168] / das esset.

Khorherr. Ir sagt was jr weldt / habt aber nit was jr welt / gůt alte
gewonheit[169] soll man nicht verachten die etwa drey oder vier
hundert jar haben gewerdt.

Schů-

---

[167] Contraction of 'euch des', with the gen. 'des' dependent on '(ge-)segnen) and referring to the 'fleisch' eaten on Fridays.

[168] Contraction of 'feil ist'.

[169] The repeated term 'gewonheit' (= NHG 'Gewohnheit') can, like its Latin counterpart 'consuetudo' mean everyday customs or habits but also legally binding case law based on previous decisions by the authority. In this sense used here as the opposite of biblical foundation and truth, as a criticism of the way in which the Catholic church framed 'tradition' as a guiding principle.

*Translation*  43

Canon: Then keep silent, but I will speak. Fasting would be the least of it, but you Lutherans eat meat on Friday. May the devil bless it for you!

Cobbler: Eating meat is also not forbidden by God, so it is not a sin, as long as one does not offend those who are weak and do not know better. Christ says in Matthew 15: What goes into the mouth does not defile anybody, but what goes out of the mouth defiles somebody, such as evil thoughts, murder, adultery, fornication, theft, false witness, blasphemy,[170] and Paul in 1 Corinthians 10: Eat everything that is for sale in the meat market.[171]

Canon: You say what you want but you do not have what you want. Good old traditions, which have lasted for three or four hundred years, should not be spurned.

Cobbler:

---

[170] Mt 15.11 *Was zum munde eingehet / das verunreiniget den Menschen nicht / Sondern was zum munde ausgehet / das verunreiniget den Menschen.* (L45). *Not that which goeth into the mouth defileth a man; but that which cometh out of the mouth, this defileth a man.* (KJV).

[171] 1 Cor 10.25 *ALles was feil ist auff dem Fleischmarckt / das esset / vnd forschet nichts / Auff das jr des Gewissens verschonet.* (L45). *Whatsoever is sold in the shambles, that eat, asking no question for conscience sake.* (KJV).

# 44 'Chorherr und Schuhmacher' (1524) German Edition

(b2v)ster. Christus spricht Johannis am viertzehenden / ich bin der weg / die warhait vnnd das lebenn / Er spricht aber nyt / ich bin die gewonhait / Derhalb můß wir der warhait anhangen / welliche das wort gottes vnnd Gott selb ist / das bleybtt ewig Mathey. xxiiij. Aber gewonhayt kumptt vonn mennschen her / wellych all lugner sein. Psalm. cxv. Darumb ist gewonhait vergencklich.

Chorherr. Lieber sagtt mir noch eins wie das jr Lutherischen nimmer Beicht / das ist noch vil ketzerischer.

Schůster. Da ist es von gott auch nit gepoten / auch nicht gemeldt weder im altten noch newen Testament.

Chorherr. Sprach doch Christus. Luce. xvij. geet hin vnd zaigt euch den priestern. &c.

Schůster. Heißt dann erzeygen beichtt / das ist mir seltzam Teutsch jr můßtt mirß hőher mit geschrifft beweysen / Solt so ein groß nőttyg vnnd haylsam ding vmb die oren beicht[172] sein / wie jr dauon sagt / so můß ers von not wegen klerer in der schrifft uerfaßt sein.

Chorherr. Ey wőlt jr dann gar nichs thůn / dann was von Got gepotten vnd in der gschrifft verfaßt ist? das ist eyn ellennde sach.

---

[172] = NHG 'Ohrenbeichte', 'auricular confession': the confession of sins to a priest in private (in his ear) rather than as part of a public service.

(b2v) Christ says in John 14: I am the way, the truth and the life.[173] But he does not say: I am the tradition. Therefore we must cling to the truth, which is the word of God and God himself, which abides forever, Matthew 24.[174] But tradition is made by people, all of whom are liars, Psalm 115.[175] Therefore tradition is transitory.

Canon: Dear man, tell me one more thing: How is it that you Lutherans never confess? That's even more heretical.

Cobbler: But it is not commanded by God, nor is it mentioned in either the Old or the New Testament.

Canon: But Christ said in Luke 17: Go and present yourselves to the priests,[176] etc.

Cobbler: Does 'to present' mean 'to confess'? That seems a strange German expression to me, you must prove it to me more convincingly in Scripture. If private confession is such a great, necessary and salutary thing, as you say, then it would have by necessity been grounded in Scripture more clearly.

Canon: Well, do you not want to do anything except what is commanded by God and written in Scripture? That is a wretched state of affairs.

---

[173] Jo 14.6 *Jhesus spricht zu jm / Jch bin der Weg / vnd die Warheit / vnd das Leben. Niemand kompt zum Vater / denn durch Mich.* (L45).

[174] Mt 24.35 *Himel vnd Erden werden vergehen / Aber meine Wort werden nicht vergehen.* (L45). *Heaven and earth shall pass away, but my words shall not pass away.* (KJV).

[175] Psalm 115 in the Vulgate numbering, 116.11 in the Protestant tradition: *Jch sprach in meinem zagen / Alle Menschen sind Lügener.* (L45). *I said in my haste, All men are liars.* (KJV). Hans Sachs had to rely for the Old Testament on the Vulgate, since the translation of the Torah and the poetic books of the Hebrew Bible was only finished in October 1524, and the prophets followed even later.

[176] Lc 17.12–14. Jesus' command to the lepers after he had cured them.

46 *'Chorherr und Schuhmacher' (1524) German Edition*

Schůster Ich kann dasselbig nit erfüllen / wie Actuum. xv. Was soll ich dann erst meer auff mich laden.

Chor*herr.* Ey es haben aber solche ding die hailigen våter in den Concilijs[177] geordnet vn*d* bestetigt.

Schů*ster.* Von wem hond sy den gwalt

Chor*herr.* Christus spricht Johannis. xvj. Ich hab euch noch vil zů sagen / Aber jr kündts yetz nit tragen / wan*n* aber yhener der geist der warhait kom*m*en wirtt / der wirt euch in alle warhait leyten / Hŏrt / hie seind die Concilia von Christo eingesetzt

Schů*ster.* Ey christus spricht daruor Johannis. xv. Der trŏster der hailig*en* gaist / welche*n* mein vater send*en* wirt in meine*m* namen / der sellbyg wyrtt euch alles leeren / vnnd euch erynnern / alles des / das ich euch gesagt hab. Hŏrt herr / er sprycht nit / er werd euch new ding leeren / welches ich euch nit gesagt hab / sonder des das ich euch gesagt hab / wirt er euch erynndern / er— kleren / auff d*as* jrs recht verstet wie ichs gemaint hab

---

[177] Latin abl. pl. (local ablative) of 'concilium' adopted for German dat. pl. Referring to the Ecumenical Councils of the Church (Jerusalem, Nicaea, Constance…).

Cobbler: I cannot even fulfil that much as Acts 15[178] states, so why should I take even more upon myself?

Canon: Yes, but the holy fathers have ordered and confirmed such things in the councils.

Cobbler: Who gave them this power?

Canon: Christ says in John 16: I have yet many things to say to you, but you cannot bear them yet. But when he, the Spirit of truth, comes, he will guide you into all truth.[179] Listen, here the councils are appointed by Christ.

Cobbler: Well, Christ says before this in John 15: The Comforter, the Holy Spirit, whom my Father will send in my name, he will teach you all things and remind you of everything I said to you.[180] Listen, Sir, he does not say that he will teach you new things that I have not told you, but that he will remind you of what I have told you and explain it, so that you may understand rightly what I meant.

---

[178] Act 15.10 *Was versucht jr denn nu Gott / mit aufflegen des Jochs auff der Jünger helse / welches weder vnser Veter / noch wir haben mügen tragen?* (L45). *Now therefore why tempt ye God, to put a yoke upon the neck of the disciples, which neither our fathers nor we were able to bear?* (KJV).

[179] Jo 16.13 *Wenn aber jener / der Geist der warheit komen wird / der wird euch in alle warheit leiten. Denn er wird nicht von jm selber reden / sondern was er hören wird / das wird er reden / vnd was zukünfftig ist / wird er euch verkündigen.* (L45). *Howbeit when he, the Spirit of truth, is come, he will guide you into all truth: for he shall not speak of himself; but whatsoever he shall hear, that shall he speak: and he will shew you things to come.* (KJV).

[180] Jo 15.26–27 *wenn aber der tröster komen wird / welchen ich euch senden werde vom Vater / der Geist der warheit / der vom Vater ausgehet / der wird zeugen von mir. 27 Vnd jr werdet auch zeugen / Denn jr seid von anfang bey mir gewesen.* (L45). *But when the Comforter is come, whom I will send unto you from the Father, even the Spirit of truth, which proceedeth from the Father, he shall testify of me: 27 And ye also shall bear witness, because ye have been with me from the beginning.* (KJV).

48  *'Chorherr und Schuhmacher' (1524) German Edition*

(b3r) Also maindt ers auch hernach / da er spricht. Er würdt euch in alle warheit leyten.

Chor*herr*. So halt jr von keinem Concilio?

Schůst*er*. Ja / von dem das die Apostel zů Jerusale*n* hielten.

Chor*herr*. Haben dann die Appostel auch ein conciliu*m* gehalten?

schůst*er*. Ja / hond jr ein Bibel.

Chor*herr*. Ja / Kŏchin bring das groß alt bůch herauß.

Kŏchin. Herr ists das?

Chor*herr*. Ey nein / das ist das Decretal / maculier[181] myrs nit.

Kŏch*in*. Herr ists das.

Chor*herr*. Ja kŏr[182] den staub her ab / das dich der rit[183] wasch / wolan maister hanns wa stets.

Schůst*er*. Sůchtt Actuum apostolorum. xv.

Chor*herr*. Sůcht selb / Ich bin nit vil darinn vmbgangen / ich weyß wol nützers zůlesen.

Schůst*er*. Secht da herr.

Chor*herr*. Kŏchyn merck Actuum am xv. Ich wil darnach von wunders wegen lesen / w*as* die alten gesellen gůts gemacht habe*n*.

Schů*ster*. Ja leßt / jr werdt finde*n* das man die burdt des alten gesetz / den Cristen nit aufladen sol / ich geschweig d*as* man yetzund vil neüer gepot vnd fünnd erdencken / vnd die christen mit beschwert / daru*m* sein wir euch nit schuldig zů hŏren.

---

[181] 'makulieren' = to discard a book, to turn something into wastepaper because it is outdated (from Latin 'macula' = flaw), here more in the sense of handling a book carelessly.

[182] ENHG 'köhren' is a variant of 'kehren', 'to swipe, brush'.

[183] ENHG 'ritte' = cold fever; personified as a mischievous being; the curse more often in the form 'dass dich der Ritt schütt' (may the cold fever make you shake); the 'wasch' is similarly used also in other works by Hans Sachs and in Shrovetide plays. The canon uses it for the cook who has not dusted the Bible and presumably made his hands dirty when he touched it.

Translation   49

(b3r) He also means the same thing later, when he says: He will guide you into all truth.

Canon: So you do not respect any council?

Cobbler: Yes, the one the apostles held in Jerusalem.

Canon: Did the apostles also hold a council?

Cobbler: Yes, do you have a Bible?

Canon: Yes, cook, bring out the big old book!

Cook: Sir, is that it?

Canon: Oh no, that's the Decretal; don't damage it!

Cook: Sir, is that it?

Canon: Yes, brush off the dust! May the cold fever drench you! Go on, Master Hans, where is it written?

Cobbler: Look for Acts 15![184]

Canon: Look for yourself, I am not that familiar with it, I know of more useful things to read.

Cobbler: Look there, sir!

Canon: Cook, note Acts chapter 15, I will read later for amusement what the good old fellows were up to.

Cobbler: Do read it! You will find that the burden of the old law should not be imposed on Christians. I won't mention that currently many new commandments and inventions are being devised and Christians burdened by them; therefore we are not obliged to listen.

---

[184] Act 15.5–9. *Da tratten auff etliche von der Phariseer secten / die gleubig waren worden / vnd sprachen / Man mus sie beschneiten / vnd gebieten zu halten das gesetz Mosi. 6 Aber die Apostel vnd die Eltesten kamen zusamen / diese rede zu besehen. 7 DA man sich aber lange gezancket hatte / stund Petrus auff / vnd sprach zu jnen / Jr Menner / lieben Brüder / Jr wisset / das Gott lang vor dieser zeit / vnter vns erwelet hat / das durch meinen mund / die Heiden das wort des Euangelij höreten vnd gleubten. 8 Vnd Gott der Hertzkündiger zeugete vber sie / vnd gab jnen den heiligen Geist / gleich auch wie vns / 9 vnd macht kein vnterscheid zwischen vns vnd jnen / Vnd reinigete jre Hertzen durch den glauben.* (L45).

# 50  'Chorherr und Schuhmacher' (1524) German Edition

Chor*herr*. Sprycht doch christus Luce .x. Wer euch hŏrt / der hŏrt mich / wer euch veracht / der verachtt mich / ist das nit klar genůg.

Schů*ster*. Ja wan*n* jr das Euangelion / vnnd das wort gottes lauter sagt / so soll wir euch hŏren wie Cristum selbs / Wa jr aber eur eigen fündt vnnd gůtgeduncken[185] sagt / sol man euch gar nicht hŏren / wan*n* Christus sagt Math*ei* .xv. vergeblich dienen sy mir / dieweil sy leren solche leer / die mensch*en* gepot seind / vn*d* weiter / ein yede pfla*n*tzu*n*g die got mein him*m*lischer vatter nit pflantzet hat / wirt auß gereüt.[186]

Chor*herr*. Seind dann die concilia auch mennschen leer?

Schů*ster*. Wann man im grund daruon reden will / so haben die Concilia mercklicher schaden zwen inn der Christenhayt thon.

Chor*herr*. Welche? zaigt an.

Schů*ster*. Zům erste*n* die gebot der an zal vnd maß ist / wie jr wyßt / vnd d*as* noch bŏßer ist schier alle mit dem ban*n* besteet[187] / vnd doch der meyst tail in der schrifft nit gegrünt / Solche eure gepot hatt man dann hoch

---

[185] = NHG 'Gutdünken', literally something which is devised because it is subjectively believed ('dünken', etymologically related to 'think') to be good ('gut') but not based on evidence or authority.

[186] ENHG 'ausreuten' = NHG 'ausjäten': to weed, eradicate, pluck out.

[187] ENHG 'bestehen' = NHG 'belegen' in the sense of being set up, linked to (Fnhd.Wb. s.v. 17: schuldig sein).

Canon: But Christ says in Luke 10: He who hears you hears me; he who despises you despises me, is that not clear enough?[188]

Cobbler: Yes, when you speak the gospel and the word of God purely, we shall listen to you as to Christ himself. But when you speak your own inventions and fabrications, you shall not be heard at all; since Christ says in Matthew 15: They serve me in vain, because they teach such doctrines as are human commandments;[189] and further: Every plantation that God, my heavenly Father, has not planted will be rooted out.[190]

Canon: Are the councils also human doctrine?

Cobbler: If you want to get to the heart of the matter, the councils have done conspicuous damage to Christianity in two ways.

Canon: Which ones? Show me!

Cobbler: Firstly, the commandments, which are innumerable and immeasurable, as you know, and - what is even more evil – they are almost all enforced by ban, and yet most of them are not founded in Scripture. Such commandments of yours have been highly

---

[188] Lc 10.16 *Wer euch höret / der höret Mich / Vnd wer Euch verachtet / der veracht Mich / Wer aber Mich verachtet / der verachtet Den / der mich gesand hat.* (L45). *He that heareth you heareth me; and he that despiseth you despiseth me; and he that despiseth me despiseth him that sent me.* (KJV).

[189] Mt 15.8–9 *Dis Volck nahet sich zu mir mit seinem Munde / vnd ehret mich mit seinen Lippen / Aber jr Hertz ist ferne von mir / Aber vergeblich dienen sie mir / die weil sie leren solche Lere / die nichts den menschen Gebot sind.* (L45). *This people draweth nigh unto me with their mouth, and honoureth me with their lips; but their heart is far from me. But in vain they do worship me, teaching for doctrines the commandments of men.* (KJV).

[190] Mt 15.13 *Aber er antwortet vnd sprach / Alle Pflantzen die mein himlischer Vater nicht pflantzet / die werden ausgereut.* (L45). *But he answered and said, Every plant, which my heavenly Father hath not planted, shall be rooted up.* (KJV).

## 52 'Chorherr und Schuhmacher' (1524) German Edition

(b3v) auffgeblasen / vnd der menschen gewissen darmit verstrycktt vnd verwickelt / das sy den waren gottes gepoten gleich geacht seind geweßt / vnd in fürgetzogen / dadurch die gepot gots verechtlich bey den mennschen gemacht / Solche leut hat Paulus verkündiget mit jren gepoten .i. Timotheon .iiij. das inn den letsten zeyten werden etlich vom glauben abtredten / vnd anhangen den irrigen geystern / vnd lern der teufel / durch die so in gleyßnerey lugenreder seind / vnd brantmal in irem gewissen haben / vnd verbieten eelich zů werden / vnd zů meyden die speyß die got geschaffen hat zů nemen myt dancksagung den glaubigen / vnd denen die die warhait erkant haben.

Korherr. Wa ist das geschehen / mit welchem gepot?

schůster. Flaysch essen am freytag hat man für grôsser sünd geacht / denn eebrechen / vnnd so ein pfaff ein recht eeweyb het gehabt / hat man für grôsser sünd gehalten / dann so er ein hůren oder zwů het.

Korherr. Wol verston[191] spricht der walch[192] / was ist dann der annder schad.

---

[191] = NHG 'wohl verstanden', used as a proverbial saying.
[192] ENHG 'walch / welsch' is used for any speaker of a Romance language, particularly French or Italian; from the 16th cent. mainly Italian.

(b3v) inflated and have ensnared and entangled men's consciences by being put on a par with the true commandments of God and even given more prominence than them, thereby making the commandments of God contemptible among people. It was about such people and their commandments that Paul preached in 1 Timothy 4[193] that at the end of days some will depart from the faith, following deceitful spirits and the teaching of devils, through those who are slanderers, bearing a brand on their conscience, and forbidding people to get married, and telling them to avoid the food which God created to be taken with thanksgiving by the faithful and by those who have recognised the truth.

Canon: Where did that happen? With which commandment?

Cobbler: Eating meat on Friday was considered a greater sin than committing adultery; and if a priest had a lawful wife, it was considered a greater sin than if he had a whore or two.

Canon: Point taken, as the Italians say.[194] And what is the other harm?

---

[193] 1 Tim 4.1–3 *DER Geist aber saget deutlich / Das in den letzten Zeiten / werden etliche von dem Glauben abtretten / vnd anhangen den verfürischen Geistern / vnd leren der Teufel / 2 Durch die / so in gleisnerey Lügenreder sind / vnd Brandmal in jrem Gewissen haben / 3 vnd verbieten Ehelich zu werden / vnd zu meiden die Speise / die Gott geschaffen hat / zu nemen mit Dancksagung / den gleubigen vnd denen die die warheit erkennen /.* (L45). *Now the Spirit speaketh expressly, that in the latter times some shall depart from the faith, giving heed to seducing spirits, and doctrines of devils; 2 Speaking lies in hypocrisy; having their conscience seared with a hot iron; 3 Forbidding to marry, and commanding to abstain from meats, which God hath created to be received with thanksgiving of them which believe and know the truth.* (KJV).

[194] Proverb not identified; it may indicate the only superficial conceding of a point in a debate, as a non-native speaker might do out of politeness if they have not understood the issue at hand. In any case a condescending, ironic reply by the canon.

## 54 *'Chorherr und Schuhmacher' (1524) German Edition*

schůster. Zům andern hat man vil neuer gotzdienst angericht / vnd gůte werck genendt / Darmit dann am allermeysten / münich / nunnen vnd pfaffen vmbgond / vnd ist doch (wann man auffs hôchst daruon will reden) eyttel eusserlych laruenwerck[195] / daruon got nichs gehayssen hat / vnnd haben dardurch (vnnd wir sampt inen) die recht christlychen gůten werck verlassen / die vnns got beuolhen hatt.

Khorherr. Was seind dann recht christliche gůte werck.

schůster. chrystus leret vns Mathei .vij. alles das ir welt / das euch die menschen tůn das thůt auch in / das ist das gantz gesetz vnd propheten / vnd Mathei .xxv. leeret er vns den hungrigen speysen / den durstygen drencken[196] / den armen herbrigen[197] / den nackenden klaiden / den krancken heymsůchen / den gefangnen trôsten.

Khorherr. Seind das allein christliche gůtte werck eines gantz christlychen lebens.

schůster. Ja ein recht christglaubiger / welcher widerumb geporen ist auß dem wasser vnd geyst / wie Joanni .iij. dienet got allein im geist vnd in der warhait / vnd seinem nech-

---

[195] ENHG 'larve' = 'mask', Fnhd. Wb. s.v. 'larve' 1 defines it as 'sanctimony' or 'hypocrisy' ('auf Äußerlichkeiten und nicht auf das Wesentliche bedachte Scheinheiligkeit; Werkheiligkeit').

[196] = NHG 'tränken', the weak factitive verb derived from the strong verb 'trinken', in modern German only used for giving water to animals.

[197] = NHG '(be)herbergen', 'to provide shelter'.

Translation    55

Cobbler: Secondly, a lot of new forms of divine service have been instituted and declared good works, which is what monks, nuns, and priests in particular practise, and yet (if one wants to sum it up) it is vain superficial mummery, none of which God has commanded; by this, they (and we together with them) have abandoned the truly good Christian works that God has ordered us to do.

Canon: What, then, are truly Christian good works?

Cobbler: Christ teaches us in Matthew 7: Whatever you want people to do to you, do to them as well; this is the whole of the law and the prophets.[198] And in Matthew 25 he teaches us to feed the hungry, to give water to the thirsty, to house the poor, to clothe the naked, to heal the sick, to comfort the captive.[199]

Canon: Are these the only Christian good works of a completely Christian life?

Cobbler: Yes, a true believer in Christ, who is born again of water and the Spirit, according to John 3,[200] serves God alone in spirit and in truth and their

---

[198] The Golden Rule Mt 7.12 *Alles nu / das jr wöllet / das euch die leute thun sollen / Das thut jr jnen / Das ist das Gesetz vnd die Propheten.* (L45). *Therefore all things whatsoever ye would that men should do to you, do ye even so to them: for this is the law and the prophets.* (KJV).

[199] The works of mercy, Mt 25.35–36 *Denn ich bin Hungerig gewesen / vnd jr habt mich gespeiset. Jch bin Durstig gewesen / vnd jr habt mich getrencket. Jch bin ein Gast gewesen / vnd jr habt mich beherberget. Jch bin Nacket gewesen / vnd jr habt micht bekleidet. Jch bin Kranck gewesen / vnd jr habt mich besucht. Jch bin Gefangen gewesen / vnd jr seid zu mir komen.* (L45). *For I was an hungred, and ye gave me meat: I was thirsty, and ye gave me drink: I was a stranger, and ye took me in: Naked, and ye clothed me: I was sick, and ye visited me: I was in prison, and ye came unto me.*

[200] Jo 3.5 *Jhesus antwortet / Warlich / warlich / Jch sage dir / Es sey denn / das jemand geboren werde / aus dem Wasser vnd Geist / so kan er nicht in das reich Gottes komen /* (L45). *Jesus answered, Verily, verily, I say unto thee, Except a man be born of water and of the Spirit, he cannot enter into the kingdom of God.* (KJV).

56 *'Chorherr und Schuhmacher' (1524) German Edition*

(b4r)sten mit den wercken der lieb / das ist die summa einen[201] christlichen wesen / Aber dise werck geen gar in der still zů / da henckt
man weder schilt / helm noch wappen an[202] / so meinen dann die
werckhailigen[203] / solche christen thůn gar nichs mer / so sy mit
irem larfenwerck[204] nimmer vmbgend.

Korherr. Mayndt ir dann vnser singen vnd lesen gelt nichs.

schůster. Chrystus wyrtt ye sunst nichs fodern von vns dann die
werck der barmmhertzygkeit im letsten vrtayl. Mathei xxv. Da
werdt ir Münnych vnnd pfaffen besten / wie die Rincklerin[205] / die
ließ die oren am pranger.

Korherr. Ir habtts wol droffen[206] / geedt zům offen vnnd wermbt
euch / leeret euch Luther sollich dant theding[207].

schůster. Neyn.

Korherr. Lyeber was haldt jr von dem Luther.

Schůster. Ich haldt inn für einen Chrystlichen leerer (welchen ich
achtt) Seydt der Appostel zeyt nye geweßtt ist.

chorherr. Lyeber was nutz hatt er / doch geschafftt inn der christenn-
hait.

---

[201] First edition has grammatically correct 'eines'.

[202] 'helm', 'schild', and 'wappen' refer to the practice of showing by the display of
heraldic devices who endowed or donated a monument, or also showing one's
colours during a tournament.

[203] 'Werkheilige' (literally 'work-based saints') is coined by Martin Luther to
denounce relying on good works instead of faith to become justified, used
synonymously with hypocrites.

[204] see above – mummery by employing masks.

[205] 'rinklerin' might be the wife of a 'ringler', a locksmith producing chainmail (made
out of rings forged together) or simply a woman married to a Mr Ringler, a family
name common in Nuremberg area (see the map on namenforschung.net s.v.).

[206] = NHG 'getroffen' in the sense of 'have been placed in a good situation'. Probably
in the sense that by not feeling obliged to complete any works to achieve salvation,
the cobbler can relax.

[207] ENHG 'tand-teiding' is a compound of 'tand' = 'useless stuff' and 'teiding' = 'legal
advice' but also 'useless talk, gossip', see also DWb 'narrentheiding'.

(b4r) neighbour with works of love, that is the sum total of a Christian existence. But these works are done in silence, not by putting up shield, helmet or coat of arms. And so those who base their saintliness on works believe that such Christians are not doing anything at all if they stop engaging in mummery.

Canon: Then do you think our singing and reading counts for nothing?

Cobbler: Christ will never ask anything else of us but the works of mercy in the last judgement, Matthew 25.[208] Then you monks and clergymen will stand like Mrs Rinckler[209] who lost her ears in the pillory.

Canon: You are lucky, go to the stove and warm yourselves! Does Luther teach you such legalistic nonsense?

Cobbler: No.

Canon: Dear man, what do you think of Luther?

Cobbler: I consider him to be a Christian teacher (whom I respect), the like of whom has not been seen since the time of the apostles.

Canon: Dear man, what good has he done in Christianity?

---

[208] For the works of mercy, see the list above. Mt 25.40 *Vnd der König wird antworten / vnd sagen zu jnen / Warlich ich sage euch / Was jr gethan habt einem vnter diesen meinen geringsten Brüdern / Das habt jr mir gethan.* (L45). *And the King shall answer and say unto them, Verily I say unto you, Inasmuch as ye have done it unto one of the least of these my brethren, ye have done it unto me.* (KJV).

[209] This was a well-known Nuremberg case of wrong-doing by this woman who was punished by cutting off the ears of the accused. In response to Martin Luther's 'Ursache und Antwort' (1523), Johann Dietenberger's 'Antwort' (1523) claims that Luther will fare in the eyes of God and the world as well as Mrs Rinckler did in the Nuremberg pillory where she lost her ears ('Ja, Luther, du besteest vor gott vnd der welt / wie die rincklerin / die zu Nürenberg die oren am pranger ließ.').

58   *'Chorherr und Schuhmacher' (1524) German Edition*

schůster. Da hatt er eur menschen gepot / leer / fund vnnd auff satzung an tag gepracht / vnnd vns daruor gewarnet / Zům anndern hat er vnns in die hailigen gschryfft geweyset / darinn wir erkennen das wir alle vnder der sünnd beschlossen vnnd sünder seynd Rőmern .v. Zům anndern / das Christus vnnser einige erlősung ist wie zůn .i. Corinth*ios* .i. vnnd dise zway stuck treybt die schrifft schyer durch vnnd durch / Darinn erleern wyr vnnser einige hoffnung / glauben vnd vertrawen in Chrysto zů setzen / welchs dann ist das recht gőtlich werck zů der seligkait wie Christus spricht Johannis am sechsten.

Kor*herr*. darff man kains wercks dartzů / Sprichtt doch cristus Mathei v Last ewer liecht leuchten vor dem menschen / das sy eur gůte werck sehen / vnd ewern vatter im himmel preyßenn

schůster. Paulus spricht Roma*norum* .v. Wir halttens das der mennsch gerechtuerttigt werd allain durch den glaube*n* / on zůthůu*n*g der werck des gesetz / Vnd zů Rőmern am erstenn / Der gerecht wirt seines gelauwben lebenn.

Korherr. Spricht

*Translation*  59

Cobbler: He has brought to light your human commandments, doctrines, inventions, and doctrines, and warned us against them. Secondly, he has pointed us to Holy Scripture, in which we recognise that we are all locked into sin and are sinners, Romans 5;[210] and further, that Christ is our only salvation, as in Corinthians 1.[211] And these two topics are treated in Scripture over and over again. In them we learn to put our hope, faith and trust in Christ, which is then the right divine work for salvation, as Christ says in John 6.[212]

Canon: Is there no work demanded to make it valid? For Christ says in Matthew 5: Let your light shine before the people, that they may see your good works and glorify your Father in heaven.[213]

Cobbler: Paul says in Romans 5: We hold that a person is justified by faith alone without the works of the law,[214] and to in Romans 1: A just person shall live by their faith.[215]

Canon: But James says

---

[210] The chapter is a key text for Protestant doctrine, explaining the justification by faith alone (see further down the quotation from Rom 5.1), despite all people being sinners, Rom 5.12 *Derhalben / wie durch einen menschen die Sünde ist komen in die Welt / vnd der Tod durch die sünde / vnd ist also der Tod zu allen Menschen durch gedrungen / die weil sie alle gesündiget haben.* (L45).

[211] The opening chapter speaks about Christ being made our salvation, see 1 Cor 1.30 *Von welchem auch jr her kompt in Christo Jhesu / Welcher vns gemacht ist von Gott zur Weisheit / vnd zur Gerechtigkeit / vnd zur Heiligung / vnd zur Erlösung.* (L45).

[212] The chapter speaks of Christ as bread of life, see Jo 6.47 *Warlich / warlich / Jch sage euch / Wer an Mich gleubet / der hat das ewige Leben.* (L45).

[213] Mt 5.16 *Also lasst ewer Liecht leuchten fur den Leuten / Das sie ewre gute Werck sehen / vnd ewren Vater im Himel preisen.* (L45)

[214] Wrong chapter number: Rom 3(!).28 *So halten wir es nu / Das der Mensch gerecht werde / on des Gesetzes werck / alleine durch den Glauben.* (L45). Therefore we conclude that a man is justified by faith without the deeds of the law. (KJV).

[215] Rom 1.17 *Sintemal darinnen offenbaret wird die Gerechtigkeit / die fur Gott gilt / welche kompt aus glauben / Wie denn geschrieben stehet / Der Gerechte wird seines Glaubens leben.* (L45). *For therein is the righteousness of God revealed from faith to faith: as it is written, The just shall live by faith.* (KJV).

60 *'Chorherr und Schuhmacher' (1524) German Edition*

(b4v) doch Jacobus .ij. Der glaub on die werck ist todt

Schůster. Ein rechter gôtlicher glaub der feyret nit / Sonnder bryngt steets gůtte frücht / dann Christus spricht Matthey am .vij. Ein gůtter boum kan kain bôß frucht bringen / Aber solliche gůte werck geschehen nicht den hymel zů verdienen / welchen vns Christus verdiendt hat / Auch nitt auß forchtt der helle zů entpflyehen / vonn der vnns Christus erlôßt hat / auch nit vmb eer / wann alle eer soll man got geben. Mathey an dem vierdten. Sonder auß gôtlicher lieb / got zů eyner danncksagung / vnd dem nechsten zů nutz / Wolan herr wie gefelt euch nun des Luthers frucht.

Chorherr. Ist er dann so gerecht Wye das im dann so wenyg geleertter / vnnd mechtiger herren annhangen? Allayn der grob vnuerstånndyg hauff.

Schůster. Christo hyeng weder Pilatus / Herodes / Cayphas noch Annas ann / auch nitt die Phariseyer / Sonnder widerstůnden im / allain das gemein volck hieng im an / Darumb erfrewet sich Jesus im gayst / Luce am zehenden / vnnd sprach / Vatter ich sag dir dannck / das du dise ding hast verborgen vor den weysen diser welt / vnd hast sy geoffennbart den klainen.

Translation   61

(b4v) chapter 2: Faith without works is dead.[216]
Cobbler: A true divine faith does not rest, but always bears good fruit; for Christ says in Matthew 7: A good tree cannot bear evil fruit.[217] But such good works do not occur in order to earn heaven, which Christ has earned for us, nor for fear of escaping the hell from which Christ has redeemed us, nor for honour, since all honour should be given to God, Matthew 4,[218] but out of divine love, to give thanks to God and for the good of our neighbour. Well then, Sir, how do you like Luther's fruit?
Canon: If he is so just why then do so few learned and mighty gentlemen follow him? Only the rough, unintelligent rabble?
Cobbler: Neither Pilate, nor Herod, nor Caiphas, nor Annas, nor the Pharisees followed Christ, only the common people followed him. Therefore, Jesus rejoiced in the Spirit, Luke 10, and said, 'Father, I thank you that you have hidden these things from the wise people of this world, and have revealed them unto the little ones.[219]

---

[216] Luther banished the letter of James to the end of the New Testament in his translation and called it a 'straw epistle' since he regarded precisely the passage which the canon is quoting as dangerous as it deflects from the justification by faith alone. Iac 2.18 *Aber es möchte jemand sagen / Du hast den glauben / vnd ich habe die werck / Zeige mir deinen glauben mit deinen wercken / So wil ich auch meinen glauben dir zeigen mit meinen wercken.* (L45). *Yea, a man may say, Thou hast faith, and I have works: shew me thy faith without thy works, and I will shew thee my faith by my works.* (KJV).
[217] The cobbler counters with a different understanding of works: not as gaining salvation but as growing out of it. Mt 7.18 *Ein guter Bawm kan nicht arge Früchte bringen / Vnd ein fauler Bawm / kan nicht gute Früchte bringen.* (L45).
[218] Referring to the temptation by the devil to worship him, Mt 4.10.
[219] Lc 10.21 *ZV der stund frewet sich Jhesus im geist / vnd sprach / Jch preise dich Vater vnd HERR Himels vnd der Erden / Das du solchs verborgen hast den Weisen vnd Klugen / Vnd hast es offenbart den Vnmündigen. Ja Vater / also war es wolgefellig fur dir.* (L45). *In that hour Jesus rejoiced in spirit, and said, I thank thee, O Father, Lord of heaven and earth, that thou hast hid these things from the wise and prudent, and hast revealed them unto babes: even so, Father; for so it seemed good in thy sight.* (KJV).

## 62 'Chorherr und Schuhmacher' (1524) German Edition

Chor*herr*. Ey lieber / der gemaynn hauff gybtt auch des wenyger tayl dem Luther recht.

Schůster Das machen euer lum*m*pen prediger / die schreyen es sey ketzerey vnd das on all geschrifft. Christus hat aber den klainen hauffen verkündt Mat*hei* .v.[220] Get ein durch die engpfort / wan*n* die pfort ist weyt / vnd der weg breyt der zů der verdam*m*nus fůret / vnd jr sünd vil die darauff wandeln / vnd Mat*hei* xxij. Vil seyndt berůfft / aber wenig seind außerwelt.

Chor*herr*. Solylch wort treibe*n* ir[221] im wirtzhauß am marckt vnd überall / wie die narren / vnnd gehört nit ann solliche ort.

Schůst*er*. Christus sprach Mat*hei* x. Was ich euch ins or sag / das predigt auff den dechern.

Chorherr. Wan*n* ich die warheit soll sagen / so haldt ich den Luther für den grösten ketzer / der syder Arrius zeyt*en* ist gweßt / vnd jr seyt sein nachfolger / an haut vn*d* har[222] entweicht[223]

---

[220] 'v' is a mistake for 'vij' either by Sachs or the typesetter of the first edition.

[221] Missed out word, put in from the first edition.

[222] 'Haar' (hair, fur) in the legal formula together with 'Haut' to denote the full person, analogue to 'Leib und Leben'.

[223] ENHG 'entwicht' from the MHG 'enwicht, niwiht' = 'rotten, useless', first about meat and food, then used more generally.

Canon: Well, dear man, but also of the common people only a minority agrees with Luther.

Cobbler: That is because of your rag-tag preachers, who cry out that it is heresy, and do so that without any scripture. But Christ proclaimed about the little crowd, Matthew 5: Enter through the narrow gate, since the gate is wide and the way broad that leads to perdition, and there are many who walk on it![224] And Matthew 22: Many are called, but few are chosen![225]

Canon: You discuss these beliefs like fools in the inn, at the market and everywhere, but they don't belong in such a place.

Cobbler: Christ said in Matthew 10: What I say in your ear, preach on the housetops.[226]

Canon: If I am to tell the truth, I consider Luther to be the greatest heretic, who has ever been since the time of Arius, and you are his successors, rotten from head to toe,

---

[224] Mt 7[!].13 *GEhet ein durch die enge Pforten / Denn die Pforte ist weit / vnd der weg ist breit / der zur Verdamnis abfüret / Vnd jr sind viel / die drauff wandeln.* (L45). *Enter ye in at the strait gate: for wide is the gate, and broad is the way, that leadeth to destruction, and many there be which go in thereat:.* (KJV).

[225] Mt 22.14 *Denn viel sind beruffen / Aber wenig sind aus erwelet.* (L45). *For many are called, but few are chosen.* (KJV).

[226] Mt 10.27 *Was ich euch sage im finsternis / das redet im liecht / Vnd was jr höret in das ohre / Das predigt auff den Dechern.* (L45). *What I tell you in darkness, that speak ye in light: and what ye hear in the ear, that preach ye upon the housetops.* (KJV).

# 64 'Chorherr und Schuhmacher' (1524) German Edition

(c1r) als vil eur ist / vnd nichts gůtts ist in euch / nichts gůtts kumpt von euch / wißt jr nun? den tittel gib ich dem Lutther vnd euch zůsamen.

Schůster. Da habt jr ein mal eins erradtten / wann niemandt ist gůt dann got / Mathei .xix. Wann vnser nattur ist gar in vnns verboßt / wie Genesis .viij. Des menschen hertz ist zů boßhait genaiget von jugent auff / welche man můß tåglych mit dem kreutz dempffen / das sy den gaist nit fel / wann sy ladt jr dück nit[227] / ob schon der gaist durch den glauben gerechtferttiget ist / wann es steet Prouerbiorum .xxiiij. Der gerecht feldt[228] im tag syben mal / Deßhalb bitt wir alltag / vergyb vnns vnser schuld. Mathei .vj. Vnd Paulus zůn Rômern am vij. daz gůt das ich wil / thů ich nicht / sonder das bôß / das ich nit wil / das thů ich / vnd schreyt darnach. O ich ellender mensch / wer wirt mich erlôsen von dem leyb des todts? Zaygt damit ann / das wir sünder sein biß in todt / Seyt jr aber on sünd[229]? So werfftt den ersten stain auf vns / Joanni .viij.

Chorherr. Ir seyt halt vnnutz leüt / kündt vil gespayß[230] / ich hoff aber man soll euch bald den laymen klopffen[231] / es hilfft doch sunst nichts.

---

[227] = NHG 'lässt ihre Tücke nicht'.

[228] = NHG 'fällt'.

[229] Typo in the original edition: 'süud'.

[230] ENHG 'gespei' = 'vomit, useless talk'.

[231] = NHG 'jmdn. den Lehm klopfen, auf den Putz hauen', working the clay used for building projects to make it pliant, idiomatic expression for 'to knock somebody about'.

# Translation 65

(c1r) the lot of you, and there is nothing good in you, nothing good comes from you. Do you know what? I give the title to you and Luther jointly.

Cobbler: You have figured out one thing correctly, for no one is good except God, Matthew 19.[232] Since our nature is completely turned bad in us, as in Genesis 8: The human heart is inclined to wickedness from youth on,[233] which must be daily subdued through the cross, so that nature does not fell the spirit, since it does not let go of its malice, even though the spirit is justified by faith, when it says Proverbs 24: The righteous falls seven times a day.[234] Therefore, we ask every day: Forgive us our debts, Matthew 6.[235] And Paul to the Romans, chapter 7: The good that I want I do not do, but the evil that I do not want I do. And then cries out: O I wretched person, who will deliver me from the body of death?[236] He shows by this that we are sinners unto death. But are you without sin? Then throw the first stone at us, John 8.[237]

Canon: You're just useless people, you know a lot of idle talk but I hope they'll knock you back into shape; there's nothing else for it.

---

[232] Mt 19.17. Part of Jesus' answer to the rich young man about what it means to be good: *Er aber sprach zu jm / Was heissestu mich gut? Niemand ist gut / denn der einige Gott. Wiltu aber zum Leben eingehen / so halt die Gebot.* (L45).

[233] God's reflection after the flood: Gn 8.21 *das tichten des menschlichen Hertzen ist böse von Jugent auff.* (L45). Sachs use of 'bosheit', not 'böse' is closer to the Latin phrasing: *cogitatio humani cordis in malum prona sunt ab adolescentia sua:* (VLC).

[234] Prv 24.16 *Denn ein Gerechter felt sieben mal vnd stehet wider auff* (L45). *Septies enim cadet justus, et resurget.*(VLC).

[235] Part of the Lord's Prayer, Mt 6.12; Luther's translation which Sachs quotes is closer to 'debt' than to 'sin' or 'trespass': *Vnd vergib vns vnsere Schulde / wie wir vnsern Schüldigern vergeben.* (L45).

[236] Rom 7.19 *Denn das Gute das ich wil / das thu ich nicht / Sondern das Böse / das ich nicht wil / das thu ich.* (L45).

[237] Jesus' encounter with the woman caught in adultery, Jo 8.7 *Als sie nu anhielten jn zu fragen / richtet er sich auff / vnd sprach zu jnen / Wer vnter euch on sunde ist / der werffe den ersten stein auff sie.* (L45).

# 66 'Chorherr und Schuhmacher' (1524) German Edition

Schůster. Wie wolt jr mit dem schwert daran? es stett euch gaistlichen nit zů.

Chorherr. Warumb nit? Hat doch Cristus Luce .xxij. zway schwert eyngesetzt / das gaistlich vnd das weltlich.

Schůster. Verbot doch christus Petro Mathei .xxvj.[238] vnnd sprach / Wer mit dem schwert fycht / wirt am schwert verderben.

Chor Hilfft syeß[239] nit / so můß aber sawr helffen / wann dye ketzerey hat groß vberhand genommen / vnd ist hochezeyt dareyn zů schlagen.

Schůster. O nein / sonder volgt dem radt Gamallicus. Actuum .v. Ist die leer auß den menschen würt sy on alle schwert schleg fallen / ist sy aber von got so kündt irs nit dempffen / auff das ir nit sehen werdt / als die wider gott streytten wöllen.

Chorherr. Es wirt nit anders darauß.

Schůster. Wolan herr dein wil gescheh Mathey an dem .vj. Der junger ist nit vber den mayster. Johanni .xv. Haben sy mich veruolgt sy weren euch auch veruolgen / vnd Luce .vj. Selig seytt jr wann

---

[238] The edition has 'xvj' which is a typographical error; correct in the first edition.
[239] = NHG 'süß'. Idiomatic contrast of sweet and sour.

Cobbler: What, do you want to take a sword to it? That's not for you clergymen.

Canon: Why not? According to Luke 22,[240] Christ instituted two swords, the spiritual and the secular.

Cobbler: But Christ forbade Peter, Matthew 26, saying: Who fights with the sword shall perish by the sword.[241]

Canon: If sweetness does not help, then sourness must do the trick, for heresy has got out of hand and it is high time to strike.

Cobbler: Oh no, but follow the advice of Gamaliel, Acts 5:[242] If it is human doctrine, it will fall without any blows of the sword, but if it is of God, you will not be able to restrain it. Lest you be seen as those who would contend against God.

Canon: There is no other way out.

Cobbler: So be it, Lord, your will be done, Matthew 6.[243] The disciple is not above the master, John 15.[244] If they have persecuted me, they will also persecute you, and Luke 6: Blessed are you when

---

[240] Jesus' answer to the disciples offering to defend him before he went to the garden Gethsemani and was arrested, Lc 22.38 *Sie sprachen aber / HErr / Sihe / hie sind zwey Schwert. Er aber sprach zu jnen / Es ist gnug* (L45). Understood by medieval doctrine to signify the two powers of ecclesiastical and secular authority.

[241] Jesus' instructs Peter to put the sword away after he hit the servant of the high priest, Mt 26.52 *Denn wer das Schwert nimpt/ Der sol durchs Schwert vmbkomen.* (L45).

[242] Act 5.34 *DA stund aber auff im Rat ein Phariseer mit namen Gamaliel / ein Schrifftgelerter / wol gehalten fur allem Volck / vnd hies die Apostel ein wenig hin aus thun / 35 vnd sprach zu jnen / Jr Menner von Jsrael / nemet ewer selbs war an diesen Menschen / was jr thun sollet.* (L45). Then stood there up one in the council, a Pharisee, named Gamaliel, a doctor of the law, had in reputation among all the people, and commanded to put the apostles forth a little space; 35 And said unto them, Ye men of Israel, take heed to yourselves what ye intend to do as touching these men. (KJV).

[243] The opening of the Lord's Prayer, Mt 6.10.

[244] From the farewell discourses of Jesus to his disciples, Jo 15.20 *Gedencket an mein wort / das ich euch gesagt habe / Der Knecht ist nicht grösser denn sein Herr. Haben sie mich verfolget / Sie werden euch auch verfolgen. Haben sie mein wort gehalten / So werden sie ewers auch halten.* (L45).

## 68 'Chorherr und Schuhmacher' (1524) German Edition

(c1v) euch die menschen hassen / verwerffen vnd schelten von meynes namen wegen.

Chorherr. Es wirt maniger schweigen der yetzund schreyt.

Schůster. Cristus Mathei .x. Wer mich bekennet vor den menschen / den will ich bekennen vor meinem hymelischen vater.

Chorherr. Es wirt schweigens gelten[245] oder hynder dem kopff hyngeen.[246]

Schůster. Cristus Mathei .x. Fürcht die nicht / die euch den leyb tödtenn / der seele künnen sy nicht thon / O herrgott / hye wer gůt sterben von deynes namens wegen.

Chorherr. Es wer verdienter lon. Einen ketzer mag man nach dreyen warnungen hynrichten.

Schůster. Ir můst vns vor zů ketzer machen / vnd beweysen auß der hayligen schrifft

Chorherr. Das mügen wir gar leychtiklich thon.

Schůster. Ey so wirt got vnser plůt von eurn henden den[247] erfordern / das ir vns (die armen scheflein christi) so lanng handt verfůren lassen vnd habt so uil prediger diser leer / also lang mit disputierenn vnangefochten gelassen.

---

[245] ENHG 'hinter dem Kopf hergehen' ('walk behind one's head') metaphorical for beheading; refers perhaps to the belief that after a beheading the corpse is still able to walk.

[246] ENHG 'gelten' with genitiv.

[247] 'den' not in the first edition, probably an accidental repetition of the preceding syllable.

# Translation 69

(c1v) the people hate, reject, and reproach you because of my name.[248]

Canon: There will be many who fall silent who shout now.

Cobbler: Christ, Matthew 10: Those who shall confess me before the people, those I will confess before my heavenly Father.[249]

Canon: This will mean keeping silent or walk away headless.

Cobbler: Christ, Matthew 10: Fear not those who kill your body; they shall not hurt your soul.[250] O Lord God, it would be good to die here for your name's sake.

Canon: It would be a deserved reward. A heretic may be executed after three warnings.

Cobbler: You must turn us into heretics first and prove it from Holy Scripture.

Canon: We can do that easily.

Cobbler: Well then, God will then demand our blood from your hands for having let us, the poor lambs of Christ, be deceived for so long, and for having left so many preachers of this doctrine unchallenged in disputations for so long.

---

[248] The end of the Beatitudes, Lc 6.22 *Selig seid jr / so euch die Menschen hassen / vnd euch absondern / vnd schelten euch / vnd verwerffen ewern namen / als einen boshafftigen / vmb des menschen Sons willen.* (L25).

[249] Jesus' promise to his disciples, Mt 10.32 *DArumb / Wer mich bekennet fur den Menschen / Den wil ich bekennen fur meinem himlischen Vater.* (L45)

[250] Directly preceding this, Mt 10.28 *VND fürchtet euch nicht fur denen / die den Leib tödten / vnd die Seele nicht mögen tödten. Fürchtet euch aber viel mehr fur dem / der Leib vnd Seele verderben mag / in die Helle* (L45) *And fear not them which kill the body, but are not able to kill the soul: but rather fear him which is able to destroy both soul and body in hell.* (KJV).

# 70 'Chorherr und Schuhmacher' (1524) German Edition

Chor*herr.* Es wirt bald / wir habenn vnser spech[251] (alle predig[252]) gůt auf sy.

Schů*ster.* Ja ist d*as* war Ir erfült den spruch Math*ei* .xxij. Vnd die phariseyer gienge*n* hyn vnd hyeltten radt / wie sy in verstrickten in seinen worte*n* vnnd sandten zů im ir dyener mitsampt des Herodes diener

Chor*herr.* Warumb nit? man můß die ketzer also erschleychen wann sy seynd lüstig / das man sy darnach kolb.

Schů*ster* O gott dise prediger wolten vns all gern zů Cristo füre*n* nyemand außgenom*m*en. So wolt ir sy / mitsampt vns / gern zům hencker füren / Ir wolt geren das fewr von himel auff vnns fellen. Luce .ix. Hŏrt cristu*m* der spricht. Wißt ir nit wŏlliches gaistes kinder ir seyndt? Des menschenn sun ist nicht kom*m*en der menschen seelen zů uerderbe*n* / sonder zů erhalte*n* .ij. Cor*inthios* .xiij. Mir hat der herr gewalt geben nitt zů uerderben sunder zů besserung.

Chor*herr.* Ey wir wŏllenn auch also.

Schů*ster.* Ey feür vn*d* schwert reympt[253] sy*ch*[254] aber nit dartzů sonder d*as* wort gotes zů Hebreere*n* .iiij. Wŏlches durchdringender ist dan*n* ein zwyschneydent schwert Derhalb seyt ir auß gott / so verfechte*n*

---

[251] ENHG 'spech' = NHG 'spähen, achtgeben'.

[252] ENHG 'predig(t)' from Latin 'praedicare', the end-t being added under the influence of the noun 'praedicatio'. The phrase here probably means that the preachers from the elevated point of the pulpit keep an eye out for any disturbance to the service which happened frequently in these early Reformation years.

[253] ENHG 'reimen' = 'to rhyme, to complement, be in harmony with each other'.

[254] The Augsburg edition is missing the ending; supplied from the first edition (Bamberg 1524).

Canon: It will be soon; we keep a keen eye on them (at every sermon).

Cobbler: Yes, is that true? You fulfil the verse in Matthew 22: And the Pharisees went and took counsel how they might entangle him in his words, and sent to him their servants along with Herod's servants.[255]

Canon: Why not? One needs to creep up on the heretics, since they are cunning, in order to club them afterwards.

Cobbler: O God, these preachers would like to lead us all to Christ, with no exception, while you would gladly lead them and us to the executioner. You would gladly bring down the fire from the sky upon us, Luke 9. Listen to Christ, who says: Do you not know of which spirit you are the children? The Son of Man has not come to destroy people's souls, but to preserve them.[256] 2 Corinthians 13: The Lord has given me power not to destroy but to correct.[257]

Canon: Well then, we want to do this, too.

Cobbler: Well then, fire and sword do not chime with this, but the word of God does, Hebrews 4, which is more penetrating than a double-edged sword.[258] Therefore, if you are from God, defend

---

[255] Mt 22.15–16, the start of the Passion narrative.

[256] Jesus orders the disciples who want to punish those who have not given shelter to them, not to invoke heavenly punishment, Lc 9.54–56 *Da aber das seine Jünger / Jacobus vnd Johannes sahen / sprachen sie / HErr wiltu / So wollen wir sagen / das fewer vom Himel falle / vnd verzere sie / wie Elias thet? Jhesus aber wandte sich / vnd bedrawet sie / vnd sprach / Wisset jr nicht / welches Geistes kinder jr seid? Des menschen Son ist nicht komen / der menschen Seelen zuuerderben / sondern zu erhalten.* (L45).

[257] Free rendering of Cor 13.10: *Derhalben ich auch solchs abwesend schreibe / Auff das ich nicht / wenn ich gegenwertig bin / scherffe brauchen müsse / Nach der macht / welche mir der HErr zu bessern / vnd nicht zu verderben / gegeben hat.* (L45)

[258] Heb 4.12 *Denn das wort Gottes ist lebendig vnd krefftig / vnd scherffer / denn kein zweischneidig Schwert / Vnd durch dringet / bis das scheidet seele vnd geist / auch marck vnd bein / vnd ist ein Richter der gedancken vnd sinnen des hertzen /* (L45). *For the word of God is quick, and powerful, and sharper than any twoedged sword, piercing even to the dividing asunder of soul and spirit, and of the joints and marrow, and is a discerner of the thoughts and intents of the heart.* (KJV).

72 *'Chorherr und Schuhmacher' (1524) German Edition*

(c2r) ewre leer vnd wesen / mit dem wort gotes / wôlches ist die kraft gottes .j. Corinthios .j.

Chorherr. Ya es hilfft aber nichts.

Schûster. Ya ir braucht sein nit / wann gottes eere sůcht yr nit zů schützen Sunder ewern gewalt / eere / vnd reychtumb / darwider ist dz wort gottes darumb veruolgt jrs / da leytz[259] als mit eynander

Chorherr. Ya ir kündt nichtz dann die leutt außrychtten[260] / wenns hertz vol ist so geet der mund vber Luce .vj

Schûster. Euch ist wie cristus sagt / Luce vij. vergleicht[261] den kynnder / dye am marckt sitzen / růffen / wir handt euch pfyffen / vnd ir hand nit tantzt / wir hand euch klagt vnd yr hand nit gewaynt / Also auch jr / sagt man euch das wortt gottes trôstlich. so verspot yrs / sagt man euchs ernstlich so zürnt yr.

Chorherr. Wenn yr sungt als eyn zeyßlin so macht ir mich nit annders.

---

[259] = NHG 'leidet es'.

[260] ENHG 'ausrichten' = 'verbally attack, mock, confront, reprimand' (Fnhd. Wb. s.v. 5).

[261] ENHG 'vergleicht' = NHG 'gleich'.

# Translation 73

(c2r) your doctrine and your nature with the word of God, which is the power of God, 1 Corinthians 1.[262]

Canon: Yes, but it doesn't help.

Cobbler: Yes, you don't need it, since you don't seek to protect God's honour, but your own power, honour, and wealth. The word of God is against this, therefore you persecute it, and everything suffers jointly.

Canon: Yes, you can do nothing but mock the people. When the heart is full, the mouth overflows, Luke 6.[263]

Cobbler: You behave, as Christ says, Luke 7, like the children sitting at the marketplace, calling: We have played the pipes for you, and you have not danced; we have lamented for you, and you have not wept.[264] You are the same: when the word of God is spoken to you comfortingly, you mock it; when it is spoken to you earnestly, you are angry.

Canon: Even if you sang like a goldfinch, you won't change me.

---

[262] 1 Cor 1.24–25 speaks about Christ as God's word being stronger than secular wisdom for those who are called: *Denen aber die beruffen sind / beide Jüden vnd Griechen / predigen wir Christum / göttliche Krafft vnd göttliche Weisheit. Denn die göttliche Torheit ist weiser denn die Menschen sind / vnd die göttliche Schwacheit ist stercker denn die Menschen sind.* (L45).

[263] Here the canon quotes Luther (probably not meant as a statement, just because Sachs had the Luther translation at hand). The phrase 'wes das Herz voll ist, geht der Mund über' is given by Luther in his 'Sendbrief vom Dolmetschen' (1530) as an example of idiomatic German translation, instead of the Latin phrase 'ex abundantia cordis os loquitur' (literally: Out of the abundance of heart the mouth speaks), see the discussion in Jones 2022. Also used in the Dialogue on Greed, c1v.

[264] Lc 7.32 *Sie sind gleich den Kindern / die auff dem Marckte sitzen / vnd ruffen gegen ander / vnd sprechen / Wir haben euch gepfiffen / vnd jr habt nicht getantzet. Wir haben euch geklaget / vnd jr habt nicht geweinet.* (L45).

## 74 'Chorherr und Schuhmacher' (1524) German Edition

Schůster. Euer hertz ist verhert wie dem künig Pharaoni. Exodi. vom vij. biß inß xv. capittel. Der weder wunnder noch plag annnam / vnd maynet ye die kinder von Ysrael solten zyegel prennen das er mit seynem volck feyren[265] mȯcht / Also auch yr halt vns weyl yr vns halten mügt.

Chorherr. Wett frytz[266] / Es ist eins erradten.

Schůster. Ya / Es dunckt mich wol / euch sey wie dem falschen amptman Luce .xvj. Sprechent / was soll ich thon / meyn herr nymmpt das ampt von mir / Ich mag nit graben / vnnd schem mich zů beetlen / Eben das selbig fürcht yr gaystlichen auch / darumm hilfft weder straffen noch ermanen ann euch.

Chorherr. Ey wißt ir nicht Cristus spricht. Johannes vj. Nyemant kumpt zů mir / der vatter zyech in dann / zeyt bringt rosen wer wayßt welcher den andern bekert.

Schůster. O herr die wort hȯr ich gern / es steet Johan .xv. On mich kündt yr nichts thon / vnd weytter / ir hand mich nit erwȯllet / ich han euch erwȯllet / darumb ligt an vns nicht got můß vns bekeren das wünsch ich euch allen von grund meines hertzen.

Chorherr. Man leütet in Khor / Kechin lang den Korrock[267] her / wol an lieber mayster zyecht hin im frid es wirt leicht noch als gůt /

Schůster. Ob gott will / wol an alde[268] / der fryd sey mit euch lie-

---

[265] ENHG 'feiern' = 'to take a break, not work'.

[266] 'Wett Fritz', an ENHG interjection; 'wett' (of unclear etymology) as expression of astonishment (mostly referencing the devil) in combination with the short form of the name 'Friedrich', which is used, like the short forms 'Hinz' ('Heinrich') or 'Kunz' ('Konrad') as a generic male name, DWb s.v. 'wett'.

[267] 'Chorrock' = large liturgical garment worn over the cassock during service in the 'Chor' (choir).

[268] ENHG alternative form to 'ade' for French 'adieu', 'farewell'.

Cobbler: Your heart is hardened like that of King Pharaoh, Exodus chapters 7 to 15,[269] who accepted neither miracles nor plagues, and kept thinking that the children of Israel should bake bricks so that he could rest with his people. So you, too, keep us for as long as you can keep us.

Canon: Good grief, you guessed it.

Cobbler: Yes, it does seem to me that you are like the dishonest steward, Luke 16, saying: What shall I do? My master is taking my office from me; I do not like to dig and am ashamed to beg.[270] You clergymen fear exactly the same thing, so neither punishment nor admonition will help you.

Canon: Well, don't you know, Christ says, John 6: Nobody comes unto me if the Father does not draw them.[271] Time brings roses; who knows who will convert the other?

Cobbler: Dear sir, I love to hear these words. It says in John 15: Without me you can do nothing;[272] and again: You have not chosen me, I have chosen you.[273] Therefore it is not up to us, God must convert us. I wish this for you all from the bottom of my heart.

Canon: The choir bell is ringing. Cook, pass me the cope! Well then, dear master, go in peace! It might still turn out well.

Cobbler: God willing! Well adieu, peace be with you,

---

[269] The report of the exodus from Egypt talks repeated about the 'hardening' of Pharaoh's heart, e.g. Ex 7.3 *Aber ich wil Pharao hertz verherten / das ich meiner Zeichen vnd Wunder viel thu in Egyptenland.* (L45) *Sed ego indurabo cor ejus, et multiplicabo signa et ostenta mea in terra Ægypti* (VLC).

[270] Lc 16.3 *Der Haushalter sprach bey sich selbs / Was sol ich thun? mein Herr nimpt das Ampt von mir / Graben mag ich nicht / So scheme ich mich zu betteln.* (L45).

[271] Jo 6.44 *Es kan niemand zu mir komen / es sey denn / das jn ziehe der Vater / der mich gesand hat / vnd ich werde jn aufferwecken am Jüngstentage.* (L45)

[272] Jo 15.5 *JCh bin der Weinstock / Jr seid die Reben / Wer in mir bleibet / vnd ich in jm / der bringet viel frucht / Denn on mich künd jr nichts thun.* (L45)

[273] Jo 15.16 *JR habt mich nicht erwelet / Sondern ich habe euch erwelet / vnd gesetzt / Das jr hin gehet vnd Frucht bringet / vnd ewre Frucht bleibe / Auff das / so jr den Vater bittet in meinem Namen / das ers euch gebe.* (L45)

76 *'Chorherr und Schuhmacher' (1524) German Edition*

(c2v)ber herr hand mir nichts verübel / vnd verzeycht mir.

Chor*herr*. Verzeych vns gott vnser sünd.

Schůster. Amen.

Chor*herr*. Secht nur an liebe kôchin / wie rede*n* die layen so gar freflich gegen vns geweychtten / Ich mayn der teuffel sey in dem
schůster verneet[274] / er hat mich inn harnasch gejagt[275] / Vnd wer
ich nit so wol geleert / er het mich auff den esel[276] gesetzt / darumb
wil ich im nicht mer zů arbayte*n* geben / sonder dem hans Zobel /
der ist eyn gůtz einfeltigs mendlin[277] / macht nit vil wort mit der
hailigen gschrifft / vn*d* Lutherischen ketzerey / wie dan*n* den
layen nit zymlich ist / noch gepürt mit jren seelsorgern zů disputiern / wan*n* es sagt Salomon / Wôlcher eyn eynfelttig wandel
fůrt / der wandelt wol / Ey disen spruch solt ich dem dolle*n*
schůster fürgeworffen han / so wer er vileicht darob erstumbt.

Kôchin. O herr / ich hett ymmer sorg nach dem yr in mit der schrifft
nit vberwinden kündt / jr wurd in mitt den panttoffel schlahen.

Chor*herr*. Ich hab nur vonn der gemayn eyn auffrůwr besorgt / sunst
wolt ich im die panttoffel in sein antlitz geschmeist[278] haben / im
het Cristus oder Paul*us* in dreyen tagen nit abgewischt / wiewol
er all sein vertrauwen auff sy setzt.

---

[274] = NHG 'eingenäht': to hide by sewing into a cover, in this case to sew the devil
into the skin of the cobbler.

[275] ENHG 'harnasch, -nisch, -nesch' = 'armour'. Phrase 'in den Harnisch jagen' = to
make somebody angry, literally to send somebody into their armour.

[276] The 'esel' in this case is a donkey-shaped wooden construction on which
offenders have to sit as form of punishment and humiliation, Fnhd. Wb. s.v. 4.

[277] = NHG 'Männlein', diminutive form for 'man'.

[278] ENHG 'schmeißen' has strong and weak forms; NHG only 'geschmissen'.

(c2v) dear sir, do not count it against me and forgive me.

Canon: May God forgive us our sin.

Cobbler: Amen.

Canon: Look here, dear cook, how the lay-people speak so impudently against us who are ordained! I think the devil is sewn up inside the cobbler; he had me up in arms, and if I had not been so well taught, he would have put me on the donkey. Therefore, I will not give him any more work, but rather Hans Zobel[279], who is a good simple-minded man, does not say much about Holy Scripture and Lutheran heresy, which is just not right for the laity, nor is it proper to argue with their spiritual leaders, since Solomon says: Those who lead a simple life, live well.[280] Well, if I had thrown this verse at the mad cobbler, he might have been struck dumb by it.

Cook: Oh, Sir, I was worried the whole time that, since you could not overcome him with scripture, you would beat him with your slippers.

Canon: I was only worried about a riot from the congregation, as otherwise I would have thrown the slippers in his face, Christ or Paul would not have wiped it off him in three days, even though he puts all his trust in them.

---

[279] Possibly a dig at a local competitor of Hans Sachs, but the name is not attested in Nuremberg records, so more likely to be a made-up name, possibly playing with the literal meaning of the name as a small animal ('zobel' = sable).

[280] Possibly Prv 16.19 *Es ist besser nidriges gemüts sein mit den Elenden / Denn Raub austeilen mit den Hoffertigen.* (L45). *Better it is to be of an humble spirit with the lowly, than to divide the spoil with the proud.* (KJV). *Melius est humiliari cum mitibus quam dividere spolia cum superbis.* (VLC). It might be part of Sachs's strategy to show up the canon in that he is using a vague proverb, attributing it to Solomon as author of the Book of Proverbs, rather than quoting properly, including giving a precise chapter number, as the cobbler does for his Biblical references.

78 *'Chorherr und Schuhmacher' (1524) German Edition*

Kŏchin. Mich nimpt groß wunder / wie die layen so geschickt werden.

Chorherr. Wilt wissen was macht? Man gybt vmb die gaistlikait nichts mer / vorzeitten het der haylig vatter der Bapst / vnnd die Bischoff (solchen als Luther vnnd ander mer / die auff sein geygen predigen) das predig amptt auffgehebt nach laut des gaistlichen rechten / Vnd zů wyder růffen benŏttiget / wie mit dem Johannes huß zů Costentz geschehen ist / Wenn man nur die Euangelischen prediger kund schweygen machen / so wurts alles gůtts / Aber wenn man sy haist schweigen / so kommen sy vnd wŏllen mit dem bapst vnd bischoffen disputiern / wellichs vnerhårt[281] bey der welt / das eyner mit dem allerhayligisten will disputiern / der nitt genůgsam vnd wirdig ist mit seiner hailigkait zů reden / Aber es wyl besser werden / wenn die prediger nit wellen / so můssen sy schwei

---

[281] = NHG 'unerhört'

Cook: I am greatly astonished by how the laypeople are becoming so skilful.

Canon: Do you want to know what is causing this? Nobody cares any longer for the clergy. In the past, the Holy Father, the pope and the bishops would, for Luther and those others who preach to the tune of his fiddle, have revoked the preaching office according to ecclesiastical law and would have been required to revoke it, as happened with Jan Hus in Constance.[282] If only the Protestant preachers could be silenced, all would be well. But when they are told to be silent, they come and want to argue with the pope and bishops, which is unheard of anywhere in the world, that someone wants to argue with the Holy of Holies, who is not sufficient or worthy to speak with His Holiness. But it will get better. If the preachers do not behave, they must remain silent, even though they are

---

[282] The reformer Jan Hus was burned as a heretic at the Council of Constance in 1415. Martin Luther referenced him frequently and wrote prefaces to his works. He even claimed that Hus had predicted his teaching, writing in 1531: 'Sanct Johannes Hus hat von mir geweissagt, da er aus dem gefegnis jnn Behemerland schreib, Sie werden jtzt eine gans braten (denn Hus heisst eine gans), Aber uber hundert jaren werden sie einen schwanen singen hören, Den sollen sie leiden. Da sols auch bey bleiben, ob Gott will.' (WA 31, 387). St John Hus prophesized of me when he wrote from imprisonment in Bohemia: They will now fry a goose (for 'Hus' means goose in Czech), but in hundred years they will hear a swan sing and will have to endure it. Thus it shall come to pass, God willing.' (my translation), leading to the frequent iconography of Luther with a swan.

80 *'Chorherr und Schuhmacher' (1524) German Edition*

(c3r)gen wie wol sy sant Paulus schrift fürzyechen / Vnd wenn sy sein schwert dartzů hetten / so můsten sy darnyder ligen / wenns der hailig vater der Bapst thon will / dann so můsten dye layen auch schweigen / vnnd wir wurden zů vnsern wirden widerumb kommen.

Kechin. Es wer für war herr gůt / wann yederman veracht euch / wie dann yetzund auch der Schůster thon hat.

Chorherr. Vorzeytten het wir ein sollichen inn Bann verkündt / Aber yetzund můssen wir von den layen hören vnd lernen / wie die Phariseyer von Cristn. Liebe kechin růff vnserm Calefactor[283] / der lißt vil in der Bybel / vnd villeicht der schrifft baß bericht ist dann ich / Er můß mir von wunders wegen ettlich sprüch sůchen.

Kechin. Heinrice[284] / Heinrice. gee[285] auff her zům herrn.

Calefactor. Wirdiger herr was wôltt jr?

Chorherr. Vnser schůster hat mich lang vexiert / vnd vil auß der Bybel angetzaigt / wie dann der Lutherischen brauch ist / du můst im etlich Capitel nach sůchen / ob er gleich hab zů gesagt / auff das ich in in der schrifft fahen môcht.

---

[283] 'Calefactor': Latin loanword, literally the person who makes the room warm, is responsible for heating. Meaning a low-ranking servant for running errands. Here picked as the strongest possible contrast to the high-ranking canon.

[284] 'Henrice': Latin vocative of 'Heinrich'.

[285] Use of the informal singular between the servants of the same household.

*Translation* 81

(c3r) quoting from Saint Paul's writings, and if they also had his sword,[286] they still would have to lie down if the Holy Father, the pope, so wishes. Then the laity must also remain silent, and we will come back to our honours.

Cook: That would indeed be good, sir, since everyone despises you, as the cobbler has done just now.

Canon: In times past, we would have proclaimed the ban over somebody like this! But now we have to hear and learn from the laity like the Pharisees from Christ. Dear cook, call the servant boy, who reads a lot in the Bible and is perhaps better informed of the Scripture than I am. He must find me some biblical sayings for amusement.

Cook: Henry, Henry, come over to the master!

Boy: Reverend sir, what do you want?

Canon: Our shoemaker has been vexing me for a long time and has quoted much from the Bible, as is the Lutheran custom. You must look up several chapters which he used, whether he has spoken correctly, so that I may catch him out with Scriptures.

---

[286] Since Paul was beheaded, his signature attribute is the sword.

82  *'Chorherr und Schuhmacher' (1524) German Edition*

Calefactor. Ir solt es billich selbst wissen / yr hand lang die geweychten exammiern helffen.

Chorherr. Ja daselbs braucht man nur schůllerische leer /[287] was die menschen haben geschriben vnd gemacht vnd gar wenig das gaistlich recht / wŏlchs die hailigen vetter in den Concilijs beschlossen haben.

Calefactor. Es leg an dem nicht das die vetter in Concilijs beschlossen / vnd die menschen so nach in kommen sein geschriben vnd gehaltten haben wo dieselben gesetz / leer vnd schrifft auß dem wort vnd gaist gotes weren / wann die propheten / Apostel vnd Euangelisten seind auch menschen geweßt.

Chorherr. Ey / so haben sy auch yrren mügen / Aber die Lutherischen wellen das nit glauben

Calefactor. Nayn / Wann Petrus spricht .ij. Petri .j. Es ist noch nye kain weissagung auß menschlichem wyllen herfür bracht / sonder die hailigen menschen gottes hand geredt / getriben / von dem hailigen gaist / Vnnd eben darnach verkündt Petrus / die falschen Prophetten / die vil verderblicher seckten

---

[287] Referring to theology teaching at university.

*Translation*  83

Boy: You should by rights know that yourself: You have been helping to examine those who are ordained for a long time.

Canon: Well, all that is needed for this is scholastic teaching, what people have written and made, and a little bit of canon law, which the holy fathers have decreed in the councils.

Boy: It is not because the fathers in councils decreed, and the people who came after them wrote and kept them, that the law, doctrine, and texts were from the word and spirit of God, since the prophets, apostles and evangelists were also men.

Canon: Well, then they too may have been wrong, but the Lutherans don't want to believe that.

Boy: No, since Peter says, 2 Peter 1: No prophecy has ever been brought forth by human will, but the holy people of God have spoken, driven by the Holy Spirit.[288] And directly after that, Peter predicts false prophets, who will introduce many pernicious sects

---

[288] 2 Pt 1.20 *Vnd das solt jr fur das erste wissen / Das keine Weissagung in der Schrifft geschicht aus eigener auslegung.* (L45). *Knowing this first, that no prophecy of the scripture is of any private interpretation.* (KJV).

# 84 'Chorherr und Schuhmacher' (1524) German Edition

(c3v) ein werden fůren / Bedeut ewrn gaistlichen standt / Ordenn[289] Regel vnd alle menschen sünd (ausserhalb dem wort gotes) darmit ir yetz vmbgeet.

Khorherr. Ya es ist aber auff vnns nitt geredt / sonder auff die alten vnd lengst vergangen.

Calefactor. O yr thoren vnd tregs hertzen zů glauben / alle dem / das ye Prophettenn geredt haben. Luce .xxiiij.

Kechin. Herr haißt euch den hanen mer kreen / von mir lydt yrs nit.

Khorherr. O du lausiger bachant[290] / wilt du mich auch rechtuertigen[291] vnd leeren Bist auch der Lutherischenn bőßwychter einer / Troll dich nur bald auß dem hauß / vnd kumm nit wyder du vnuerschamtes thyer.

Calefactor. Es thůt euch and[292] / das euch der schůster das rodt pyrret[293] geschmåcht hatt / Laßt euch nit wunndern / wann im alten gesetz / hat gott die hyrtten seyn wort lassenn verkünden / also auch yetz můssen (euch phariseer) die schůster leeren / Ya es werden euch noch die stayn in die oren schreyen Alde ich schaid mit wissenn.

---

[289] Typographical mistake in the edition of 'u' instead of 'n'.

[290] Loanword based on Bacchus, the Roman god of drunkenness.

[291] ENHG 'rechtfertigen' normally of the work of God to justify humans. Here in the sense of making somebody 'recht', i.e. 'to correct'.

[292] ENHG 'ande' = ridicule, contempt; 'and tun' = to rile.

[293] = NHG 'Barret', the red soft cap worn by the higher clergy, see above.

*Translation* 85

(c3v) that is, your spiritual state, order, rule, and all human sins (outside the word of God), with which you are now involved.

Canon: Yes, but it was not spoken of us, but of the ancients, who have long since passed.

Boy: Oh, you fools, and slow of heart to believe all that the prophets have spoken! Luke 24.[294]

Cook: Sir, just encourage the rooster to crow more for you![295] You wouldn't suffer it from me.

Canon: Oh, you lousy drunkhead, do you want to correct and teach me too? Are you also one of those Lutheran villains? Get out of this house at once and don't come back, you shameless animal!

Boy: It pains you that the cobbler has slandered your red cap. Let it not surprise you, since in the old law, God let the shepherds proclaim his word. So even now the cobblers must teach you, the Pharisees. Yes, even the stones will be shouting in your ears. Adieu, I depart with this knowledge.

---

[294] Luke 24.25 *VND er sprach zu jnen / O jr Thoren vnd treges hertzen / zu gleuben alle dem / das die Propheten geredt haben* (L45) *then he said unto them, O fools, and slow of heart to believe all that the prophets have spoken:* (KJV).

[295] The cook is mocking the canon who has involuntarily encouraged the boy ('rooster') to loudly announce ('crow') all the criticism, after forbidding criticism from anybody else.

86 *'Chorherr und Schuhmacher' (1524) German Edition*

Kechin. Euch geschycht recht mich wundert das ir[296] mit den groben filtzen reden mügt. Sy schonen weder ewer noch der hailigen weych.

Khor*herr*. Ich wil mich nun woll vor in hůttenn / verprents künd / fürcht fewer[297] Woll an ich wil in Khor / so gee an marckt / kauff eyn krammetvogel[298] oder zwelff / Es wirt nach essen meines gnedigen herren Caplan / mit etlichen herren kommen / vnd ein pangett haltten. Trag die Bibel auß der stuben hynauß / vnd sich ob die stayn vnd würffel all im bretspyl seyn / vnd das wir eynn frysche kartten oder zwů haben.

Kechin. Es soll seyn. Herr werdt ir von stund an nach dem vmmgang heymher gen?

Kor*herr*. Ya schaw das essen beraytt sey.

Paulus. Ir bauch ir gott.
M D XXiiij.

---

[296] Typographical error 'it' in the edition, correct in the first edition.

[297] Proverbial saying = NHG 'Verbranntes Kind scheut das Feuer', literally: once burnt, a child fears the fire.

[298] Literally a bird that eats juniper berries ('krammet'), indicating small birds like quails served in fine dining.

Cook: Serves you right. I'm surprised that you have to talk to these coarse beasts. They spare neither you nor the holy orders.

Canon: I will now stay well clear of them; once bitten, twice shy. Well, I will go and sit in choir. You go to the market, buy a bird or twelve! After dinner, my gracious master's chaplain will come with some gentlemen and hold a banquet. Take the Bible out of the parlour and see if the playing stones and dice are all in the board game and that we have a fresh pack of cards or two.

Cook: It will be done. Sir, will you come home immediately after the procession?

Canon: Yes, make sure the food is ready!

Paul: Their belly is their god.[299]
1524

---

[299] Phil 3.19 *welcher Ende ist das verdamnis / welchen der Bauch jr Gott ist / vnd jre Ehre zu schanden wird / Dere / die jrdisch gesinnet sind.* (L45) *Whose end is destruction, whose God is their belly, and whose glory is in their shame, who mind earthly things.)* (KJV).

# b) Dutch: *Schoenmaker ende Coorhere*

*Een fchoon | difputacie van eenē Euā-|geliffchen Schoenmaker | ende van eenē Papistigen | Coo2heere / met twee | ander perfonagiē | ghefchiet tot | Norēborch. | Ghed2uckt by my Magnus | vanden Merberghe.*
[s.l.:] Magnus van den Merberghe, [c.1545].

Collation: A1-4, B1-4, C1-8, D1-8, 8°.

> University Library Greifswald, 542/Fv 28 adn9, with a microfilm copy in The Hague.

Transcription: Christina Ostermann, footnotes: Johanneke Sytsema

The copy is part of a 'Sammelband' of twelve Dutch Reformation pamphlets in the University Library Greifswald, starting with Willem de Volder, *Een troost ende Spiegel der siecken ende der ghenen die in lijden sijn*, Antwerp c.1540, 542/Fv 28. There are two reprints, in 1565 (a copy in the Stadtbibliothek Nuremberg, Will 3, 800 8°, Spriewald (1970), p. 49) and in 1614.

To make the Dutch and Tudor English versions comparable to the German model of the text, the page breaks follow those of the German copy in the Taylor Institution Library. The folio numbering of that copy have been added in with lower case letters at the top of each page, e.g. '(a2r)'. Folio numbers with capital letters, e.g. '(A2r)' are referring to the Dutch and English edition.

Nasal bars and other abbreviations have been expanded *in italics*, line breaks have been removed. The word division and the suspension abbreviations with a dot have been preserved.

## c) English: *Shomaker and Parson*

*A goodly | dyſputacion betwene a Ch2i-|ſten Shomaker / and a Popyſſhe Par-|son with two other parſones more, | done within the famous Citie | of Norembourgh. | Translated out of ẙ Germayne | tongue into Englyſſhe. By | Anthony Scoloker.*
London: Anthony Scoloker and Wyllyam Seres, 1548.

Collation: A1-8, B1-8, C1-8, 8°.

> Bodleian Library, Vet. A1 f. 237. Partly washed ownership mark on the titlepage and on fol. A1r, reading 'James Lowe His B[ook]'

> Bodleian Library, Douce Fragm. f. 22 (only quire C)

Transcription: David Hirsch, footnotes: Jacob Ridley

Online edition available as
https://editions.mml.ox.ac.uk/editions/shoemaker/

(a1r) (A1ʳ) Een schoon disputacie van eenen Euangelisschen Schoenmaker ende van eenen Papistigen Coorheere / met twee ander personagien
gheschiet tot Norenborch.

Ghedruckt by my
Magnus vanden Merberghe.

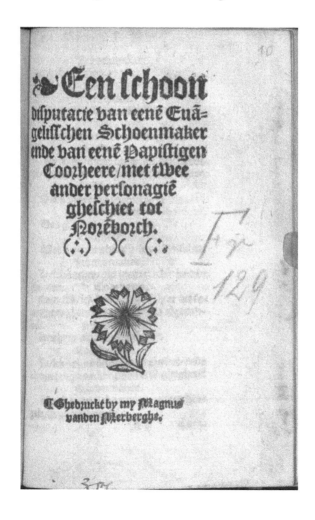

(a1r) (A1r) A goodly dysputacion betwene a Christen Shomaker / and a Popysshe Parson with two other parsones more, done within the famous Citie of Norembourgh.

Translated out of the Germayne tongue into Englysshe. By Anthony Scoloker.

Imprynted at London by Anthony Scoloker. And Wyllyam Seres. Dwellynge wythout Aldersgate. Anno. 1548.
¶ Cum Gratia et Priuilegio ad Imprimendum solum.

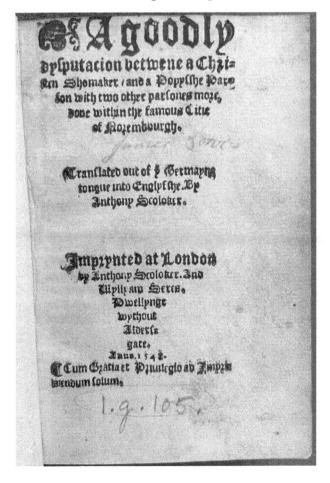

## 92 'Schoenmaker & Coorhere' (c. 1545) Dutch Edition

(A1ᵛ) (a1v) ***blank***
(a2r) (A2ʳ)

Schoenmaker.[1] BOnus dies.[2]

Kochin. Semper quies. Sijt willecome meester Hans.

Schoenmaker. God dancke v[3] / waer is v Heere.

Kochin. Hy is int somer huys / ick wil hem roepen / Heere heere / die Schoenmaker is hier.

Coorheere. Bene veneritis magister[4] Hans.

Schoenmaker. Deo gratias.

Coorheere. Wat brenget ghi my / die pantoffelen?

Schoenmaker. Ja / ick dachte / ghi waert in die kercke ghegaen.

Coorheere. Neen ick / ick hebbe daer achter int somerhuys gheweest / ende ic hebbe afgerabbelt.

Schoenmaker. Hoe hebt ghy afgherabbelt.[5]

Coorheere. Ja / ick hebbe mijn horas ghebet / ende altemet mijn nachtegalen teten ghegheuen

---

[1] Other than in the German (G) version, in the Dutch (D) and English (E) editions speech prefixes are centred and speeches indented but have been typeset here analogous to the German edition above. There were not yet settled conventions for typesetting dialogues (see Introduction 2).

[2] Like in the German version, the opening dialogue uses textbook Latin greeting formulas, see footnotes there. The English version keeps the Latin for the exchange with the priest.

[3] Like in G, D uses the formal form of address (2 ps pl) throughout. In E, it starts as formal ('you'), but then later switches without an apparent reason to the informal 'thou'.

[4] G 'mayster', for an artisan, is turned in D to 'magister', the Latin honorific for a learned man, and E keeps this formula.

[5] D 'afgerabbelt' (literally: 'unravelling') for G 'abgedroschen' ('threshing'). E 'Mumbled' does not literally translate either, but keeps Sachs's polemical sense of thoughtless, mechanical speech. Mumbling can either mean 'muttering indistinctly' (from Middle English 'momelen') or 'chewing', usually toothlessly, and thus 'mashing up randomly', and it was often used by anticlerical writers, from the late thirteenth-century Wycliffites to the Tudor Protestant reformers, for ignorant timeserving Catholics who babble their Latin prayers without understanding them. The Shoemaker calls the Parson's prayers 'outward mumblyng' again below (B2r).

# 'Shomaker & Parson' (1548) English Edition   93

(A1ᵛ) (a1v) \*\*\*blank\*\*\*

(a2r) (A2r) ¶ The Shomaker comminge to the parsones house, speaketh to the parsons seruaunt.[6]

Shomaker. Good morrow good fellow

Seruaunt.[7] ye are welcom master Ioan[8]

Shomaker I thanke you with all my hert, Where is your master?

Seruaunt. He is in the gallery,[9] O tary a lytle I wyll go and call hym, master master your shomaker is here.

Parson.[10] Bene veneritis magister Hans.

Shomaker. Deo gratias.

Parson What bringe you there / do you brynge my slyppers?

Shomaker. Yea forsoth Syr, I thoughte you had bene in the Church.

Parson. No mary.[11] I was yonder behynde in the gallery and there haue I mumbled.

Shomaker. What saye you master Parson? haue (A2v) ye mumbled?

Parson. Yea I haue sayd my diuine seruice[12] and besydes that I haue nowe and then fedde my nyghtyngale.

---

[6] Scoloker adds a brief cue for the opening speech. This is not exactly a stage direction, as in a play, which would typically offer an instruction like 'Enter Shoemaker'. The only other extradiegetic comments occur when the parson's handmaid appears, introduced by the marginal note 'Katherin the parso[n]s handmaid' (B5r), and when he is consulting the Bible (B5r-v); there, Scoloker adds sarcastic comments in his own voice next to the speeches.

[7] The jobs have been reallocated. Here, the female cook's part is split into this male servant and later Katherine the handmaid, and at the end the Parson will summon his (male) cook, not the 'Calefactor' as in the Dutch. Scoloker's addition of a male servant might perhaps reflect the androcentric world of contemporary Tudor drama.

[8] Perhaps by Scoloker's oversight, the cobbler is first called 'John' and then 'Hans', as in the original.

[9] An indoor space, unlike the G/D 'summerhouse', a garden house typical of Nuremberg patrician houses.

[10] 'Parson' is not as specific as 'canon' (German 'Chorherr', Dutch 'Coorheere'). A parson in the English Church, before or after the Reformation, is any priest or rector 'presented to an ecclesiastical living by a patron and instituted to it by the bishop' (OED 'parson', 1.1).

[11] Variant of 'marry', an expression of surprise, outrage, astonishment, now archaic.

[12] G/D uses the Latin term 'horas'.

94 *'Schoenmaker & Coorhere' (c. 1545) Dutch Edition*

Schoenmaker. Heere / wat hebdy voor een nachtegale / singhet hy[13] noch?

(A2v) Coorheere. O neen / het is te spade opt iaer.

Schoenmaker. Jck weet eenen Schoenmaker / die heeft eenen nachtegale / die heeft ierst begonn te singhen.

Coorheere. Ey die duyuel hale die Schoenmaker met alle sinen nachtegalen / Hoe heeft hy onsen alderhoochsten vader den Paus den heylighen vader / ende onsen heerweerdichsten Heere wt geroepen als een wijnsuyper / ende een banck boeue.[14]

Schoenmaker. Ey heere / wat dinc ist dan / hi heeft toch v maniere ende Gods dienst den gemeenen man bewees / ende nv roept ghy ouer hem.[15] Js dan v wesen Euangelis oft guyghelwerck.[16]

---

[13] The gendering of the nightingale as 'he' in E might be influenced by the Dutch personal pronoun 'hy'.

[14] D 'wijnsuyper' (wine drinker) and 'banck boeue' (literally: bench boy, also meaning a heavy drinker, DWb s.v. 'bankbube').

[15] Phrase 'and now you call him out' added in D.

[16] D 'fool's work, illusion' for G 'holhüppel werk' = a fraudulent tradesman's trick.

## 'Shomaker & Parson' (1548) English Edition 95

Shomaker. Syr Iohan[17] I praye you tell me what nyghtingale is it, syngeth he yet?

Parson. No forsoth, it draweth to nygh wynter.

Shomaker I knowe a shomaker who hath a nightyngale that beginneth now fyrst to synge.

Parson. Yea, the deuell of hell[18] take that shomaker with all hys nyghtyngales, he hath so rayled on oure mooste holyest Father the pope the moost hyghest Father and reuerend lorde. yea, he hath so cryed and called hym abroade, euen as though he had bene the moost vylest and vngrationst wretche or knaue of the whole world.

Shomaker. What softe and fayre Sir[19] I praie the, he hath partely[20] declared your maner of lyuinge, and your diuine seruice to the common people, and nowe I perceaue you do nothing but rayle on him, but what shall I (A3r) saie?[21] is your behauiour and lyuinge[22] according to christes Gospell[23] / or is it apesplaye?[24]

---

[17] Sir John was a stock name for a priest in Tudor fiction, sometimes used seriously – as in John Heywood's play *Johan Johan* (c.1525), where the priest is called Sir John – or disrespectfully – as in the morality play *Hick Scorner* (c.1515), in which the vice Riot calls the virtue Charity 'Sir John' as they put Charity into the stocks).

[18] Scoloker frequently uses the common idiom 'devil of hell' for the original 'devil'.

[19] 'What, soft and fair, Sir' = 'Now, steady on, Sir' (with an ironical tone).

[20] Either 'openly/boldly' (OED), or indicating that the abuses are still only partially exposed. G has 'simply', D no equivalent.

[21] Expands the added D phrase 'and now you call him out'.

[22] The double formula 'behaviour and living' expands the German/Dutch simple 'wesen' ('being')

[23] For G/D 'evangelisch'.

[24] Scoloker substitutes his own coinage for D 'fool's work'.

## 96 'Schoenmaker & Coorhere' (c. 1545) Dutch Edition

Coorheere. Maer waer gaet alsulcken ons wesen den dul[25] Schoenmaker aen.

Schoenmaker. Het staet Exodi int .xxiij. ca. Als ghy siet ws vyants Esel ligghen gheuallen onder sinen last / so en sult ghy niet voerby gaen / maer hem opheffen[26] / hoe veele te meer sal een Christen sinen naesten helpen / die by siet ligghen in eene beswar(A3ʳ)de conscientie.

Coorheere. Hy en soude daer inne die geestelijcke ende religioenen niet ghemeynt hebben dien esel cop / si weten te voren wel wat sonde is.

Schoenmaker. Maer Ezechiel spreeckt in zijn .xxxiij. cap. Siet ghy uwen broeder sondighen / soo straft hem / oft ick sal zijn bloet van uwer hant eysschen /[27] daerom moet een Christen sinen broeder straffen / sy ghewijt oft niet.

Coorheere. Sijt ghy Euangelischs?

Schoenmaker. Ja ick Heere.

Coorheere. Hebt ghy niet ghelesen in

---

[25] D 'dul' = 'mad' (equivalent to the German 'toll').

[26] The Bible passages in the D version are translated from Sachs, not taken from an exisiting Dutch or Low German version. In the following, the German text of Luther's translation (L45) is given for comparison in the footnotes for selected Bible quotations. Ex 23.5 *Wenn du des / der dich hasset / esel sihest vnter seiner last ligen / Hüt dich vnd las jn nicht / sondern verseume gern das deine vmb seinen willen.* (L45).

[27] A summary of Ez 33.2–4.

## 'Shomaker & Parson' (1548) English Edition 97

Parson. What the deuell of hell haue these dulheaded[28] shomakers to do with oure behaueour and lyuyng[29]?

Shomaker. It is wryten. When thou seest thyne Ennemies asse fallen vnder hys Burden / thou shalt not go by but helpe him vp.[30] How muche more is a christen Man[31] bounde to helpe hys neyghbour[32] / who he seeth lyinge in an heauy conscience?

Parson. That horeson[33] assehed ought not to haue meaned spyrituall and relygious men / for they knowe well ynoughe before hand what synne is.

Shomaker. But Ezechyell speaketh yf thou seest thy brother synne, reprehend hym, or els I wyll require hys bloude, at thy handes.[34] Therfore a Christen man ought to reprehend hys brother, be he anoynted or no.

Parson. Arte thou a Gospeller[35]?

Shomaker. Yea forsothe Syr.

Parson. (A3v) Hast thow not redde

---

[28] Misunderstanding of D 'dul' and turned this into the plural form (sg in G/D).

[29] Again 'wesen' in German / Dutch.

[30] *Exod. 23.* Ex 23.5 *If thou see the ass of him that hateth thee lying under his burden, and wouldest forbear to help him, thou shalt surely help with him.* (KJV). In the 1548 edition, the abbreviated Bible citations are printed in the outer margins. They are here moved at the start of the footnotes. Bible passages are translated from the Dutch, and not taken from any of the English Bible translations published by the 1540s. In the following, the King James Version (KJV) is given in the footnotes as a comparator text for selected Bible quotations.

[31] G: 'getaufter Christ', D: 'Christen'.

[32] G: 'bruder'; D: 'naesten' (literally: nearest, used in the sense of 'neighbour').

[33] = 'whoreson'. Added by Scoloker; often used in early modern English almost like an adjectival intensifier.

[34] *Ezechi. 33.* A summary of Ez 33.2–4.

[35] G/D: 'evangelisch' ('Protestant').

## 98 'Schoenmaker & Coorhere' (c. 1545) Dutch Edition

(a2v) Mattheus Euangelie int .vij. cap. Ghy ensult niet oordeelen / soo en wort ghy niet gheoordelt[36] / maer ghy Lutherianen en neemt alsulcken sprake niet ter herten / ghy en soeckter niet na / want si zijn v teghen.

Schoenmaker. Straffen ende oordelen is tweerley / wy en onderwinden ons niet te oordeelen dat God aen gaet / als Paulus seyt tot den Romeynen int .xiiij. capit. Niemant en sal eenen anderen sinen knecht (A3v) oordeelen / maer straffen[37] / ende vermanen ghelijck door den Prophete Esaiam int lviij .capit. spreckt / Screyt ende en hout niet op / ende als een basuyne soo verheft v stemme te vercondighen mijn volck haer misdaet / &c.[38]

Coorheere. Daer staet ooc Exod. int .xxiiij. Ghy en sult die ouersten onder v volc niet beschamen.[39]

Schoenmaker. Wie is die ouerste onder dat volc / ist niet die Keyser / ende daer na die Vorsten Grauen ende Princhen / met haer Ruyters ende wereltlijcke ouerheyt.

Coorheere. Neen / die Paus een Vicarius Christi daer nae Cardinalen / Bisschoppen met den gheheelen gheestelijcken staet / als gheschreuen staet / Solite de maioritate & obedientia. Sy beduyden die Sonne / ende dat weerlijcke ghewalt / beduyt die Mane / ende des seluen is die Paus veele machtigher dan die Keyser / welcken hem zijn voeten cussen moeten.

---

[36] Mt 7.1 1 *RJchtet nicht / Auff das jr nicht gerichtet werdet.* (L45).

[37] Rom 14.4 *Wer bistu / das du einen frembden Knecht richtest?* (L45).

[38] Is 58.1 *RVffe getrost / schone nicht / Erhebe deine stim wie eine Posaune / vnd verkündige meinem Volck jr vbertretten / vnd dem hause Jacob jre sunde.* (L45).

[39] Ex 22.27 *DEn Göttern soltu nicht fluchen / Vnd den Obersten in deinem Volck soltu nicht lestern.* (L45).

'Shomaker & Parson' (1548) English Edition  99

(a2v) the gospel of S. Mathew in the vij. Chapter. Thou shalte not Judge to thyntente[40] thou be not iudged?[41] But ye Lutheryans[42] passe nothyng at all vppon suche Sayinges / neyther do ye seke for them / for they are playne agaynst you.

Shomaker. To iudge and reprehend, is to be vnderstande two maner of wayes, we take not vppon vs to iudge that thynge which only aperteineth to god. As Paule sayth No man shall Iudge the seruaunt of an other man,[43] but ought, to reprehend and exhorte hym. As the prophet Esaye saythe Call without Ceasynge, and exalte youre voice lyke a trompett[44] to declare my people theyr offenses. et cetera.[45]

Parson. Ther is also written. Thou shalte not make the chefest of the people ashamed.[46]

Shomaker. Who is the chefeste, amonge the people / is it not the Emperour, kynges / prynces, Dukes / Earles, with theyr knygtes esquires and worldly power?

Parson. Nay, nay. The pope is Christes vicare, and next vnder hym, Cardynals, Bys-(A4r)shops with all the spiritualte / as it is written. Solite de maioritate et obediencia. These spirytuall men represent the sunne and the worldly powers represent only the moone. Wherout doth folowe that the pope must nedes be of greater power then the Emperour, who is faine to kysse hys fete.

---

[40] 'to the intent' (Middle English 'entent') = 'in order that'.

[41] *Math. 7.* Mt 7.1 *Judge not, that ye be not judged.* (KJV).

[42] Taken from the Dutch 'Lutherianen'. The more familiar 'Lutheran' was still perhaps not a common word, though the OED cites one English example from 1521 and one from 1530.

[43] *Roma. 14.* Rom 14.4 *Who art thou that judgest another man's servant?* (KJV).

[44] G/D 'Posaune' = trombone.

[45] *Esay. 58.* Is 58.1 *Cry aloud, spare not, lift up thy voice like a trumpet, and shew my people their transgression, and the house of Jacob their sins.* (KJV).

[46] *Exod. 22.* Ex 22.28 *Thou shalt not [...] curse the ruler of thy people.* (KJV)

## 100 'Schoenmaker & Coorhere' (c. 1545) Dutch Edition

Schoenmaker. Js die Paus een soo ghewaldeghen Heere / so en is hy certeynlick gheen stadthouder Christi / want Christus spreeckt Joannis int .xviij. capit. Mijn rijck en is niet (A4ʳ) niet van deser werelt.[47] Ende Joannis int vi. cap. vloet Christus daermen hem tot eenen Coninck maken woude.[48] Ooc sprack Chrisus tot sinen Jongheren Luce int xxij. cap. Die weerlijcke Coninghen domineeren / ende die gheweldighe heetmen ghenadighen heer / maer ghi niet alsoo / wane die onder v wil wesen die grootste die sal zijn als die minste / ende die ouerste als een dienaer.[49] Daerom is die Paus ende ghy gheestelijcke / als dienaers der Christelijcker ghemeynten / ist sake das ghy anders wt God zijt / ende daerom machmen v wel straffen.

Coorheere. Die Paus ende die zijne en zijn niet schuldich die gheboden Gods ghehoorsaem te zijne / als in die geestelijcke rechten staet. C. Solite de maioritate et obedientia / wt dien sluyten iuy dat die Paus gheen sondaer en is / maer die alderheylichste / ende in dier manieren onstraffelick.

Schoenmaker. Daer staet gheschreuen Joannis int .i.

---

[47] Jo 18.36 *Jhesus antwortet / Mein Reich ist nicht von dieser welt.* (L45).

[48] Jo 6.15 *Da Jhesus nu mercket / das sie komen würden / vnd jn haschen / das sie jn zum Könige machten / entweich er abermal / auff den Berg / er selbs alleine.* (L45). *When Jesus therefore perceived that they would come and take him by force, to make him a king, he departed again into a mountain himself alone.* (KJV).

[49] Lc 22.25 *Er aber sprach zu jnen / Die weltlichen Könige herrschen / vnd die Gewaltigen heisset man gnedige Herrn. 26 Jr aber nicht also / Sondern der Grössest vnter euch / sol sein wie der Jüngste / vnd der Furnemest wie ein Diener.* (L45).

## 'Shomaker & Parson' (1548) English Edition 101

Shomaker. Is the pope such a puyssaunt[50] lorde? truly then is he not Christes vicare. For Christ sayth, my kyngdome is not of thys worlde.[51] And Iohn. 6. Christ (when he sawe that men wolde make hym kyng) went hys wayes.[52] Christ also sayd vnto hys dysciples. Worldely prynces haue dominion and beare Rule, and the Myghtye of the earthe are called Lordes / but let it not be so amonge you. For who of you wyll be the greatest shalbe the leaste, and the chefest as a Seruaunt,[53] and therfore the pope and ye spyrytuall men are but mynysters vnto the Christians (in case ye be of God) and therfore menne maye reprehende you well Inoughe.

parson. The pope with hys, is not bounde to obeye the commaundement of God. As it is written in the spirituall lawe. C. Solite de maioritate et obediencia out of the whych (A4v) we do conclude that the pope is no sinner but the most holyest and in all thyng inreprehensible.

Shomaker. It is wrytten,

---

[50] = 'powerful/mighty' (from Old French *poissant*).

[51] *Iohan. 18.* Jo 18.36 *Jesus answered, My kingdom is not of this world:* (KJV).

[52] *Iohan. 6.* Jo 6.15 *When Jesus therefore perceived that they would come and take him by force, to make him a king, he departed again into a mountain himself alone.* (KJV).

[53] *Luke. 22.* Lc 22.25 *And he said unto them, The kings of the Gentiles exercise lordship over them; and they that exercise authority upon them are called benefactors. 26 But ye shall not be so: but he that is greatest among you, let him be as the younger; and he that is chief, as he that doth serve.* (KJV).

# 102 *'Schoenmaker & Coorhere' (c. 1545) Dutch Edition*

(a3r) in zijn ierste Epistels / die seyt dat hi sonder sonde is / die is een lueghenaer[54] / ende niet die alderheylichste / mer te straffen.

Coorheere. (A4ᵛ) Ey lieue / ende oft die Paus so quaes ware / dat hy ontallijcke vele volcs met grooten hoopen ter hellen voerde / so en machmen hem niet straffen / dat staet geschreuen in onsen rechten. Dis .xl. Si Papa / hoe behaecht v dat.

Schoenmaker. Wel soo staet int Euangelio Matth. int .xviij. Jst dat v broeder sondicht teghen v / soo gaet henen ende straft hem tusschen v ende hem / hoort hy v / so hebe ghy zijn siele ghewonnen.[55] Ghebruyckt die Paus sulcken salighen werck.

Coorheere. Jst dat broederlijcke gestraft / also int openbaer wt te roepen.

Schoenmaker. Ey daer staet noch breeder in den text / ist dat uwe broeder niet en hoort / soo neemt noch een oft twee tot v / ende hoort hy v noch niet / so segghet der ghemeynten / hoort hy die ghemeynte oock niet / soo laet hem gaen ghelijck een Heyden[56] / ghelijck ghy heer domine.

---

[54] 1 Jo 1.8 *So wir sagen / Wir haben keine sünde / So verfüren wir vns selbs* .... (L45).

[55] Mt 18.15 *SVndiget aber dein Bruder an dir / so gehe hin / vnd straffe jn zwischen dir vnd jm alleine. 16 Höret er dich / so hastu deinen Bruder gewonnen.* (L45).

[56] Mt 18.16 *Höret er dich nicht / so nim noch einen oder zween zu dir / Auff das alle Sache bestehe / auff zweier oder dreier Zeugen munde. 17 Höret er die nicht / so sage es der Gemeine. Höret er die Gemeine nicht / So halt jn als einen Heiden vnd Zölner.* (L45).

## 'Shomaker & Parson' (1548) English Edition   103

(a3r) who so ever sayth that he is wythout synne, is a lyer,[57] oute of the whiche followeth that the Pope muste nedes be a sinner or a lier (if he be not both) and not the most holyest / but is greatly to be reprehended.

Parson. What I say[58] / although the pope were so wycked, that he dyd bryng a great multytude of people into hell, yet may no man reprehende him. For it is wrytten in oure lawes dyst. xl. Si papa.[59] Howe doth that please the?[60]

Shomaker. It is written in the gospell of Mathew if thy brother do synne reprehend him betwene hym and the / and if he heare the, then hast thou wonne him.[61] Doth the pope vse such Godly actes?

Parson. Doest thou call this to reprehende after a brotherly sorte, to cry and call it out so openly?

Shomaker. It is further written in the same text, (A5r) in case thy brother heare the not / then take one or two wyth you / and if he heare you not then, then tell it to the congregacion, and let him go lyke a heathen and infidell,[62] euen as thou art sir domine.[63]

---

[57] *Iohan. 1.* 1 Jo 1.8 *If we say that we have no sin, we deceive ourselves.* (KJV).

[58] In G/D a friendly address 'Ei lieber' (Well, my dear).

[59] *distinct. 40.* Friedberg, Vol. I, Distinctio 40, c. 6. p. 146, see full footnote in the translation of the German text.

[60] The formal second person plural of the Dutch is made singular and informal, typical of the more tetchy and disrespectful tone of the English dialogue.

[61] *Math. 18.* Mt 18.15 *Moreover if thy brother shall trespass against thee, go and tell him his fault between thee and him alone: if he shall hear thee, thou hast gained thy brother.* (KJV).

[62] Mt 18.16 *But if he will not hear thee, then take with thee one or two more, that in the mouth of two or three witnesses every word may be established. 17 And if he shall neglect to hear them, tell it unto the church: but if he neglect to hear the church, let him be unto thee as an heathen man and a publican.* (KJV).

[63] In G a challenge to the parson: 'What about that, Sir canon?' Seems to be a literal translation of D 'ghelijck ghy heer domine'.

## 104 'Schoenmaker & Coorhere' (c. 1545) Dutch Edition

Coorheere. Lieve wat is dat profijt / dat hy ons so langhe teghen roepe / ghelijck sprinchanen wy en keeren ons niet daer na / ende houden toch onsen Decretalen. (B1ʳ)

Schoenmaker. Waerom spreeckt Christus Matthei int .x. capit. Jst datmen niet en hoort / soo schuddet den stof van uwen voeten / tot een ghetuy ghenisse / dat hem dat rijcke Gods na is gheweest / want het sal Sodomam ende Gomorrham verdrachgelijcker wesen in den dach des oordeels / dan sulcken volcke /[64] hoe salt v dan gaen / als ghi gheen straffenisse en wilt aennemen

Coorheere. Nv ick laet dat goet zijn / want geleerde verstandighe lieden waren / maer den leeken en betamet niet.

Schoenmaker. Een Esel strafte toch den Prophete Balaam. Numeri int .xxij. ca. Waerom ensout niet betamen eenen leeken te straffen eenen gheestelijcken.

Coorheere. Eenen Schoenmaker behoert met leer ende met swerten om te gaen / ende niet met der heylighen schriftueren.

Schoenmaker. Met welcken schriftueren wilt ghyt by brenghen / dat een Christen menschen niet in der schriftueren ondersoecken / lesen ende schrijuen sal / want Christus spreect Joan. int .v. cap. Doorsoeckt die schrijft/ (B1ᵛ) want sy gheuet ghetuyghenisse van my[65] / ende noch soo spreeckt die Psalmist .i. Salich is die man die hem dach ende nacht oeffent

---

[64] Mt 10.14 *VND wo euch jemand nicht annemen wird / noch ewer Rede hören / So gehet eraus / von dem selben Hause oder Stad / vnd schüttelt den staub von ewren Füssen. 15 Warlich / Jch sage euch / dem Lande der Sodomer vnd Gomorrer wird es treglicher ergehen am jüngsten Gericht / denn solcher Stad.* (L45).

[65] Jo 5.39 *SVchet in der Schrifft / … sie ists / die von mir zeuget / ….* (L45).

*'Shomaker & Parson' (1548) English Edition*   105

Parson. I praye the what preuayleth it that thou doest call vs thus abroad lyke greshoppers[66], consyderyng we passe nothyng for it. For we holde vs by our decrees?

Shomaker. Therfore sayth Chryst, in case men do not heare you, then shake the dust from your fete for a wytnes that the Kyngdome of God hath bene nygh vnto them. For theyr Iudgement shall be greater at the day of dome, then to Sodoma and Gomorra.[67] In what case shalt thou be then; seing thou wylt not be reprehended?

Parson. I wolde graunte it to be so / in case they were learned men, but it becommeth not the laye people to reprehend the spiritualte

Shomaker. An asse reprehended Balaam the prophet. Wherfore then is it not lawfull. For a lay man to reprehende a spirituall man?

Parson. A shomaker ought to meddle with grea-(A5v)sing of his lether and clouting of his showes, and not with holy scripture.

Shomaker. Howe can ye proue that by scripture / that a Christen man may not rede, wryte and search in the scriptures? For Chryste sayth, search the Scriptures for she beareth witnes of me.[68] And the psalmograph[69] sayth also. Blessed is the man that studyeth nyght and daye

---

[66] In G 'market crier', in D 'sprinchanen', literally: jumping cockerel, a term for 'grashopper'.

[67] Mt 10.14 *And whosoever shall not receive you, nor hear your words, when ye depart out of that house or city, shake off the dust of your feet.15 Verily I say unto you, It shall be more tolerable for the land of Sodom and Gomorrha in the day of judgment, than for that city.* (KJV).

[68] Jo 5.39 *Search the scriptures [...] and they are they which testify of me.* (KJV).

[69] Literally: 'Psalm-writer' (G/D 'Psalmist'); a rare word to describe David as author of the psalms.

## 106 'Schoenmaker & Coorhere' (c. 1545) Dutch Edition

(a3v) in die Wet des Heeren /[70] ende noch soo spreckt Petrus in zijn ierste Epistel int .iij. ca. Sijt altijt bereyt om altijt antwoorde te gheuen eenen yeghelijcken / dye gront eysschet des hopinghen die in v is /[71] ende alsoo leert Paulus die Ephesien int .vi. capi. Vechtet teghen den aenloop des duyuels / met den woorde Gods / welcke hy een sweert noemet /[72] Heere / hoe sullen wy moghen wederstaen als wy de scriftueren niet en wisten.

Coorheere. Ghelijck die gansen int water.

Schoenmaker. Ghy spot wel / die Joden weten haer Wet wtwendich / sullen wy Christenen niet oock weten dat Euangelium Jesu Cristi / welcke is die cracht Gods allen die daer salich sullen werden / ghelijck Paulus seyt .i. Cor .i.[73]

Coorheere. Ja ghy sult weten / ghelijck Christus v seyt Mat .xxiij. Op Moyses stoel hebben he in gheset die gheleerden ende Phariseen / al wat si v segghen dat doet /[74] dat beduyt die daghelicxse prekinghe / hebt ghi leeken niet ghenoech daer aen? (B2[r])

Schoenmaker. Ey daer staet aen die selue plaetschs[75] Mat. int .xxiij. Sy binden sware ondrachlijcke lasten op der menschen schouderen[76] ende sulcke lasten beduyden sekerlijcke ende sonder twijfel der menschen geboden / daer mede ghy ons leeken dringhet ende dwinghet ende maect ons quade conscientien / waerom souden wy v volghen.

---

[70] Ps 1.1 *WOl dem der ... 2 ... hat lust zum Gesetz des HERRN / Vnd redet von seinem Gesetz tag vnd nacht.* (L45).

[71] 1 Pt 3.15 *Seid aber allezeit bereit zur Verantwortung jederman / der grund foddert der Hoffnung / die in euch ist* / (L45).

[72] Eph 6. 11 *Ziehet an den harnisch Gottes / Das jr bestehen künd gegen die listigen anlauff des Teufels.* (L45).

[73] Paraphrase of 1 Cor 1.23–24.

[74] Mt 23.2 *Auff Moses stuel sitzen die Schrifftgelerten vnd Phariseer / 3 Alles nu was sie euch sagen / das jr halten sollet / das haltet vnd thuts* / (L45).

[75] The final letters on this page smudged in several places.

[76] Mt 23.4 *Sie binden aber schwere vnd vntregliche Bürden / vnd legen sie den Menschen auff den hals* / (L45)

## 'Shomaker & Parson' (1548) English Edition   107

(a3v) in the lawes of the lord,[77] And Peter sayth also Prepare your selues to answere euery man / the grounde requyreth the hope whiche is in you,[78] and in lyke maner Paule teacheth the Ephesians to fyght agaynst the assaultes of the deuell, with the swerde of Gods woorde.[79] Oh lord howe were it possyble for vs to resyst, if we knewe nothing of the scripture?

Parson. Euen lyke a heape of gise[80] in the water.

Shomaker. Mocke at your pleasure. The Iewes knowe theyr lawe by roote or wythoute the boke, shal not we that are Christians know the gospell of Iesus Chryst? whiche is the power of God to as manye as shal be saued / as Paule sayth.[81]

Parson. Yea, thou shalt know it as Christ hath (A6r) tolde. The scribes and pharizees haue set them vppon Moses seat. What so euer they teach you, loke you do the same[82] which signifieth the dayly preachinges / doth not this suffise the laye people?

Shomaker. Ther is also written in the same chapter They laye heauy and vnbearable burdens vppon mennes neckes,[83] and such sygnifye the tradicions and commaundementes of men wherby ye dryue and oppresse vs laye people, bryngyng vs in heauy consciens / wherfore shulde we then folowe you?

---

[77] Ps 1.1 *Blessed is the man* [...] 2 [...] *his delight is in the law of the LORD; and in his law doth he meditate day and night.* (KJV).

[78] *1. Petri. 3.* 1 Pt 3.15 *be ready always to give an answer to every man that asketh you a reason of the hope that is in you with meekness and fear:* (KJV).

[79] *Ephesi. 6.* Eph 6. 11 *Put on the whole armour of God, that ye may be able to stand against the wiles of the devil.* (KJV).

[80] = geese. It is not clear that Scoloker has understood the original proverb 'like geese in bad weather', meaning: easily, naturally.

[81] *1. Corin. 1.* Paraphrase of 1 Cor 1.23–24.

[82] *Math. 22.* Typographical error for '23': Mt 23.2 *The scribes and the Pharisees sit in Moses' seat: 3 All therefore whatsoever they bid you observe, that observe and do;* (KJV).

[83] Mt 23.4 *For they bind heavy burdens and grievous to be borne, and lay them on men's shoulders.* (KJV). No marginal note, perhaps because the translator could not locate it in the same chapter since it is one chapter further on.

108 *'Schoenmaker & Coorhere' (c. 1545) Dutch Edition*

Coorheere. Hoe wilt ghy daer mede schrift bewijsen.

Schoenmaker. Christus spreeckt in dat voorgeseyde cap. Wee v ghy ypocriten *ende* Phariseen die dat rijck der hemelen toe sluyt voor den menschen / ghi en wilt er niet in gaen ende ghy belet die daer in gaen willen.[84]

Coorheere En sulck heeft Christus tot die Priesteren der Joden gheseyt / maer met onse Priesters / ist wel anders ghestelt.

Schoenmaker. Ey Heere /ghi hebt v ierst de*n* nae*m* der Phariseen aengenome*n* / die op den stoel Moysi sitten / &c. al ist van v Papen ende Monicken ghesproke*n* / alst oock daer is / alsoo ist oock van v ghesproken / want v wercken gheue*n* ghetuy genissen / wa*n*t ghy versloct der weduwe*n* huysen / als de*n* selvue*n* (B2ᵛ) text voorder verclaert / Heere ghy hebt v vergrepen.

Coorheere. Fij[85] / hoe zijn die Luterianen soo nueswijs / ghy hoort dat gras wasschen / wa*n*neer uwer een / een sprake oft twee

---

[84] Mt 23.13 *WEh euch Schrifftgelerten vnd Phariseer / jr Heuchler / die jr das Himelreich zuschliesset fur den Menschen / Jr kompt nicht hinein / vnd die hinein wöllen / lasset jr nicht hin ein gehen.* (L45).

[85] Simplified for G 'pi pa pu'.

*'Shomaker & Parson' (1548) English Edition* 109

parson. How canst thou proue that by scripture?

Shomaker. Chryst sayth in the before named chapter. Wo be vnto you ye hipocrites and pharizees, that shut vp the kyngdome of heauen for the people / thou wylte not entre into it thy selfe, nor yet suffre any other to enter.[86]

parson. Yea that was spoken to the priestes of the Iewes, and not to our priests.

Shomaker. Mary.[87] Syr ye haue fyrst taken the name of pharizees vppon you Which sytte vppon moses seate etc. Although it be spo-(A6v)ken of the Priestes of the Iewes (as the trueth is) euen so it also spoken of you. For your workes beare witnes / thou eatest the widdowes houses / as the text further doth declare, in good fayth sir domine you haue taken your selfe by the nose.[88]

Parson. Fye on the. Howe do these horeson lutherians reioyce and laughe in their fyst, when they can fynde some sayings

---

[86] Mt 23.13 *But woe unto you, scribes and Pharisees, hypocrites! for ye shut up the kingdom of heaven against men: for ye neither go in yourselves, neither suffer ye them that are entering to go in.* (KJV). Again no marginal reference, probably for the same reason.

[87] Variant of 'marry', an expression of surprise, outrage, astonishment, now archaic.

[88] Instead of the Dutch 'you have a wrong grip', Scoloker substitutes this common idiom for catching someone out, or leading them blindly. The Catholic speaker in the Protestant debate *A dialogue* [...] *betwene two neighbours* (1554; STC 10383) is called Sir Nicholas Noseled. In G/D a nose-related expression comes in the next sentence where the Lutherans are accused of being 'naßweiß' / 'nueswijs' (use the nose for sniffing = being forward and insolent).

110 *'Schoenmaker & Coorhere' (c. 1545) Dutch Edition*

(a4r) wt de*n* Euangelien heeft / soo verceert e*nde* quelt ghy eenen yeghelijcken daer mede.

Schoenmaker. Ey heere vertoorent v niet / ick meyne in goede.

Coorhere. Jck en vertoorne my niet / mer ic moet v segghen / het en behoort den leeke*n* niet toe met der schrijft om te gaen.

Schoenmaker. Ende Christus spreeckt toe Matthei int .vij. Huet v voor den valschen Propheten /[89] ende Paulus tot den Philippe*n*sen int .iij. Sijt op v hoede.[90] Soude ons die schriftuere niet behooren te lesen oft te weten / hoe souden wy dan sulcken dinck bekennen.

Coorheere. Alsulcke*n* hoort den Pausdom[91] toe / gelijck Paulus tot Timot. int .i. staet / Ghi sult se scerpelijcke straffen die verleyders[92]

Schoenmaker. Ja si en doens niet / maer daerteghen / (B3ʳ) alsoot claer is.

Coorheere. Daer laet se om sorghen.

Schoenmaker. Neen niet alsoo / willen si niet / soe behooret ons selue / daer nae hem te schouwen / want gheen en sal des anders last draghen.

Coorheere. Ey lieue / segghet wat ghi wilt / het en behoort de leeken niet toe / met der scrift om te gaen / ghelijck Paulus seyt .i. Cor. int .vij. een yeghelijck ghelijck hem die Heere gheroepen heeft / soo wandele hy[93] hoort ghy nv wel / ghy hebt te vooren schrift begheert.

---

[89] Mt 7.15 *SEhet euch fur / fur den falschen Propheten* (L45).

[90] Phil 3.2 *Sehet auff die Hunde / sehet auff die bösen Erbeiter / sehet auff die Zurschneitung* (L45).

[91] G 'bischoffen' (bishops), replaced by 'papacy', a neutral term. Turned in E into the derogatory term 'papistry'.

[92] Tit (!) 1.10–11 *DEnn es sind viel frechen / vnd vnnütze Schwetzer vnd Verfürer* […] *welchen man mus das maul stopffen.* (L45). The Dutch translator or typesetter mixed up the abbreviations for the letters to Timotheus and Titus. Titus is correct.

[93] 1 Cor 7.20 *Ein jglicher bleibe in dem ruff / darinnen er beruffen ist.* (L45).

## 'Shomaker & Parson' (1548) English Edition 111

(a4r) out of the scripture / they trouble and vexe one therwith, without ceasyng.

Shomaker. Syr I pray the be not discontented for in good fayth I speake of a good zeale.

Parson. I am not angry, but I am bounde to tell it the, it beco*mm*eth not the laye People to meddle with the scripture.

Shomaker. Chryst sayth. Beware of false prophetes[94] and Paule to the Philippi*ans*. iij. take hede.[95] If we myght not be suffered to rede the scriptures, how shulde we the*n* know these thynges.

Parson. The same apperteyneth to the papistry[96] as Paule sayth to Timoth*y*. 1. ye shall correct the seducers with all extremitie.[97] (A7r)

Shomaker. Yea they do it not, but do manifestly agaynst it as it daylie doth apere.

parson Let them care for that.

Shomaker. No syr not so / we wyll not esteme it so lyght / if they wyll not, then muste we take hede that we folow not them / for no man shall beare an others burden.

parson. Saye what ye lyst,[98] it apperteyneth not to the laye people to meddel with the scripture as Paule saythe. 1. Cor*inthians*. 7. Let euery man walke accordynge to the lordes callyng.[99] Howe sayest thou nowe? thou woldest haue scripture, and now I haue scriptured[100] the I trow.

---

[94] *Math. 7.* Mt 7.15 *Beware of false prophets.* (KJV).

[95] *Philipi. 3.* Phil 3.2 *Beware of dogs, beware of evil workers, beware of the concision.* (KJV).

[96] 'Papistry' was a derogatory Protestant word for Catholicism (a 'papist' is a Roman Catholic), first attested in the 1540s (OED). Either Scoloker, or typesetter, meant to write 'papacy', or the Parson has made a Freudian slip.

[97] Tit (!) 1.10–11 *For there are many unruly and vain talkers and deceivers, [...] Whose mouths must be stopped.* (KJV). Wrong attribution taken over from D.

[98] = 'what you like' (informal 2 ps sg of Middle English 'listen', 'to want').

[99] *1. Cor. 7.* 1 Cor 7.20 *Let every man abide in the same calling wherein he was called.* (KJV).

[100] G/D: 'it was you who wanted Scripture'. Scoloker uses verbing of 'Scripture' in the sense of the Bible for comic effect; neologism.

## 112 'Schoenmaker & Coorhere' (c. 1545) Dutch Edition

Schoenmaker. Ja Paulus spreeckt van den wtwendighen staet ende handelinghe / van knechten ende vrijen / ghelijck aen die selue plaetse ende capittel claer staet / maer hier is dat woort Gods noch eene yeghelijcken onuerboden te handelen.

Coorheere. Ey hoort ghy niet / ghy moest te voren door die heylige wijinghe gheroepen zijn ende daer na vander ouerheyt vercoren werden / anders en betamet nieman met der heyligher schrift om te gaene.

Schoenmaker. (B3ᵛ) Christus spreeckt Lu. int .x. Den oost is groot / maer die arbeyders zyn weynich bidt den Heere des oosts dat hy arbeyders seynde in sinen oosts.[101] Ende daerom moet die roepinghe inwendich van God zijn / ende niet wtwendich / Wtwendich zijn alle Prekaers gheroepen / alsoo wel die valsche / alsoo wel als die rechte.

Coerheere. Ey het is sots werck met uwen clappen.

Schoenmaker. Het is met v als metten iongeren. Luce int .ix. die verdrooten dat die andere oock die duyuelen wtwerpen in Cristus name / maer Christus sprack / belettet haer niet want wie niet teghen v en is / die is met v /[102] in dien ghy rechte Christen waert / so sout ghy v verblijden

---

[101] Lc10.2 *Die Erndte ist gros / der Erbeiter aber ist wenig / Bittet den Herrn der erndten / das er Erbeiter aussende in seine erndte.* (L45).

[102] Lc 9.50 *Weret jm nicht / Denn wer nicht wider vns ist / der ist fur vns.* (L45).

## 'Shomaker & Parson' (1548) English Edition   113

Shomaker Yea paule speaketh that of the outward conuersacion[103] and lyuinge, of boundemen and Fremen / as in the same Chapter it is clearley specifyed. But here doth he forbid no man to searche the worde of God.

Parson. Doest thou not here? ye muste fyrste be called throughe the holy oyntment / and after that / be chosen of the higher powers other wyse is it not laufull for any man to meddell with the scrypture. (A7v)

Shomaker. Chryst sayth. The haruest is great, but ther are very fewe labourers, pray to the lorde of the haruest to send labourers into his haruest,[104] wherby the callyng muste nedes be inwardlye of God / and not outwardely. For outwardly are all preachers called, as well the false as the true.

Parson. Tush.[105] It is but folyshnes to reason with such pratlers.

Shomaker

It is euen so with you, as it was with the discyples / whiche were offended that other men cast oute[106] deuelles in Chrystes name, as wel as they. But Christ sayd forbydde them not. For whosoeuer is not agaynste you is with you.[107] And if ye were true Chrystyans / ye shulde euen reioyce

---

[103] Not only how one speaks and acts, but also the social company one keeps (OED, 'conversation' 2).

[104] *Luke. 10. Lc10.2 The harvest truly is great, but the labourers are few: pray ye therefore the Lord of the harvest, that he would send forth labourers into his harvest.* (KJV).

[105] A common interjection, dismissive in tone. German 'Ach', Dutch 'Ey'.

[106] Printed 'castoute'.

[107] *Luke. 9. Lc 9.50 And Jesus said unto him, Forbid him not: for he that is not against us is for us.* (KJV).

# 114 'Schoenmaker & Coorhere' (c. 1545) Dutch Edition

(a4v) / dat men oock leeken vonde die God woort wisten ende verstonden.

Coorhere. Wat gaet v den noot aen.

Schoenmaker. Daeromme dat wy den duyuel in dat doopsel versaeckt hebben / daerom zyn wy neerstich teghen hem / ende teghen zijn rijck te vechten met den woorden Gods / ende oock te waghen lijf ende goet.

Coorheere. Siet daer na ghy leeken hoe ghy lieben (B4ʳ) wijf ende v kinderen gheneeren mocht.

Schoenmaker. Christus verbiet Matthei int .vi. cap. ende spreeckt / Sorghet niet wat ghi eeten ende drincken ende aendoen sult / om sulcke din ghen sorghen die Heydenen / maer soeckt eerste dat rijcke Gods / ende zijn gherechticheyt / dat ander sal v van selfs toe gheworpen worden[108] / ende Petrus .i. Epistele. int .iiij. Worpt alle v sorghe op den Heere / want hy sorghet voor v.[109] En de oock Christus Mat. int .iiij Die menschen en leeft niet alleene vanden broode / maer van eenen yeghelijcken woorde dat daer gaet wt den mont Gods.[110]

Coorheere. Laet v daer met ghenoeghen ende en backt niet.

---

[108] Mt 6.31 *DArumb solt jr nicht sorgen / vnd sagen / Was werden wir essen? Was werden wir trincken? Wo mit werden wir vns kleiden? ... / Denn ewer himlischer Vater weis / das jr des alles bedürfft.* (L45).

[109] 1 Pt 5.7 *Alle ewer sorge werffet auff jn / Denn er sorget fur euch.* (L45). The wrong chapter number 4 is taken over from the German.

[110] Mt 4.4 *Der Mensch lebet nicht vom Brot alleine / Sondern von einem jglichen wort / das durch den mund Gottes gehet.* (L45).

'Shomaker & Parson' (1548) English Edition 115

(a4v) that the lay people do vnderstand & know the worde of God.

Parson. What grefe is it to you?

Shomaker. Because we haue forsaken the deuell in our baptym, therfore are we thus dilygent to fyght with Gods worde agaynst him & his kingdom, yea and to auenture[111] and Ieoparde both body and goods.

Parson. It were better for ye lay people to study howe to get the lyuing of your wyues and chyldren. (A8r)

Shomaker. Chryst forbiddeth and sayth, take no thought what ye shall eate and drinke or what clothes ye shal put on, for suche thinges do the heathen seke, but seke fyrst the kingdom of God. &c. And it shal be[112] geuen you aboundauntly.[113] The man lyueth not onely by breade, but of euery word which procedeth out of the mouth of God.[114]

Parson. Satisfye and content your selfe therwith / and bake neuer a whitte.[115]

---

[111] = 'hazard/risk' (from Middle French *aventurer*). G/D 'fechten' (to fight).

[112] Printed 'shalbe' (a common elision).

[113] *Math. 6.* Mt 6.31 *Therefore take no thought, saying, What shall we eat? or, What shall we drink? or, Wherewithal shall we be clothed? ... for your heavenly Father knoweth that ye have need of all these things.* (KJV). The English translation skips the following quotation from 1 Pt 5, perhaps because of being unable to locate the quotation due to the wrong chapter number being given.

[114] *Math. 4.* Mt 4.4 *But he answered and said, It is written, Man shall not live by bread alone, but by every word that proceedeth out of the mouth of God.* (KJV).

[115] = 'boast not a bit'. Directly taken over from G 'bachen/pochen' /D 'baken' = boast, insist on something. Usually in English 'to brag'.

## 116 *'Schoenmaker & Coorhere' (c. 1545) Dutch Edition*

Schoenmaker. Wy sullen arbeyden ghelyck[116] Adam gheboden is / Genesis int .iij. ende Job int v. Die mensche is gheboren te arbeyden ghelijck den voghel tot den vlieghen /[117] ende wy en sullen niet sorghen / maer God betrouwen / daerom moghen wy wel den woorde Gods aenhanghen / welcke is dat beste deel. Luce int .x.[118]

Coorheere. Waer sout ghijt leeken geleert hebben / uwer sommighe en can niet een lettere. (B4ᵛ)

Schoenmaker. Christus spreeckt Joannis. Sy sullen al van God gheleert werden.[119]

Coorheere. Daer moeste oock conste zijn / waer voor zijn die hoghe scholen.

Schoenmaker. Op welcker hogher scholen heeft Joannes ghestaen / die soo hooghe ghescreuen heeft (Jn beghinsel was dat woort) ende dat woort was by God / &ce. Joannis .i.[120] Hy was doch nv een vischer / ghelijck Marci .i. staet.[121]

Coorheere. Lieue dese heeft den heylighen gheest ghehadt / ghelijck Actuum int .ij. staet.

Schoenmaker. Daer staet toch Johelis int .ij. Ende het sal gheschien inden lesten daghen spreect God / Jck wil wt ghieten van mijnen geest op alle vleesche / hoe meynt ghy niet dat van ons gheseyt is?

Coorheere. Neent / het is van den Apostelen geseyt / ghelijck als Petrus betuyghet / Actuum int .ij. Daerom swyghet met den gheest.

Schoenmaker. Christus spreect Joannis int .vij.

---

[116] Typesetting error 'gheluck' (luck) instead of 'ghelyck' (similar to). G: 'wie'.

[117] Sachs's translation follows the Latin Job 5.7 *Homo nascitur ad laborem, et avis ad volatum.* (VLC). The Dutch in turn follows his translation rather than the Hebrew as given in the Luther-Bible *Der Mensch wird zu vnglück geborn / wie die Vögel schweben empor zufliegen.* (L45).

[118] Lc 10.42 Jesus praises Mary for having 'chosen the good part', listening to him.

[119] Jo 6.45 *Sie werden alle von Gott geleret sein.* (L45).

[120] Jo 1.1 *JM anfang war das Wort / Vnd das wort war bey Gott* (L45).

[121] Mk 1.19 tells of Christ calling the disciples directly from their fishing boats.

'Shomaker & Parson' (1548) English Edition   117

Shomaker. We must labour, as it was commaunded to Adam.[122] The men are borne to labour lyke the byrdes to flye.[123]

> **Shomaker.**
> We must labour, as it was commaun= Gene. 3. ¶
> ded to Joā. The mē are boʒne to labour Job. 5.
> lyke the byʒdes to flye.       Parson.
> Where shuld you and other laye people

Parson. Where shuld you and other laye people haue learned it? some of them knowe neyther A nor B.[124]

Shomaker. Chryst sayth. They shal all be taught of God.

Parson. But there nedeth also learning, wherfore are the vniuersities els ordeyned?

Shomaker. In what vniuersitie (I pray the) dyd Ioan studye? Who wrote so profoundly In the beginning was the worde and the (a8r) worde was God. &cete.[125] For he was but a fyssher as it is wrytten.

Parson. What man / he was illuminate wyth the holy gost.

Shomaker. It is wrytten. And it shall happen in the later daies, sayth God, I wyl power out my spyrite vppon all fleshe. What meane ye? thynke ye that thys is not spoken of vs?[126]

Parson. No, it is spoken of the Apostles, as peter witnesseth. Therfor hold thy peace and speake no more of the spyrite.

Shomaker. Chryste sayth

---

[122] *Gene. 3.* Gn 3.19, God's prediction that Adam will have to work 'in the sweat of his face'. The following quotation from Lc 10.42 is missed out, perhaps because the translator could not verify the verse since it is a free paraphrase.

[123] *Iob. 5.* [joined to the previous marginal note *Genesis.3.* with &] Job 5.7 *Yet man is born unto trouble, as the sparks fly upward.* (KJV) – see footnote of D for the difference in translation.

[124] G/D 'not a letter'.

[125] Jo 1.1 *In the beginning was the Word, and the Word was with God, and the Word was God.* (KJV). The St John's Prologue held a special status in the Middle Ages, often used as charm.

[126] *Actes. 2.* Acts 2.14–17, Peter's sermon at Pentecost.

## 118 'Schoenmaker & Coorhere' (c. 1545) Dutch Edition

(b1r) Wie aen my ghelooft (ghelijck die scrift leyt) Van zijn leuen sullen vlieten vloeden des (C1ʳ) leuende waters dat (spreeckt die Euangelist[127] (welcke hi spreeckt van den heylighen gheest / welcke ontfanghen souden die aen hem gheloouen.

Coorheere. Hoe / ick meyne ghi stinct na Mantuano den ketter / met den heylighen gheest.

Schoenmaker. Paulus spreeckt .i. Cor. int .iij. Weet ghy niet dat ghy den tempel Gods zijt / ende die gheest Gods in v woont.[128] Ende Galathas int .iiij. die wijle ghi nv kinderen zijt / heeft God sinen gheest ghesent in uwer herten / die roept Abba lieue Vader.[129] Ende Timot. int .iij. na zynder Bermherticheyt maect hi ons salich / door dat badt der wedergheboorten / ende der vernieuwinghe des heylighen gheest / dwelc hy wtghegoten heeft rijckelijcke in ons.[130] Ende tot den Romeynen int .viij. So nv den gheest in v woont / die Jesum heeft op verwect van der doot.[131]

Coorheere. Jck en vinde gheenen heylighen gheest in my / ghy ende ick en zijn niet daer toe edel ghenoech.

---

[127] Jo 7.38 *Wer an mich gleubet / wie die Schrifft saget / von des Leibe werden ströme des lebendigen Wassers fliessen.* (L45).

[128] 1 Cor 3.16 *WJsset jr nicht / das jr Gottes tempel seid / vnd der geist Gottes in euch wonet?* (L45).

[129] Gal 4.6 *Weil jr denn Kinder seid / hat Gott gesand den geist seines Sons in ewre hertzen / der schreiet / Abba / lieber Vater.* (L45).

[130] Tit (!) 3.5 *nach seiner Barmhertzigkeit / machet er vns selig / Durch das Bad der widergeburt / vnd ernewerung des heiligen Geistes* (L45). Again a mistake reading Timothy instead of Titus.

[131] Rom 8.11 *So nu der Geist / des / der Jhesum von den Todten aufferwecket hat / in euch wonet / So wird auch derselbige der Christum von den Todten aufferwecket hat / ewre sterbliche Leibe lebendig machen / vmb des willen / das sein Geist in euch wonet.* (L45). The incomplete sentence of G in quoting only the first half verse is preserved.

## 'Shomaker & Parson' (1548) English Edition   119

(b1r) who so beleueth on me out of his bodye shall flowe streames of lyuing water.[132] Whych is expou*n*ned by the Euangelist, that he speaketh the same of the holy gost[133] whych all they shuld receyue that beleue in him.

Parson. What I saye my thynke[134] that thou smellest after Ma*n*tuanus[135] that heretyke / wyth thy holy ghost.

Shomaker. Paule speaketh. Do ye not knowe that ye are the te*m*ple of God; and *that the* spyryte of God dwelleth in you?[136] And to the (B1r) Gallath*ians*. 4. Seynge ye are nowe become chyldren, God hathe sente his spirite in to your hartes, who calleth. Abba, that is, beloued father.[137] He maketh vs ryghtuous accordyng to his mercy, through the bath of renouacion / and the renewyng of the holy ghost / whiche he hath powred habou*n*dauntly in vs.[138] And to the Romaynes in the. 5. chapter. As the spirite nowe dwelleth in you, who hath raysed Iesus Christe from death.[139]

parson. I fynde no holy spirite in me, you nor I are not noble inough therto.

---

[132] *Iohan. 7.* Jo 7.38 *He that believeth on me, as the scripture hath said, out of his belly shall flow rivers of living water.* (KJV).

[133] Printed 'holygost'. The print is inconsistent in leaving a space in this word; I have normalised it as two words throughout.

[134] = 'methinks/it seems to me'.

[135] A mistake for Montanus, the second-century Phrygian heretic and founder of Montanism, who taught spontaneous inspiration by the Holy Spirit. The mistake is carried over here from the original German. The spelling is perhaps by confusion with the Italian Carmelite poet Mantuan (d. 1516), who was popular with Protestants.

[136] *1. Cor. 3.* 1 Cor 3.16 *Know ye not that ye are the temple of God, and that the Spirit of God dwelleth in you?* (KJV).

[137] *Gallat. 4.* Gal 4.6 *And because ye are sons, God hath sent forth the Spirit of his Son into your hearts, crying, Abba, Father.* (KJV).

[138] *Timot.* (!) *4.* Tit 3.5 *according to his mercy he saved us, by the washing of regeneration, and renewing of the Holy Ghost.* (KJV). Wrong attribution taken over from D.

[139] *Roman. 5.* Rom 8.11 *But if the Spirit of him that raised up Jesus from the dead dwell in you, he that raised up Christ from the dead shall also quicken your mortal bodies by his Spirit that dwelleth in you.* (KJV). Keeping the incomplete phrase of G/D.

## 120 'Schoenmaker & Coorhere' (c. 1545) Dutch Edition

Schoenmaker. Waerom heet ghy die gheestelijcke als ghy den gheest Gods niet en hebt / (C1ᵛ) ghy sout heeten die gheesteloosen.

Coorheere. Het zijn al ander luyden dan ghi zijt / die den heylighen gheest Gods hebben.

Schoenmaker. Ghi en dorft niet om sien na die. God en is gheen aensiender der persoonen. Actuum int .x.[140] Het staet Esaie .lxvi. Die gheest Gods sal rusten op een gebroken oft verplet herte.[141]

Coorheere. Thoont my een.

Schoenmaker. Paulus spreect met ronden woorden tot den Romeynen int .viij. Wie Cristus gheest niet en heeft / die en is niet sine.[142]

Coorheere. O eenen armen gheest / die ghi Luterschen hebt / ick ghelooue hi is coolswart / lieue wat doet toch uwen heyligen gheest by v / ick ghelooue / hy slaept nacht ende dach by v / want men en spuert of en verneemt hem niet.

Schoenmaker. Christus spreect Matth. int .vij. Ghy en sult uwen heylichdom niet de honden gheuen / noch den peerlen voor dye verkens worpen / op dat dye selue dat niet met voeten en treden.[143] (C2ʳ)

Coorheere. Lieuer / schaemt ghi v niet sulcken grouen woorden wt te spreken voor my.

Schoenmaker. Ey lieue Heere en vertoorent v niet / het is die heylighe schriftuere.

Coorheere. Ja / ia / ia / ghy Lutersche segghet vele van twoort Gods / ende het wert nv / hoe

---

[140] Act 10.34 *Nu erfare ich mit der warheit / das Gott die Person nicht ansihet* (L45).

[141] Paraphrase of Is 66.2. *Jch sehe aber an / den Elenden vnd der zubrochens Geists ist / vnd der sich fürchtet fur meinem wort.* (L45).

[142] Rom 8.8 *Wer aber Christus geist nicht hat / Der ist nicht sein.* (L45).

[143] Mt 7.6 *JR solt das Heiligthum nicht den Hunden geben / vnd ewre Perlen solt jr nicht fur die Sew werffen / Auff das sie die selbigen nicht zutretten mit jren Füssen.* (L45).

## 'Shomaker & Parson' (1548) English Edition 121

Shomaker. Wherfore are ye then called spiritual seyng you haue not the spyrite of God? ye ought with good right to be called spyrytelease.[144]

parson. They be other maner of people then eyther you or I am whiche haue the spiryte of God.

Shomaker. Ye ought not to haue respect vnto them. For God is no accepter[145] of parsons.[146] It is also written. The spirite of God shal rest vpon a broken or weake harte.[147]

Parson. (B1v) shewe me one, I praye the.

Shomaker. Paull speaketh openly. Whosoeuer that hath not the spyrite of Chryst, perteyneth not to hym.[148]

Parson. Oh / trulye it is a very poore and myserable spirit / which ye Lutherians haue, I thinke he is as blacke as a cole. I praye the tell me what make ye wyth your holy ghost? I beleue verely that he slepeth both nyght and daye by you, for men can not so much as ones spye hym.

Shomaker. Christ sayth, Geue not that whych is holy to dogges, neyther cast ye your pearles before swyne, leaste they treade them vnder theyr fete.[149]

Parson. What, are ye not ashamed to speake such Rude and Vncommelye woordes before me?

Shomaker. I pray the sir domine be not displeased for it is the saying of holy scripture.

parson. yea, yea, yea, ye Lutherians speake much, of Goddes woorde, and it waxeth

---

[144] = 'spiritless'.

[145] = 'respecter'.

[146] *Actes. 10.* Act 10.34 talks about the expansion of the mission to the gentiles, with Peter conceding: *I perceive that God is no respecter of persons.* (KJV).

[147] *Esay. 66.* Is 66.2 *to this man will I look, even to him poor and of a contrite spirit.* (KJV).

[148] *Rom.an8.* The form might come about because the '8' looks like a final 's'. Rom 8.8 *Now if any man have not the Spirit of Christ, he is none of his.* (KJV).

[149] *Math. 7.* Mt 7.6 *Give not that which is holy unto the dogs, neither cast ye your pearls before swine, lest they trample them under their feet.* (KJV).

## 122 'Schoenmaker & Coorhere' (c. 1545) Dutch Edition

(b1v) langher hoe argher / ic en mercke aen geenen / gheen beteringhe.

Schoenmaker. Christus spreect Luc. int .xvij. Dat rijcke Gods en coemt niet wtwendich / oft met opsien / dat men mochte spreken / siet hier oft daer ist / maer het is inwendich in v / dat is soo vele / het en staet niet in wtwendighe wercken.[150]

Coorheere. Dat merckt men aen de Gods dienst wel / ghy en bidt niet / noch ghy en soeckt die kercke niet / noch die daechsgetijden / oft schier gheheel niet. Js dan een sulcken rijck Gods in v Luterschen / Jck ghelooue het is dat duyuelsrijck.

Schoenmaker. Christus spreeckt Joannis int .iiij. Die tijt sal comen en is nv / datmen niet mere en sal bidden op dese berch / noch tot Hie(C2ᵛ)rusalem den Vader / maer die warachtighe aenbidders sullen den Vader aenbidden inden gheest / ende in der waerheyt.[151] Hier mede leyt daer neder alle kercken gaen / ende v daechs ghetijden / ende vor alle ghebet na dat ghetal / welcke sonder alle gheest ende waerheyt aenbidden / maer vele meer aenstaet dat ghetal ende dat wtwendich gherabbel / daer af Christus spreeckt Matth. int .xv. Dit volck eert my metten lippen / maer haer herte is verre van my. [152]

Coorheere. Ende Christus spreeckt Luc .xviij. ghi sult sonder ophouden bidden.[153]

---

[150] Lc 17.20–21 *Das reich Gottes kompt nicht mit eusserlichenGeberden / Man wird auch nicht sagen / Sihe hie / oder da ist es. Denn sehet / Das reich Gottes ist inwendig in euch.* (L45).

[151] Jo 4.21 & 23. *Es kompt die zeit / das jr weder auff diesem Berge / noch zu Jerusalem werdet den Vater an beten. Aber es kompt die zeit / vnd ist schon jtzt / Das die warhafftigen Anbeter werden den Vater anbeten / im Geist vnd in der Warheit.* (L45)

[152] Mt 15.8 8 *Dis Volck nahet sich zu mir mit seinem Munde / vnd ehret mich mit seinen Lippen / Aber jr Hertz ist ferne von mir /* (L45).

[153] Lc 18.1 *ER saget jnen aber ein Gleichnis dauon / Das man alle zeit beten vnd nicht lass werden solt.* (L45).

## 'Shomaker & Parson' (1548) English Edition   123

(b1v) the lenger the worse / I can not spye any amende(B2r)ment in none of you all.[154]

Shomaker. Christ saythe Luk*e*. 19. The kyngdome of God co*mm*eth not outwardly / or wyth lokyng vp / that men myght poynt it wyth fyngers, to saie here in thys or in that place is it / but it is inwardly in you. that is, it standeth not in outwarde workes.[155]

Parson. Men may perceaue that by your deuine seruyce. Ye praye not, nether go ye to the Churche / nor to the dayly seruice, nor in a maner to nothynge at all that good is Is then suche kyngdom Gods kyngdom, amongest you Lutherians? I beleue it is the great deuell of helles kyngdome.

Shomaker. Christ speaketh, The tyme shall come / and is euen nowe, that men shall praye no more vpon this mou*n*tain nor at Ierusale*m*, but shall praye only in spyryte and veryte[156] Thys casteth downe and condempneth your daylye seruice with also your numbred prayers. For Chryste wholy and all abhorreth youre nombred prayers wyth youre outward mumblyng. Where as he saythe Math*ew* xv. Thys people worshyp me wyth theyr lyppes, but theyr harte is farre from me.[157] (B2v)

parson. And Christ sayth, ye shall praye without ceasyng.[158]

---

[154] = 'any of you all'. Double negatives are common in medieval and early modern English for emphasis, and do not change the positive sense.

[155] *Luke. 19.* Lc 17(!).20–21 *The kingdom of God cometh not with observation: Neither shall they say, Lo here! or, lo there! for, behold, the kingdom of God is within you.* (KJV). A misreading of the chapter number either by the translator or the typesetter.

[156] *Math.* (!) *4.* Jo 4.21 & 23. *Jesus saith unto her, Woman, believe me, the hour cometh, when ye shall neither in this mountain, nor yet at Jerusalem, worship the Father. But the hour cometh, and now is, when the true worshippers shall worship the Father in spirit and in truth.* (KJV). Wrong attribution to the gospel of Matthew by the translator or typesetter in the margin, the text has the correct John.

[157] *Math. 15.* Mt 15.8 *This people draweth nigh unto me with their mouth, and honoureth me with their lips; but their heart is far from me.* (KJV).

[158] *Luke. 18.* Lc 18.1 *And he spake a parable unto them to this end, that men ought always to pray, and not to faint.* (KJV).

124 *'Schoenmaker & Coorhere' (c. 1545) Dutch Edition*

Schoenmaker. Ja dat bidden in de*n* gheest mach sonder ophouden gheschiede*n* / mer uwe vele bidden verworpt Christus Matthei .vi. spreckt: Ghy en sult niet vele woorden maken.[159]

Coorheere. Lieue wat is dat voor een ghebet oft Gods die*n*st in den gheest ende waerheyt leert my / soo en derf ick nemmermeer te metten gaen / oft mijn ghetijden lesen.

Schoenmaker. Leset dat boecxken Martini Luthers va*n* der Christelijcker vrijheyt / welcke by den Paus Leo toegheschickt heeft / daer (C3ʳ) vint ghyt corts beschreuen.[160]

Coorheere. Jck woude dat Luther met allen sine*n* boecken verbrant ware / ick en hebber noyt gheen ghelesen / ende ick en wille noch gheen lesen.

Schoenmaker. Ey / wat oordeelt ghy dan?

Coorheere. Hoe dat hi die heylighen nem*m*ermeer en dient.

Schoenmaker. Cristus spreeckt Matth. int .iiij. Ghi sult God

---

[159] Mt 6.7 *Vnd wenn jr betet / solt jr nicht viel plappern / wie die Heiden / Denn sie meinen / sie werden erhöret / wenn sie viel wort machen.* (L45).

[160] Martin Luther, 'De libertate christiana' (1520). On the publication history and the theological background see Taylor Editions 3, ed. Jones / Lähnemann (2020).

*'Shomaker & Parson' (1548) English Edition*   125

shomaker. yea, he meaneth, to praye without ceasynge in the spyrite, but Chryst dispyseth your prayer: saying, ye shall not make many wordes.[161]

parson. Gentle frende what is that for a prayer, to praye in spirite and veritie? teache me that same I praye the, then shall I nede no more to say my matte*n*s nor myne other seruice.

shomaker. Reade that lytle boke of Marten Luther, intituled of the Christen lybertye[162] w*hich* he dedicated to Pope Leo, and there shall ye fynde it brefely declared.

parson. I wolde rather that Luther wyth al hys bokes were burnt, I neuer in all my lyfe dyd reade none of them,[163] nor yet wyll as I am aduysed.

shomaker. What, why doest thou iudge then?

parson. Mary[164] because he worshippeth not the saintes.

shomaker. (B3r) Chryst sayth. Thou shalt onely worshyp

---

[161] *Math. 6.* Mt 6.7 *But when ye pray, use not vain repetitions, as the heathen do: for they think that they shall be heard for their much speaking.* (KJV).

[162] Martin Luther 'De libertate christiana', see the footnote in D; <u>digital edition of the Taylorian copy Open Access</u>. The pamphlet was the most sold book of the entire 16th century, first published in German but shortly afterwards in the Latin version which Luther had written first, and translated into Dutch and English from there.

[163] = 'I never read any of them'. Another emphatic double negative.

[164] Variant of 'marry', an expression of surprise, outrage, astonishment, now archaic.

# 126 'Schoenmaker & Coorhere' (c. 1545) Dutch Edition

(b2r) uwen Heere alleene aenbidden / ende hem alleene dienen.[165]

Coorheere. Ja / wy moeten voorsprekers hebben by God.

Schoenmaker. Joannes spreeckt Joan. int .i. capit. in die eerste Epistel. Ende oft yemant sondich / soo hebben wy eenen Aduocaet by God Jesum Christum / die gherechtich is / ende die selue is die versoeninge / voor onse sonden.[166]

Coorheere. Ja lieue ia / noot bringhet eysschen / oft v hant ontwee ware / sout ghi sinte Wolfgang niet aenropen.

Schoenmaker. Neen ick / Christus spreeckt Mat .xi. (C3ᵛ) Coemt hier alle tot my die belast oft beswaert zijt / ick wil v vertroosten /[167] waer willen wy dan beter hulpe soecken / ghy hebt afgoden / wt den heylighen gemaect / ende ons daer na van Christo afgheuoert.

Coorheere. Ja ick hebbe wel vernomen / hoe dat ghy Lutherianen niet meer en vast / leert v dat Luthers gheest.

Schoenmaker. Vasten en is ons van God niet gheboden / maer van God vrij ghelaten. Christus spreeckt Matth. int .vi. Wantneer ghy vasten wilt / soo laet v hooft der saluen niet ghebreken /[168] hy en spreeckt niet / ghy sult oft moet vasten / ghelijck onse stiefvader te Roomen.

---

[165] Mt 4.10 *Da sprach Jhesus zu jm / Heb dich weg von mir Satan / Denn es stehet geschrieben / Du solt anbeten Gott deinen HERRN / vnd jm allein dienen.* (L45).

[166] Jo 1.1-2 *Vnd ob jemand sündiget / So haben wir einen Fursprecher bey dem Vater / Jhesum Christ / der gerecht ist / Vnd derselbige ist die versönung fur vnser sünde.* (L45).

[167] Mt 11.28 *Kompt her zu mir / alle die jr müheselig vnd beladen seid / Jch wil euch erquicken.* (L45)

[168] Mt 6.17 *Wenn du aber fastest / so salbe dein heubt / vnd wassche dein angesicht /* (L45).

'Shomaker & Parson' (1548) English Edition    127

(b2r) thy lorde God, and serue him onelye.[169]

Parson. Yea, we must haue intercessours to god

Shomaker. Iohn sayth, If any man haue synned we haue a mediatour by God / whiche is Iesus Chryst, who is ryghtuous, who is also the peacemaker for oure sinnes.[170]

Parson. Yea thou speakest fayre wordes good fellowe, but nede compelleth a man to begge yf thy legge were broken / woldest thou not go to saint Wolfgange? or if thou haddest the tothache woldest thou not pray to saint Apolonia?[171]

shomaker. No trulye. Chryst sayth, come vnto me al ye that labour and are laden, and I wyll ease you.[172] Where then wyll we seke better helpe, ye haue made Idoles of the saintes and so ye haue seduced and brought vs from Chryst.

Parson. Yea, I haue hearde wel Inough of you Lutherians that ye do neuer fast / doth Luthers holy ghost teache you that?

shomaker. We are not commaunded of God to (B3v) fast, but God hath lefte it free. Chryst saith when thou wylt faste, annoint thy head and wasshe thy Face,[173] he sayth not, thowe shalt or thou must faste, lyke our Romysh stepfather doth.

---

[169] *Math. 4.* Mt 4.10 *Then saith Jesus unto him, Get thee hence, Satan: for it is written, Thou shalt worship the Lord thy God, and him only shalt thou serve.* (KJV).

[170] *1. Iohn. 1.* 1 Jo 1.1-2 *And if any man sin, we have an advocate with the Father, Jesus Christ the righteous: And he is the propitiation for our sins.* (KJV).

[171] Scoloker adds the passage on Apollonia, the third-century Alexandrian martyr who had all of her teeth pulled out and thus became the patron saint of dentistry. He may have added this for English relevance: whereas the tenth-century Swabian bishop Wolfgang was a distinctively German saint, Apollonia was frequently represented in medieval English churches. Her cult was one of those defended by the Catholic Sir Thomas More (himself martyred in 1535) in his *Dialogue concerning Heresies* (1530): 'as for your tethe I wene if they aked well / ye wolde your selfe thynke it a thynge worthy and not to symple to aske helpe of saynt Appolyn and of god to.' (*A dyaloge of Syr Thomas More knyghte* ([William Rastell], 1530; STC 18085), book 2 chapter 11, [o6]v.)

[172] *Math. 11.* Mt 11.28 *Come unto me, all ye that labour and are heavy laden, and I will give you rest.* (KJV)

[173] *Math. 6.* Mt 6.17 *when thou fastest, anoint thine head, and wash thy face* (KJV).

# 128  'Schoenmaker & Coorhere' (c. 1545) Dutch Edition

Coorheere. Ja / maer ghi en vast nemmermeer.

Schoenmaker. Jck ghelooue / recht te vasten / dat doen die hantwerckers meer / al ist sake dat sy viermael inden dach eten / dan alle Monicken / Nonnen / ende Papen / die in dat gheheel Duytsche Lant zijn / het is openbaer / ick en derf niet meer daer af segghen.

Coorheere. So swijghet / so wil ic spreken / aen tvasten ist weynichste ghelegen / maer ghi Lutherianen eet vleesch / daer toe op den vrij(C4$^r$)dach / dat v die duyuel seghene.

Schoenmaker. Vleesch te eten en is van God niet verboden / ende daerom en ist gheen sonde / als men die crancken niet en arghert. Cristus spreeckt Matth .xv. All wat inden mont gaet en besmet den mensche niet / maer dat wt den monde gaet / als hoerije / moort / ouerspel / diefte / valsche ghetuy ghenisse / lasteringhe[174] /[175] en Paulus i. Cor .x. Al wat op die merct oft vleeshhuys veyl is / dat etet.[176]

Coorheere. Ghi segt wat ghi wilt / goede oude gewoonten en sal men niet verachten / dye schier drie oft vier hondert iaer hebben geweest.

Schoenmaker.

---

[174] Typographical error: 'lachteringhe' instead of 'lasteringhe', G: 'lesterung'.

[175] Mt 15.11 *Not that which goeth into the mouth defileth a man; but that which cometh out of the mouth, this defileth a man.* (KJV).

[176] 1 Cor 10.25 *ALles was feil ist auff dem Fleischmarckt / das esset / vnd forschet nichts / Auff das jr des Gewissens verschonet.* (L45).

## 'Shomaker & Parson' (1548) English Edition   129

Parson. Yea, but ye neuer do fast.

Shomaker I beleue that the[177] handycraftes menne do faste better (yea although they eate. 4. tymes in a daye) then all the pryestes and shauelyngs[178] of the realme. It is manyfeste Inough. I nede not to speake any more therof.

Parson. Holde thy peace then, and let me speake, as concernyng fastinge that is the least faute, but ye Lutherians eate flesshe on the fryday, that the deuell of hell mought[179] blysse you.

Shomaker. It is not forbydden of God to eate flesh, and therfore is it not sinne / so farre fourth as the weake people are not therby offended. Chryst saith. That which goeth into the Mouthe, defyleth not the Manne / but that which commeth oute of the mouth defyleth the Manne / as whooredome, murther, aduoutye,[180] theft, false wytnesse (B4r) bearing, bacbyting. &c.[181] And Paule: 1 Corinthians What soeuer is sold in the market that eate.[182]

Parson. yea, saye what ye lyst, but good olde customes whych haue bene kept and obserued aboue foure hondreth[183] yeres / are not to be despysed.

Shomaker.

---

[177] Original 'thathe'.

[178] A derogatory term for monks and friars (because of their distinctive shaved heads), common in Protestant polemics. Earliest OED attestation 1529.

[179] = 'might' (auxiliary verb).

[180] Misprint for 'advoutry' = adultery.

[181] *Math. 15.* Mt 15.11 *Not that which goeth into the mouth defileth a man; but that which cometh out of the mouth, this defileth a man.* (KJV).

[182] *1. Corinth* = 'You may eat whatsoever is sold in the market'. Preserves syntax of the Dutch. 1 Cor 10.25 *Whatsoever is sold in the shambles, that eat, asking no question for conscience sake.* (KJV).

[183] = 'hundred'.

130 *'Schoenmaker & Coorhere' (c. 1545) Dutch Edition*

(b2v) Christus spreeckt Joannis int .xiiij. Jc ben den wech / die waerheyt / ende dat leuen /[184] maer hi en spreeckt niet / ick ben die ghewoente / daerom moeten wy die waerheyt aenhangen / welcke dat woort Gods ende God selue is / dat blijft eewich. Mat. int xxiij. ca.[185] Maer ghewoente coemt van menschen / welcke alle lueghenaers zijn / ghelijck den .cxv. Psalme seyt /[186] daerom is die ghewoente verganckelick.

Coorheere. Lieue segghet my noch eens / hoe dat die Lutherianen nemmermeer en biechten (C4v) dat is noch veel meer ketterscher.

Schoenmaker. Dat en is oock van God niet geboden / oock niet wt ghesproken / noch int oude / noch int nieuwe Testament.

Coorheere. Nochtans sprack Christus Luce .xvij. Gaet ende vertoent v den Priesters / &c.[187]

Schoenmaker. Heet dan verthoonen biechten / dat is een wonderlijcs Duytsch / ghy moestet my hogher met schriftueren bewijsen / soude die oorebiecht so grooten bedwanc ende salighen dinghen zijn / so sout claerder in der schriftueren staen.

Coorheere. Ey / wilt ghi dan gheheel niet doen dan wat van God gheboden is / ende inder schrift begrepen is / dat is een ellendighe sake.

---

[184] Jo 14.6 *Jhesus spricht zu jm / Jch bin der Weg / vnd die Warheit / vnd das Leben. Niemand kompt zum Vater / denn durch Mich.* (L45).

[185] Mt 24.35 *Himel vnd Erden werden vergehen / Aber meine Wort werden nicht vergehen.* (L45).

[186] Ps 115.2 *Omnis homo mendax.* (VLC). Psalm 115 in the Vulgate numbering, 116 in the Protestant tradition: Ps 116.11 *Alle Menschen sind Lügener.* (L45). Hans Sachs had to rely for the Old Testament on the Vulgate since the translation of the Torah and the poetic books of the Hebrew Bible was only finished in October 1524, and the prophets followed even later.

[187] Lc 17.14 *Vnd da er sie sahe / sprach er zu jnen / Gehet hin / vnd zeiget euch den Priestern.* (L45).

## 'Shomaker & Parson' (1548) English Edition 131

(b2v) Chryst sayth Iohn in. 14. I am the waye, verytie / and the euerlastynge Lyfe /[188] but he saith not I am the custom. Their fore must we sticke and cleaue to the verytie whyche is Gods worde, and euen god hym selfe, which endureth for euer more /[189] But custome commeth of men, whyche are all lyers / as the. 115. psal. saieth,[190] which sayinge dothe whole and all ouerthrowe your customes.

Parson. Syr I pray the tell me, the Lutherians do neuer shryue[191] nor confesse them, whych is the greatest heresie of all.

Shomaker. Nether is that commanded of God, nor yet pronounced, nether in the olde nor in the newe Testament.

Parson. Dyd not Chryst saye Go and shewe thy(B4v)selfe vnto the priestes.[192]

shomaker. Doest thou call shewing shryuing, that is a wonders straunge Englysshe[193], ye must declare it better vnto me by scripture. If the same shryuing in the eare were such a great bonde and holy thyng, it shuld truely be clerer declared in the scripture.

Parson. What I say / wyll ye do nothyng els but that whyche is commaunded yow of GOD[194] in the scripture? that is a pitious case.

---

[188] *Johan. 14.* Jo 14.6 *Jesus saith unto him, I am the way, the truth, and the life: no man cometh unto the Father, but by me.* (KJV).

[189] *Math. 25.* Mt 24.35 *Heaven and earth shall pass away, but my words shall not pass away.* (KJV).

[190] *Psalm. 115.* Ps 116.11 *All men are liars.* (KJV). On the numbering, see opposite.

[191] 'to shrive' = 'take prescribed penance', here later explained as 'shriving in the ear' = to confess privately to a priest rather than part of public penance.

[192] *Math. (!) 22.* Lc 17.14 *And when he saw them, he said unto them, Go shew yourselves unto the priests.* (KJV). Wrong gospel in the margin (Mt 22 has not the story of the healing of the lepers who have to show themselves to the priests), also misunderstanding of the plural (ten lepers, addressed as 'u' = 'you') as singular (addressed as 'thou').

[193] = 'wondrously strange English', instead of 'seltzam Teutsch' ('strange German', G) / 'wonderlijcs Duytsch' ('strange Dutch', D).

[194] Capitalised in original. In many Tudor works, the name 'God' would be capitalised throughout.

## 132 'Schoenmaker & Coorhere' (c. 1545) Dutch Edition

Schoenmaker. Jck en can dat selue niet veruullen / gelijck Actuum int .xv. staet /[195] wat soude ick dan noch meer op my laden.

Coorheere. En alsulcken dinghen hebben die heylighe vaders gheordineert inden Consilio.

Schoenmaker. Van wien hebben si die macht.

Coorheere. (C5ʳ) Christus spreeckt Joan. int .xvi. ca. Jc hebbe v noch vele te segghen / dwelck ghi nv niet draghen en muecht / maer als die gheest der waerheyt coeme / die sal v alle dinck verclaren /[196] hoort hier / zijn dan dye Consilia niet van God ingheset.

Schoenmaker. Maer Christus spreeckt daer vooren Joan. int .xv. Die trooster die heylighe gheest / welcke mijn Vader senden sal in mynen name / die selue sal v alle dinck leeren / ende v vercondighen van alle dat ick v gheseyt hebbe /[197] hoort / hy en spreeckt niet hy sal v nieuwe dinghen leeren / welcke ic v niet gheset en hebbe / mer dat ick v geset hebbe / dat sal hy v verclaren. Op dat ghy recht verstaet / als ic ghemeynt hebbe /

---

[195] Act 15.10 *Was versucht jr denn nu Gott / mit aufflegen des Jochs auff der Jünger helse / welches weder vnser Veter / noch wir haben mügen tragen?* (L45).

[196] Jo 16.13 *Wenn aber jener / der Geist der warheit komen wird / der wird euch in alle warheit leiten. Denn er wird nicht von jm selber reden / sondern was er hören wird / das wird er reden / vnd was zukünfftig ist / wird er euch verkündigen.* (L45). *Howbeit when he, the Spirit of truth, is come, he will guide you into all truth: for he shall not speak of himself; but whatsoever he shall hear, that shall he speak: and he will shew you things to come.* (KJV).

[197] Jo 15.26–27 *wenn aber der tröster komen wird / welchen ich euch senden werde vom Vater / der Geist der warheit / der vom Vater ausgehet / der wird zeugen von mir. 27 Vnd jr werdet auch zeugen / Denn jr seid von anfang bey mir gewesen.* (L45). *But when the Comforter is come, whom I will send unto you from the Father, even the Spirit of truth, which proceedeth from the Father, he shall testify of me: 27 And ye also shall bear witness, because ye have been with me from the beginning.* (KJV).

'Shomaker & Parson' (1548) English Edition 133

shomaker. I can not fulfyll the same, as it is declared /[198] what nede I to lay any more burthen vpon me?
parson. Such thynges haue the holy fathers ordeyned in their councels.
shomaker. Who gaue them Auctoritie?[199]
parson. Chryst sayth I haue yet many thyngs to say vnto you, but ye can not beare it awey[200] now: Howe sayst thou? Are not than the councels instituted of God?
Shomaker.[201] But Chryst speaketh before that, I shall (B5r) send the comforter (which is the spyrite of trueth which procedeth of the father) and he shall declare you all thynges whiche I haue tolde you.[202] Marke, he sayth not, he shall teache you new thinges, whych I haue not tolde you, but the same thynges which I haue tolde you, euen the same shall he declare vnto you:

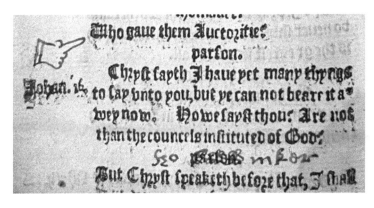

Manicule and correction in Bodleian Library, Vet. A1 f. 237, B4v

---

[198] *Actes. 15.* Act 15.10 *Now therefore why tempt ye God, to put a yoke upon the neck of the disciples, which neither our fathers nor we were able to bear?* (KJV).
[199] Manicule in the Bodleian copy, see illustration above.
[200] *Iohan. 16.* See left for KJV.
[201] The edition has 'parson.' as speaker; in the Bodleian copy crossed out by a contemporary reader and corrected, see illustration above.
[202] *Iohan. 15.* See left for KJV.

## 'Schoenmaker & Coorhere' (c. 1545) Dutch Edition

(b3r) alsoo meynt hy oock hier na / daer hy spreect / Hy sal v in alle waerheyt leyden.
Coorheere. Soo en houdy van dat Consilium niet.
Schoenmaker. Ja ick / van dien dat die Apostelen hielden te Hierusalem.
Coorheere. Hebben die Apostelen oock een Consilium ghehouden.
Schoenmaker. Ja sy / hebdy een Bibel? (C5ᵛ)
Coorheere. Ja / Kochin / brenghet dat groote oude boeck hier op.
Kochin. Heere is dat?
Coorheere. Ey neent / dat is dat Decretal / maeckes niet onreyn.
Kochin. Heere ist dat?
Coorheere. Jaet / veecht dat stof af dat v die rits slae / wel aen meester / waer ist?
Schoenmaker. Soeckt Actuum int .xv.[203]
Coorheere. Soecket selue / ick en ben daer niet wel in bekent / ick weet wel nuters te lesen.
Schoenmaker. Siet daer Heere.

Marginal note by way of a commentary in the English dialogue, B5v

---

[203] Act 15.5–9. *Da tratten auff etliche von der Phariseer secten / die gleubig waren worden / vnd sprachen / Man mus sie beschneiten / vnd gebieten zu halten das gesetz Mosi. 6 Aber die Apostel vnd die Eltesten kamen zusamen / diese rede zu besehen. 7 DA man sich aber lange gezancket hatte / stund Petrus auff / vnd sprach zu jnen / Jr Menner / lieben Brüder / Jr wisset / das Gott lang vor dieser zeit / vnter vns erwelet hat / das durch meinen mund / die Heiden das wort des Euangelij höreten vnd gleubten. 8 Vnd Gott der Hertzkündiger zeugete vber sie / vnd gab jnen den heiligen Geist / gleich auch wie vns / 9 vnd macht kein vnterscheid zwischen vns vnd jnen / Vnd reinigete jre Hertzen durch den glauben.* (L45).

## 'Shomaker & Parson' (1548) English Edition   135

(b3r) And sayth further hereafter / he shal leade you in all treuth

Parson. Thus holdest thou nothynge of the councels I perceaue well
Inough.

shomaker. yes verelye of that counsell whych the Apostles kepte at
Ierusalem.

Parson. Haue the apostles also kept a counsell?

shomaker. yea if you haue a byble.

parson. yea I haue one, O Katherin / brynge he ther that same great
old boke

Katherin.[204] Syr is that same it?

parson. What no / that same is the decrees, loke ye make it not
foule.[205]

Katheryn. Syr is thys it?

(B5v) Parson. Yea, make it cleane, and swepe of the dust and
cobwebbes now master shomaker where is it?[206]

shomaker. Seke in the Actes of the Apostles in the. 15. chapter.[207]

Parson. Seke your self / I am not much vsed in the same boke I knowe
other thynges which are proffytabler vnto me, then that.[208]

shomaker. There it is / beholde Syr.

---

[204] *Katherin the parsons handmayd* in the margin. Scoloker gives the girl a name which
was equally common in Germany and England, and makes her a maidservant rather
than the original cook whom he turns into a male servant.

[205] *what elses.* as marginal note. Typical of a polemical dialogue, Scoloker prints
sarcastic commentary in the margins telling us exactly what to think about the
foolish Catholic. Here he seems to be saying ironically 'Of course it's the Pope's
Decretals [and not Scripture], what else?'

[206] *o much dyd he regarde the byble.* as marginal note = 'there is so much dust on it that
he clearly never picks it up'.

[207] *Actes. 13.* [!] The number in the margin is wrong, that in the text is correct,
referring to Act 15.5–9, Peter's sermon at Pentecost. It is ironic that the typesetter
seems set to confuse any readers exactly at the point where they might want to check
a reference in the Bible for themselves.

[208] *Now he telleth truth.* as maginal note.

# 136 *'Schoenmaker & Coorhere' (c. 1545) Dutch Edition*

Coorheere. Kochin merct Actuum int .xv. Jc wilt lesen van wonders weghen / wat die oude ghesellen ghemaeckt hebben.

Schoenmaker. Ja leest / ghi sult vinden datmen die lasten des ouden Testaments op die kersten menschen niet legghen en mach / daerom en zijn wy niet schuldich v te hooren / vele meynigher int nieuwe Testament. (C6ʳ)

Coorheere. Maer Cristus spreect Luce int .x. Wie v hoort / die hoort my / die v veracht / dye veracht my /[209] is dat niet claer ghenoech.

Schoenmaker. Jaet / wanneer ghy dat woort Gods claer ende louter segt / soo salmen v hooren ghelijc Christum selue / mer waer ghi v eyghen goetduncken segghet / so en salmen v niet hooren / want Christus seyt Matth. int .xv. Vergheuelijck dienen sy my / ter wijlen si leeren menschen gheboden /[210] ende int selue / Alle plantatie die van God mijnen hemelschen Vader niet gheplant en is. die sal wtgheroeyt werden.[211]

Coorheere. Sijn dan die Consilia oock menschen leeren.

Schoenmaker. Wanneermen inden gront daer af spreken wilt / soo hebben die Consilia merckelijc twee schaden in Christenheyt ghedaen.

Coorheere. Welcke / bethoont se.

Schoenmaker. Jtem ten iersten die gheboden die sonder ghetal oft mate zijn / gelijck ghi weet ende dat noch quader is / schier al met den ban beuesticht / ende daer toe den meesten deel niet inder schrift ghegront / ende sulcke (C6ᵛ) nwe gheboden heeft men hooghe

---

[209] Lc 10.16 *Wer euch höret / der höret Mich / Vnd wer Euch verachtet / der veracht Mich / Wer aber Mich verachtet / der verachtet Den / der mich gesand hat.* (L45).

[210] Mt 15.9 *Aber vergeblich dienen sie mir / die weil sie leren solche Lere / die nichts den menschen Gebot sind.* (L45). This is missing in the English translation; it would be the *But in vain they do worship me, teaching for doctrines the commandments of men.* (KJV).

[211] Mt 15.13 *Aber er antwortet vnd sprach / Alle Pflantzen die mein himlischer Vater nicht pflantzet / die werden ausgereut.* (L45).

## 'Shomaker & Parson' (1548) English Edition   137

Parson. Katherin, rede Actum 15. nay let alone, I wyll rede it my self, and I wyll know what the same olde fellowes haue made.

Shomaker. Yea, Rede, and ye shall fynde that men may not lay the burdens of the olde Testament vppon the Christians, therfore are we not bounde to heare you in the olde, muche lesse in the new testament.

Parson. But Christ sayth. Whosoeuer heareth you, heareth me, and he that despyseth you, despyseth me,[212] is that same not cleare Inough?

shomaker. (B6r) Yea, when you do syncerlye and purelye teach Gods worde, then are men bounde to heare you euen as Chryste hym selfe. But when ye preach youre owne Imaginacyons and inuencyons, then ought no man to gyue care vnto you. For all that is not planted of God my heauenly father shalbe plucked vp by the rotes. [213]

Parson. Are the councelles then also the learnyng of men?

Shomaker. If a man shulde say the trueth, the councelles haue done great dammage in Chryhendome by two maner of wayes.

Parson. What hurt or dammage? declare them I pray the hartelye.

Syomaker. Fyrst the commaundementes which are innumerable and vnmeasurable as you your self knowe / and that which is worst of all haue bene by excommunycacyons confyrmed, and aboue that moost part are not grounded in the scrypture, and such your commaundements men haue highly

---

[212] *Luke. 10.* Lc 10.16 *He that heareth you heareth me; and he that despiseth you despiseth me; and he that despiseth me despiseth him that sent me.* (KJV).

[213] The first quotation from Matthew (see D footnote left: Mt 15.9) is left out and consequently the second quotation which refers back 'and in the same chapter' is also no marked with a marginal note. Mt 15.13 *But he answered and said, Every plant, which my heavenly Father hath not planted, shall be rooted up.* (KJV).

## 138 'Schoenmaker & Coorhere' (c. 1545) Dutch Edition

(b3v) op geheuen / ende des menschen conscientie daer mede ver-
schrickt ende verueert / dat si den warachtelicken gheboden Gods
gelijck gheacht zijn gheweest / ende die voorgeset ende die
gheboden Gods te rugge geset zijn / ende vergetelic by den
menschen ghemaeckt zijn / sulcke lieden heeft Paulus vercondicht
met haren gheboden .i. Timo. int .iiij. dat inden lesten tijden
souden comen sommighe die af souden treden vant ghelooue /
ende aenhangen den gheest der dolinghen / ende leeringhe des
duuels / door welcken zy in ypocrisie lueghen sprekers zijn / ende
branttekenen in haer conscientie hebben / ende verbieden den
houwelicken staet / ende te mijden die spijse die God gheschapen
heeft / te nemen met dancksegghinghe den gheloouighen / ende
dien dye de waerheyt bekent hebben.[214]

Coorheere Waer ist / is dat gheschiet / met welcken gheboden.

Schoenmaker. Vleesch te eten op eenen vrijdach / heeftmen voor een
groote sonde gheacht / dan ouerspel / ende soude een Paep een
echte wijf ghehadt hebben / dat heeftmen voor groote sonde ghehouden / dan oft hy een hoere oft twee ghehouden hadde. (C7ʳ)

Coorheere. Wel verstaen spreect die Wale / was is dan die ander
schade.

Schoenmaker. Ten anderen hebben sy vele nieuwe Gods diensten
opgherecht / ende goede wercken ghenoemt / daer mede alle
ander Monicken / Nonnen ende Papen om gaen ende tis toch
(alsmen dat alderhoochste daer af spreken wille /)[215] sommighe
wtwendighe sotswerck /[216] daer God niet af ghesproken en heeft /
ende hebben daer dore / ende wy alte samen mede / die rechtighe
goede wercken verlaten / die ons God beuolen heeft.

---

[214] 1 Tim 4.1–3 … / *Das in den letzten Zeiten / werden etliche von dem Glauben
abtretten / vnd anhangen den verfürischen Geistern / vnd leren der Teufel / 2 Durch die /
so in gleisnerey Lügenreder sind / vnd Brandmal in jrem Gewissen haben / 3 vnd verbieten
Ehelich zu werden / vnd zu meiden die Speise / die Gott geschaffen hat / zu nemen mit
Dancksagung / den gleubigen vnd denen die die warheit erkennen /.* (L45).

[215] The closing bracket is missing, inserted following the German version.

[216] The work of a 'sot' = fool. In G 'Larvenwerk' (= mummery / play with masks).

'Shomaker & Parson' (1548) English Edition 139

(b3v) estemed and therwith greatly charged mens conscyences / and haue bene reputed lyke the commaundmentes of God / yea, set before them (B6v) wherby the commaundementes of God haue bene set backe and made vnknowen to the people. Such people hath Paul declared with their commaundementes. That in the latter tymes shulde departe from the fayth, and gyue hede vnto spirites of errour / and deuelyshe doctryne of them which speake false thorow ypocrysy & haue their consciences marked with an hote yron, forbyddyng to marry, and commaundyng to absteyne from meates which God hathe created to be receyued wyth thankes geuyng of them which beleue and know the truth.[217]

Parson. How is that come to passe, with what commaundementes I pray the?

Shomaker. To eate flesh on the fryday, hath bene taken for a greater synne, then to kepe a whore or two.

parson. I vnderstande you very well, what dammages are there more?

Shomaker. Secondarely they haue brought forth many straunge Gods seruises / and called them good workes, which is nothyng elles (if a man shulde saye sothe) but verye (B7r) apesplay and outward folysshnes /[218] Wherof God neuer spake one worde / wherby both we and they / haue neglected, and not regarded the good woorkes whych God hath commaunded vs.[219]

---

[217] *1. Timo. 4.* 1 Tim 4.1–3 ... *that in the latter times some shall depart from the faith, giving heed to seducing spirits, and doctrines of devils; 2 Speaking lies in hypocrisy; having their conscience seared with a hot iron; 3 Forbidding to marry, and commanding to abstain from meats, which God hath created to be received with thanksgiving of them which believe and know the truth.* (KJV).

[218] 'apesplay' is also used above, A2v. In G 'play with mask', in D 'a public fool's play'.

[219] Scoloker omits the original passage about monks, nuns, and popes – perhaps because none of these social estates any longer existed in England in the 1540s, after Henry VIII's split with Rome in 1534 and his dissolution of the nation's monasteries and nunneries in 1535-40. Good works, however, were still affirmed as necessary in Henry's conservative Church of England, so the Shoemaker's other point was still a controversial one.

# 140   'Schoenmaker & Coorhere' (c. 1545) Dutch Edition

Coorheere. Wat zijn dan rechte Cristelicke wercken?

Schoenmaker. Christus spreect Matthei int .vij. Alle dat ghy wout dat v die menschen doen / dat doet oock hen / dat is die gheheel Wet ende Propheten.[220] Ende Matth. int .xxv. leert hi ons die hongherighe spijsen / den dorstighen te drincken gheuen / den armen herberghen / den naeckten cleeden / den crancken te huys versoecken[221] oft visenteren / den gheuanghen troosten.[222]

Coorheere. Sijn dan alleen christelijcke wercken / ende een gheheel Christelijcke leuen. (C7ᵛ)

Schoenmaker. Ja / een recht Christelijck gheloouich mensch die weder nieuwe herboren is / ws den water ende gheest / ghelijck Joan. int iij. staet /[223] die dient God alleen inden gheest ende waerheyt / ende sinen

---

[220] The Golden Rule Mt 7.12 *Alles nu / das jr wöllet / das euch die leute thun sollen / Das thut jr jnen / Das ist das Gesetz vnd die Propheten.* (L45).

[221] Normal form would be 'besoeken'.

[222] The works of mercy, Mt 25.35–36 *Denn ich bin Hungerig gewesen / vnd jr habt mich gespeiset. Jch bin Durstig gewesen / vnd jr habt mich getrencket. Jch bin ein Gast gewesen / vnd jr habt mich beherberget. 36 Jch bin Nacket gewesen / vnd jr habt micht bekleidet. Jch bin Kranck gewesen / vnd jr habt mich besucht. Jch bin Gefangen gewesen / vnd jr seid zu mir komen.* (L45).

[223] Jo 3.5 *Jhesus antwortet / Warlich / warlich / Jch sage dir / Es sey denn / das jemand geboren werde / aus dem Wasser vnd Geist / so kan er nicht in das reich Gottes komen /* (L45).

'Shomaker & Parson' (1548) English Edition   141

parson. what are then the ryght true workes of a chrysten man?

shomaker. Chryst sayth. All what thou woldest the men shuld do to the, do euen the same vnto them / and that is the fulfilling of the whole lawe and prophetes.[224] And he doth teache vs to fede the hungry / to geue drinke to the thyrstye / to harbarrowe the harbarroules to clothe the naked, to visite the sycke, and to comforte the prisonner.[225]

parson. Are that only the workes of a Christen man, and the wholl somme of a Chrysten lyfe?

shomaker. Yea / a true and faythfull chrysten man which is borne a newe out of the water and the Spyrite (as it is written Iohan. iij. chapter)[226] serueth God onely in spyrite and Veritie, and

---

[224] *Math. 7.* Mt 7.12 *Therefore all things whatsoever ye would that men should do to you, do ye even so to them: for this is the law and the prophets.* (KJV).

[225] *Math. 15.* Mt 25.35–36 *For I was an hungred, and ye gave me meat: I was thirsty, and ye gave me drink: I was a stranger, and ye took me in: 36 Naked, and ye clothed me: I was sick, and ye visited me: I was in prison, and ye came unto me.*

[226] *Iohan. 3.* Jo 3.5 *Jesus answered, Verily, verily, I say unto thee, Except a man be born of water and of the Spirit, he cannot enter into the kingdom of God.* (KJV).

# 142 *'Schoenmaker & Coorhere' (c. 1545) Dutch Edition*

(b4r) naesten met die wercken der liefden / dat is die summa een Cristelijck leuens / maer dese wercken gaen gheheel stil toe / datmen daerom noch schilt noch wapen en derf aenhanghen / ende dan meynen die werckheylighen / sulcke Christelijcke leuen en is niet oft dat die Christenen niet en doen / om dat si met gheenen ghetey kenden wercken nemmermeer om en gaen.

Coorheere. Meynt ghy dan dat ons singhen ende lesen niet en is?

Schoenmaker. Christus en sal anders niet van ons eyschen / dan die wercken der bermherticheit int leste oordeel. Matth. int .xv.[227] Dan sult ghy Papen ende Monicken staen ghelijck die Sotten die haer ooren aen den staeck ghelaten hebben.

Coorheere. Ghy hebbet wel gheraeyt / gaet totten ouen ende wermt v / leert v Luther sulke dinghen.(C8$^r$)

Schoenmaker. Neen hy.

Coorheere. Lieue / wat houdt ghy van Luther?[228]

Schoenmaker. Jc houde hem voor een Christelijcke leeraer / welcke ick achte dat sint der Apostelen tijt / noyt gheweest en is.

Coorheere. Lieue / wat profijt heeft hy toch ghedaen / int Christen ghelooue.

---

[227] The works of mercy as referenced in Mt 25 (!).40 *Vnd der König wird antworten / vnd sagen zu jnen / Warlich ich sage euch / Was jr gethan habt einem vnter diesen meinen geringsten Brüdern / Das habt jr mir gethan.* (L45). The typesetter obviously missed out one 'x' of 'xxv'.

[228] Literal translation from G 'was haldt jr von dem Luther'; idiomatic would be 'wat denckt ghy van Luther'. Kept exactly like that in English: 'What holdest thou of Luther?', except that the informal form of address is used.

*'Shomaker & Parson' (1548) English Edition* 143

(b4r) serueth also his Neighbour, wyth the woorkes of charitie / that is the whole summe of a Christen lyfe / but these (B7v) papistes meane that such a Chrysten lyfe is nothing at all, because the same workes haue not such an outwarde shyne as their workes do.

Parson. Thynke ye then that our syngyng and Readyng is of no worth?

shomaker. Chryste shall require nothyng elles of vs at the day of iudgement / then the workes of mercy /[229] then shal ye priestes and monkes stande lyke foles which haue left their eares at the pylory.[230]

Parson. Thou hast hyt it wonders[231] well /[232] gette you to the furnace and warme you a lyttell, doth Luther teache you suche thynges?

shomaker. No.

parson. What holdest thou of Luther? I pray the tell me.

Shomaker. I hold him for a Chrysten Doctour and I thynk there hath not been a better sens the Apostles tyme.

Parson. What proffyt hath he done in the christen fayth?

---

[229] *Math. 15.* [!] *Gene. 3. & Iob. 5.* The wrong chapter number for the works of mercy is taken over from the Dutch, see there. It is Mt 25.40 *And the King shall answer and say unto them, Verily I say unto you, Inasmuch as ye have done it unto one of the least of these my brethren, ye have done it unto me.* (KJV). The other two Bible references are added in English. Genesis 3 references the story of the fall of Adam and Eve. Why Job 5 is referenced is less clear; the chapter is part of a praise of God the creator who rescues the oppressed.

[230] A literal translation of the Dutch. The German version had referenced a local case, the 'Rincklerin' which has been generalised here.

[231] = 'wondrously'.

[232] *Luke. 10.* Additional Bible reference, not in G or D. The chapter tells of Jesus sending out his disciples to preach the good news to everybody. Perhaps an ironic comment on the itself ironic remark of the parson that the shoemaker has acquitted himself well by linking biblical teaching and contemporary politics.

144 *'Schoenmaker & Coorhere' (c. 1545) Dutch Edition*

Schoenmaker. Dat hy uwe menschelicke leere ende geboden / sonde / ende opsettinge / int licht gebrocht heeft / ende ons daer af ghewaerschout. Ten anderen heeft hy ons inder schrift ghewesen / daer in wy bekennen / dat wy alle onder der sonden besloten / ende sondaers zyn / als totten Romeynen. int .v. staet. Ten anderen / dat Christus alleene onse verlossinghe is / ghelijck .i. Corinth. int .i. staet /[233] ende die twee stucken drijft die schriftuere schier door ende door / daer in leeren wy / dat onse eenighe hope / ghelooue / ende betrouwen in Christo te setten / welcke is dat rechte goddelijck werck tot salicheyt ghelijck Cristus spreeckt / Joan. int .vi.[234]

Coorheere. Behoeft men gheen werck daertoe / ende (C8v) Christus spreeckt Matthei int .v. Laet v licht wtbersten / ende lichten voor die menschen / dat si uwe goede wercken sien / ende uwen vader inden hemel prijsen.[235]

Schoenmaker. Paulus spreeckt tot den Romeynen / int .v. Wy houden daer voor dat die mensche gherechtueerdicht wort alleen doort ghelooue / sonder toedoen der wercken /[236] ende tot den Romeynen int eerste / dye gherechtighe sal leuen wt den ghelooue.[237]

Coorheere. Jacobus spreeckt

---

[233] Rom 5.1 *NV wir denn sind gerecht worden durch den glauben / So haben wir Friede mit Gott / durch vnsern HErrn Jhesu Christ /*. and 1 Cor 1.30 *Von welchem auch jr her kompt in Christo Jhesu / Welcher vns gemacht ist von Gott zur Weisheit / vnd zur Gerechtigkeit / vnd zur Heiligung / vnd zur Erlösung.* (L45).

[234] Jo 6.47 *Warlich / warlich / Jch sage euch / Wer an Mich gleubet / der hat das ewige Leben.* (L45).

[235] Mt 5.16 *Also lasst ewer Liecht leuchten fur den Leuten / Das sie ewre gute Werck sehen / vnd ewren Vater im Himel preisen.* (L45)

[236] Rom 3(!).28 *So halten wir es nu / Das der Mensch gerecht werde / on des Gesetzes werck / alleine durch den Glauben.* (L45). The wrong chapter number already in G.

[237] Rom 1.17 *Der Gerechte wird seines Glaubens leben.* (L45).

## 'Shomaker & Parson' (1548) English Edition   145

Shomaker. (B8r) Mary,[238] fyrst, he hathe discouered and brought to lyght youre false doctryne, commaundementes, tradicions and Imagynacyons, and admonysshed and warned vs therof. Secondarely / he hath declared vs by scripture / that we shulde confesse that we are all the bondmen of synne. Thyrdely / that Chryst alone is our sauyour and redemer,[239] of which two points the whole scripture is full, wherby we learne to putt oure truste / hope and fayth onelye in Christe,[240] which is a true and godly worke to saluacion, as Christ sayth Ioan. 6[241]

And Christ sayth. Mat*thew*. 5. Let your lyght braste oute / and so shyne before the people / that they (seing your good workes) maye praise the father which is in heauen.[242]

Parson. Nedeth no worke therto?

Shomaker. Paule sayth ad Rom*anos*. 5. we hold it therfore, that man is onelye made right wes through fayth, without the workes,[243] & to the Romaynes in the last chapter. The ryghtuous shall lyue by fayth.[244]

Parson. Iames sayth

---

[238] Variant of 'marry', an expression of surprise, outrage, astonishment, now archaic.

[239] *Rom. 5.* Rom 5.1 *Therefore being justified by faith, we have peace with God through our Lord Jesus Christ.* (KJV).

[240] *1. Cor. 1.* 1 Cor 1.30 *But of him are ye in Christ Jesus, who of God is made unto us wisdom, and righteousness, and sanctification, and redemption.* (KJV).

[241] *Iohan. 11.* The text is correct, not the number in the margin. This is Jo 6.47.

[242] *Math. 5.* Mt 5.16 *Let your light so shine before men, that they may see your good works, and glorify your Father which is in heaven.* (KJV).

[243] *Roma. 5.* Rom 3(!).28 *Therefore we conclude that a man is justified by faith without the deeds of the law.* (KJV).

[244] *Rom. vlt.* = 'the last [chapter of the Epistle] to the Romans'. A misunderstanding of 'eerste' = 'first' in D. Rom 1.17 *The just shall live by faith.* (KJV).

146 *'Schoenmaker & Coorhere' (c. 1545) Dutch Edition*

(b4v) in zijn .ij. capit. Dat ghelooue sonder die wercken is doot.[245]

Schoenmaker. Een recht Christelijcke ghelooue en viert niet / maer brengt altijt goede wercken ende vruchten / want Cristus spreeckt Matth. int .vij. Eenen goeden boom en can gheen quade vrucht en voortbrenghen[246] maer sulcke goede wercken en ghescieden niet om den hemel te verdienen / want die heeft ons Christus verdient / ooc niet wt vreesen der hellen te ontvlieden / van welcke ons Christus verlost heeft / oock niet om eere / want alle eere salmen God gheuen / Als Matth. int .iiij. staet /[247] maer wt liefden / God tot een dancsegghinghe ende tot profijt des naesten / wel aen Hee(D1ʳ)re / hoe behaecht v Luthers vreese

Coorheere. Js hy dan soo gherechtich / hoe comet dan dat hem soo weynich geleerden aenhanghen / ende groote Heeren volghen / dan alleene dat grof ongheleert volck.

Schoenmaker. Christo en hinck noch Pilatus / noch Herodes / noch Cayphas / noch Annas aen / oock niet de Phariseen / maer si versonden hem / alle dat ghemeyn volck hinck hem aen / daerom verblijde hem Christus inden gheest. Luce .x. ende sprack: Vader ick dancke v / dat ghi dese dinghen hebt verborghen voor den wijsen deser weerelt / ende hebbet gheopenbaert den cleynen.[248]

Coorheere. Ey lieue / die ghemeynen hoop gheeft oock Luther dat weynichste deel recht.

---

[245] On Luther's rejection of the letter of James see p. 61. Iac 2.18 *Aber es möchte jemand sagen / Du hast den glauben / vnd ich habe die werck / Zeige mir deinen glauben mit deinen wercken / So wil ich auch meinen glauben dir zeigen mit meinen wercken.* (L45).

[246] The cobbler counters with a different understanding of works: not as gaining salvation but as growing out of it. Mt 7.18 *Ein guter Bawm kan nicht arge Früchte bringen / Vnd ein fauler Bawm / kan nicht gute Früchte bringen.* (L45).

[247] Referring to the temptation by the devil to worship him, Mt 4.10.

[248] Lc 10.21 *ZV der stund frewet sich Jhesus im geist / vnd sprach / Jch preise dich Vater vnd HERR Himels vnd der Erden / Das du solchs verborgen hast den Weisen vnd Klugen / Vnd hast es offenbart den Vnmündigen. Ja Vater / also war es wolgefellig fur dir.* (L45).

(b4v) in his. 2. chap. Fayth wi*th*out good workes is dead.[249]

Shomaker. (B8v) A true Christen fayth can neuer be Idell but bryngeth alwayes good workes and frutes forth. For Chryst sayth / A good tree can brynge forth no euell frute,[250] but such good workes ought not to be done for to meryte or deserue heauen therby / for Chryst hath merited and deserued it for vs, neyther for feare, and to a voyde the paynes of hell, for Chryst hath delyueryd vs therof, neyther for honour, for all honour shalbe geuen onely vnto God, as it is writen.[251] But ye shall do them for loue, for a thankes geuyng to God, and to the helpe and profyt of your neyghbour.

parson. If Luther be so ryghtuous and so good a doctour as you name hi*m* to be, how chau*n*ceth then that so fewe greate lords do cleaue and styck vnto his doctryne: Saue onely a heape of rude and vnlearned people?

Shomaker. Pylate, Herode, Cayphas nor Annas, cleued not to Chryst nor yet the pharizees, but the common people. Therfore Christ reioyced in spirite, a*n*d sayd. Father I thanke you, that ye haue hydden these thynges from the wyse of the world, & haue opened it to the lytle flocke.[252]

(C1r) Parson. What I saye the common people cleaue least of all to Luther and hys doctrine.

---

[249] *Iacobus. 2* Iac 2.18 *Yea, a man may say, Thou hast faith, and I have works: shew me thy faith without thy works, and I will shew thee my faith by my works.* (KJV).

[250] *Math. 7.* Mt 7.18 *A good tree cannot bring forth evil fruit, neither can a corrupt tree bring forth good fruit.* (KJV).

[251] *Math. 4.* Mt 4.10 *Then saith Jesus unto him, Get thee hence, Satan: for it is written, Thou shalt worship the Lord thy God, and him only shalt thou serve.* (KJV).

[252] *Luke. 10.* Lc 10.21 *In that hour Jesus rejoiced in spirit, and said, I thank thee, O Father, Lord of heaven and earth, that thou hast hid these things from the wise and prudent, and hast revealed them unto babes: even so, Father; for so it seemed good in thy sight.* (KJV).

148 *'Schoenmaker & Coorhere' (c. 1545) Dutch Edition*

Schoenmaker. Dat maken v botte Prekaren / die staen en roepen / het is een ketter / ende dat sonder gheschrift / maer Christus heuet den cleynen hoop vercondicht / Mat. int .v. Gaet henen door die enghe poorte / want dye poorte is wijt / ende den wech is breet der verdoemenissen / ende daer zijnder vele die daer op wandelen /[253] ende Mat. int .xxij. Vele zijnder gheroepen / weynich wtuercoren[254] (D1ᵛ)

Coorheere Sulcke woorden claptmen in die tauerne / op die merct / ende ouer al / gelijc die sotten / ende ten behoort niet aen sulcke plaetsen.

Schoenmaker. Christus spreeckt Matth. int .x. Wat ick v int heymelicke spreke / dat sult ghy preken op dat dack.[255]

Coorheere. Als ick die waerheyt soude segghen / so houde ick Luther voor den grootsten ketter die sint Arrius tijden is gheweest / ende ghy zijt zijn nauolgher /

---

[253] The wrong chapter number copied from G. It is Mt 7[!].13 *GEhet ein durch die enge Pforten / Denn die Pforte ist weit / vnd der weg ist breit / der zur Verdamnis abfüret / Vnd jr sind viel / die drauff wandeln.* (L45).

[254] Mt 22.14 *Denn viel sind beruffen / Aber wenig sind aus erwelet.* (L45).

[255] Mt 10.27 *Was ich euch sage im finsternis / das redet im liecht / Vnd was jr höret in das ohre / Das predigt auff den Dechern.* (L45).

## 'Shomaker & Parson' (1548) English Edition   149

Shomaker. Your dulheaded and folyshe preachers are cause of that /
whych without any scripture, crye and call, he is an heretyke / he
is an heretike. But Chryste hath declared to the litell flocke. Go
thoroughe the narrowe gate, for the gate is wyde and the way is
broade whyche leadeth to dampnation, and ther are many which
walke in it,[256] And ther are many called and fewe electe.[257]

Parson. Men do vse to speake suche wordes in tauernes, vpon the
market, and elles wher lyke fooles, whych ought not to be spoken
in suche places.

Shomaker. Christ sayeth / what I saye to you in secret, that shall ye
preache vppon the house toppes.[258]

parson. If I shulde saye trueth. I holde Luther for the greateste
heretyke, that euer was sence Arrius Tyme, and thou arte hys
folower,

---

[256] *Math. 5.* Mt 7[!].13 *Enter ye in at the strait gate: for wide is the gate, and broad is the*
*way, that leadeth to destruction, and many there be which go in thereat:.* (KJV).

[257] *Math. 22.* Mt 22.14 *For many are called, but few are chosen.* (KJV).

[258] *Math. 10.* Mt 10.27 *What I tell you in darkness, that speak ye in light: and what ye*
*hear in the ear, that preach ye upon the housetops.* (KJV).

# 150 'Schoenmaker & Coorhere' (c. 1545) Dutch Edition

(c1r) ende in v daer en is niet goets in / ende niet goets en coemt wt v / weet ghy nv / dien tittel gheue ick Luthere / ende v te samen.

Schoenmaker. Daer hebt ghijt eens gheraden / want niemant en is goet dan God. Matthei int .xix.[259] Want onse natuere is gheheel in ons ghecorrumpeert. Alst Genesis int .viij. staet. Des menschen herte is tot boosheyt gheneghen van ioncheyt op /[260] welcke men moet daghelicx met dat cruys dooden / op dat den gheest niet en lette / want dye natuere en laet haer tucken niet / al ist dat schoon die gheest door dat gelooue gherechtueerdicht is / want daer staet Proverbiorum int .xxiiij. Die gherechtighe (D2ʳ) valt inden dach seuen mael /[261] daerom bidden wy alle daghe / vergheeft ons onse schult. Matthei .vi.[262] ende Paulus tot den Romeynen int vij. Dat goet dat ic wille dat en doe ick niet / maer dat quaet dat ic hate ende niet en wille / dat doe ick / ende spreeckt daer nae. O ellendich mensche / wie sal my verlossen van dat lichaen des doots /[263] daer mede bewijst hy / dat wy sondaers zijn tot in die doot / maer zijt ghy sonder sonde / soo werpt den iersten steen op ons / Joannis int .viij.[264]

Coorheere. Ghi zijt alle onnutte luyden / ghi cont veele clappen / ick hope men sal v schier die lenden cloppen / ten helpe anders niet.

---

[259] Mt 19.17. *Niemand ist gut / denn der einige Gott.* (L45).

[260] God's reflection after the flood: Gn 8.21 *das tichten des menschlichen Hertzen ist böse von Jugent auff.* (L45).

[261] Prv 24.16 *Denn ein Gerechter felt sieben mal vnd stehet wider auff* (L45).

[262] Mt 6.12 *Vnd vergib vns vnsere Schulde / wie wir vnsern Schüldigern vergeben.* (L45).

[263] Rom 7.19 *Denn das Gute das ich wil / das thu ich nicht / Sondern das Böse / das ich nicht wil / das thu ich.* (L45).

[264] Jo 8.7 *Wer vnter euch on sunde ist / der werffe den ersten stein auff sie.* (L45).

## 'Shomaker & Parson' (1548) English Edition   151

(c1r) and ther is no good in you, nether commeth theyr any good from you / vnderstandeste thou that? The same ty-(C1v)tell do I gyue both to Luther and to the.

Shomaker. Veryly you haue hitte the prycke / for theyr is no man good but God only.[265] For oure nature is whole and all corrupte in vs, as it is wrytten. Gene*sis*. 8. The harte of man is inclyned to euell / euen from hys youthe /[266] whych dayly muste be mortifyed wyth the crosse, leaste it myght hinder the spirite. For nature ceaseth not to seke that thynge wherunto it is inclined, all though the spyryte be made ryghtuous throughe fayth. For it is wrytten Prouer*bs*. 24. The ryghtuous falleth seuen tymes in the daye.[267] Therfore do we daily praye. Forgiue vs our trespaces Math*ew* 6.[268] and paule to the Rom*ans*. 7. The good which I wolde I do not / and the euell whiche I hate, I do, a*n*d after that speaketh he. O miserable man / who shall delyuer me from the body of death?[269] Therwyth declareth he that we are synners euen vnto death. But syr Domine[270] / yf thou arte wyth out Synne, caste the fyrst stone vppon vs.[271]

Parson. Ye are all vnproffitable[272] people, ye can prate very well / I truste ye shal shortly be knocked vppon your boanes, for I perceaue there is none other remedye.

---

[265] *Math. 14.* A typographical mistake, reading G/D 'xix' as 'xiv'. Mt 19(!).17 *there is none good but one, that is, God:* (KJV)

[266] *Genesis. 8.* Gn 8.21 *the imagination of man's heart is evil from his youth* (KJV).

[267] *Prouerbs. 24.* Prv 24.16 *For a just man falleth seven times, and riseth up again:* (KJV).

[268] *Math. 6.* Mt 6.12 *And forgive us our debts, as we forgive our debtors.* (KJV). G/D also have 'debts' but since Tyndale (1542) the liturgical version of the Lord's Prayer has 'trespasses', also then in the 1549 Prayer Book.

[269] *Romans. 7.* Rom 7.19 *For the good that I would I do not: but the evil which I would not, that I do.* (KJV).

[270] This mocking expression, used elsewhere in the Dutch, is added here.

[271] *Iohan. 8.* Jo 8.7 *He that is without sin among you, let him first cast a stone at her.* (KJV). This marginal note is mistakenly printed next to the Parson's speech in the original.

[272] Misprinted 'vn proffitable'.

# 152 'Schoenmaker & Coorhere' (c. 1545) Dutch Edition

Schoenmaker. Hoe / woude ghi met den sweerde daer aen / dat en behoort v geestelijcke niet toe.

Coorheere. Waerom niet / Cristus heeft toch Luce int .xxij.[273] twee sweerden ingeset / dat geestelick ende weerlick.

Schoenmaker. Christus verboot toch Petro Mat. xxvi. ende sprack / Die met den sweerden staet / die sal met den sweerde vergaen.[274]

Coorheere. Ten helpet aldus niet / so moetet met (D2ᵛ) swaerder punitien helpen / want die ketterie heeft groote ouerhant ghenomen / ende het is hooch tijt daer in te slane.

Schoenmaker. O neen / maer volghet den raet Gamalielis na. Actuum int .v.[275] Js die leere van God / soo en moecht ghij se niet keeren / ende ist wt den menschen / soo salse vallen sonder eenich sweert / op dat ghy niet ghesien en wert / als die teghen God strijden willen.

Coorheere. Daer en sal niet anders af comen.

Schoenmaker. Wel aen / Heere dinen wille ghesciede. Matth. int .vi.[276] Die knecht en is niet bouen sinen meester. Joan .xv.[277] Hebben si my veruolcht / si sullen v oock veruolghen / ende Luc. int .vi. Salich zijt ghi / wanneer

---

[273] Jesus' answer to the disciples offering to defend him before he went to the garden Gethsemani and was arrested, Lc 22.38 *Sie sprachen aber / HErr / Sihe / hie sind zwey Schwert. Er aber sprach zu jnen / Es ist gnug* (L45). Understood by medieval doctrine to signify the two powers of ecclesiastical and secular authority.

[274] Mt 26.52 *Denn wer das Schwert nimpt/ Der sol durchs Schwert vmbkomen.* (L45).

[275] Act 5.34 *DA stund aber auff im Rat ein Phariseer mit namen Gamaliel / ein Schrifftgelerter / wol gehalten fur allem Volck / vnd hies die Apostel ein wenig hin aus thun / 35 vnd sprach zu jnen / Jr Menner von Jsrael / nemet ewer selbs war an diesen Menschen / was jr thun sollet.* (L45).

[276] Mt 6.10 *Dein Wille geschehe* (L45).

[277] Jo 15.20 *Der Knecht ist nicht grösser denn sein Herr.* (L45).

## 'Shomaker & Parson' (1548) English Edition    153

shomaker. (C2r) What, wolde you be in hande with the swerde? that apperteyneth not to the spyritualtie.

Parson Hath not Christ Luce. 22. ordeyned two swerdes, one spirituall and an other temporall.

shomaker. Chryst did forbydde Peter. Math*ew* 26 and sayd he that striketh with the swerd / shall perysh with the swerde.[278]

parson. It helpeth not by other meanes, therfore must it be holpen[279] / wyth a quicke punishment, for heresy hath in a maner taken t*h*e vpperhande, therfore it is hygh tyme to stryke in the flocke.

Shomaker. Oh, do not so, but rather follow the co*n*sell of Gamaliel / Actum in the 5. chapter. If the doctryne[280] be of God, ye can not for bydde nor defend it, and if it be of menne, then shall it fall without any swerde /[281] to the intent[282] ye be not take*n* as one that wyll fyght agaynst God.

parson. Ther shall come nothyng elles therof for this shalbe the ende.

(C2v) Shomaker. Nowe, O lord of heauen, thy wyll be fulfylled. Math 6.[283] The Discyple is not aboue hys master. Haue they persecuted me. they shal persecute you also /[284] and happy are ye, when

---

[278] *Math. 26.* Mt 26.52 *for all they that take the sword shall perish with the sword.* (KJV).

[279] = 'helped'. Early English past participle of 'to help', reflecting the strong verb pattern, still in German 'geholfen' (and preserved in the 'Magnificat' in the Book of Common Prayers: 'hath holpen his servant Israel').

[280] Misprinted 'ddctryne'.

[281] *Actes. 5.* Act 5.34 *Then stood there up one in the council, a Pharisee, named Gamaliel, a doctor of the law, had in reputation among all the people, and commanded to put the apostles forth a little space; 35 And said unto them, Ye men of Israel, take heed to yourselves what ye intend to do as touching these men.* (KJV).

[282] = 'in order that'.

[283] Mt 6.10 *Thy will be done* (KJV).

[284] *Iohan. 15.* Jo 15.20 *The servant is not greater than his lord.* (KJV).

154 *'Schoenmaker & Coorhere' (c. 1545) Dutch Edition*

(c1v) v die menschen haten / verworpen / *ende* schelden om mijns naems wille.[285]

Coorheere. Daer sulle*n* sommighe swijghe*n* / die nv ter tijt roepen.

Schoenmaker. Cristus spreect Matth. int .x. Wie mi bekent voor den menschen / dien wil ick bekennen voor mijnen hemelsche*n* Vader.[286]

Coorheere. Het sal v dwinge*ns* ghelde*n* / oft me*n* sal v met de*n* cop grijpe*n* / *ende* achter de*n* cop slae*n*. (D3ʳ)

Schoenmaker. Christus spreect Matth. int .x. Vreest v niet / die v dat leuen nemen mueghen / die sielen en mueghen sy niet doode*n*.[287] O Heere God / hier waert goet sterue*n* van uwen naems weghe*n*.

Coorheere. Het waer verdienden loon. Ee*n* ketter machme*n* na die derde vermaninghe dooden.

Schoenmaker. Ghy moest ons te vore*n* ketters make*n* ende bewijsen wt der heyligher schrift.

Coorheere. Dat moghen wy lichtelijck doen.

Schoenmaker. Soo sal God ons bloet va*n* uwer hant eysschen / dat ghy ons / ende die arme scapen Cristi soo langhe hebt laten verleyden / ende hebt soo vele Prekaers deser leeringhen / onbeuochten ghelaten.

---

[285] Lc 6.22 *Selig seid jr / so euch die Menschen hassen / vnd euch absondern / vnd schelten euch / vnd verwerffen ewern namen / als einen boshafftigen / vmb des menschen Sons willen.* (L25).

[286] Mt 10.32 *DArumb / Wer mich bekennet fur den Menschen / Den wil ich bekennen fur meinem himlischen Vater.* (L45)

[287] Directly preceding this, Mt 10.28 *VND fürchtet euch nicht fur denen / die den Leib tödten / vnd die Seele nicht mögen tödten. Fürchtet euch aber viel mehr fur dem / der Leib vnd Seele verderben mag / in die Helle* (L45)

'Shomaker & Parson' (1548) English Edition   155

(c1v) ye are hated / dysdayned and dispysed for my names sake.[288]

parson. Some shall then holde their peace, whych nowe do call and roare a lowde.

Shomaker. He that confesseth me before the world him wyll I knowledge and confesse before my heauenly father.[289]

Parson. Ye shall be handeled and serued lyke as heretikes ought to be serued.

shomaker. Chryst sayth feare not them whych may destroy the body only, but feare him which may destroy both body and soule.[290] O lorde God, howe good is it to dye for thy names sake?

parson. It were euen your iust rewarde / an heretyke (after the third admonicion and warning) ought to be put to death.

shomaker. But yow ought fyrste to proue or de-(C3r)fyne vs to be heretikes, wyth the holy scripture.

parson. That may we full easely do.

Shomaker. Then shall God require our bloude at youre hands / because you haue suffered vs, and the pore shepe of Chryst to haue bene thus long seduced and ledde oute of the right way. And that you haue not resysted and disputed with so many preachers of this learning.

---

[288] *Luke. 6.* The end of the Beatitudes Lc 6.22.

[289] Jesus' promise to his disciples, Mt 10.32.

[290] *Math. 10.* Directly preceding this, Mt 10.28 *And fear not them which kill the body, but are not able to kill the soul: but rather fear him which is able to destroy both soul and body in hell.* (KJV).

156 *'Schoenmaker & Coorhere' (c. 1545) Dutch Edition*

Coorheere. Het sal volleken gheschieden / wy hebben ons raet ghesloten.

Schoenmaker. Ja is dat waer / ghi veruolcht de sprake / Matth. int .xxij. Ende die Phariseen ghinghen ende hielden eenen raet / hoe sy hem mochten vanghen in sinen woorden / ende sonden toe hem dienaers / met Herodes dienaers.[291] (D3ᵛ)

Coorheere. Waerom niet / men moet die ketters alsoo wtrechten / want si zijnt wel weerd datmense daer nae cloppe.

Schoenmaker. Och God / dese Prekaren wouden ons allen gheerne tot Christum voeren / niemant wtgenomen. Soo wilt ghi ons tsamen met v seluen totten hencker voeren ghi wout gheerne dat / dat vier vanden hemel op ons viele. Luce .ix. Hoort Christum die daer spreeckt / Weet ghy niet welcke kinderen des gheests ghy zijt / des menschen sone en is niet comen die menschen sielen te verderuen / maer te behouden[292] .ij. Corin. int .xiij. My is ghewelt gegheuen / niet te bederuen / maer te beteren.[293]

Coorheere. Ey / wy willen nock alsoo.

Schoenmaker. Vier ende sweert en dient niet daer toe / maer dat woort Gods / als totten Hebr. int .iiij. welcke doordringender is dan een snijdende sweert / aen beyde syden /[294] dies haluen zijt ghy wt God / soe verhuecht

---

[291] Mt 22.15–16.

[292] Lc 9.54–56 *Da aber das seine Jünger / Jacobus vnd Johannes sahen / sprachen sie / HErr wiltu / So wollen wir sagen / das fewer vom Himel falle / vnd verzere sie / wie Elias thet? Jhesus aber wandte sich / vnd bedrawet sie / vnd sprach / Wisset jr nicht / welches Geistes kinder jr seid? Des menschen Son ist nicht komen / der menschen Seelen zuuerderben / sondern zu erhalten.* (L45). Verse 55 is probably a later addition but was part of the Greek New Testament Luther used.

[293] Free rendering of Cor 13.10: *Derhalben ich auch solchs abwesend schreibe / Auff das ich nicht / wenn ich gegenwertig bin / scherffe brauchen müsse / Nach der macht / welche mir der HErr zu bessern / vnd nicht zu verderben / gegeben hat.* (L45)

[294] Heb 4.12 *Denn das wort Gottes ist lebendig vnd krefftig / vnd scherffer / denn kein zweischneidig Schwert /* (L45).

Parson. It shal shortly come to passe, we haue taken our aduise and counsell vppon the matter.

Shomaker. Yea, is that true indede? I perceaue ye do fulfyll the sayeng of Mat. And the Pharizees went and helde a councel how they might trippe him in his wordes, and dyd send officers vnto him / with the offycers of Herode.[295]

parson. What elles? Thus ought the heretykes to be serued.

Shomaker. Oh, lorde. These true preachers wolde fayne bryng vs all to Chryste, no man (C3v) excepted. And thow woldeste bringe both vs and thy selfe to the deuell. Thou woldest fayne that the Fyre of Heauen shulde fall on vs Luk. 9.[296] Heare what Chryst sayeth. Do ye not knowe what chylderen of spyrite ye are? The sonne of man is not come to destroy the soules of men, but to saue them. 2. Corinthians. 13. He hath geuen me power (saith he) not to destroy, but to amend.[297]

Parson. What, I say, I wyll euen the same also.

shomaker. Fyre and swerde serueth not therto, but the woorde of God Hebrews. 4. Which is sherper then a two edged sworde.[298] Therfore if thou arte of God, defende

---

[295] *Math. 22.* The start of the Passion narrative Mt 22.15–16.

[296] *Luke. 9.* Jesus orders the disciples who want to punish those who have not given shelter to them, not to invoke heavenly punishment, Lc 9.54–56.

[297] *2. Corinthians. 13.*

[298] *Hebrews. 4.* Heb 4.12 *For the word of God is quick, and powerful, and sharper than any twoedged sword.* (KJV).

# 158 *'Schoenmaker & Coorhere' (c. 1545) Dutch Edition*

(c2r) v leere ende weten / met dat woort Gods / welcke is die cracht Gods .i. Corinth .i.[299]

Coorheere. Ja / het en helpt niet. (D4ʳ)

Schoenmaker. Ja / ghy en brengt dat woort niet / want Gods eere en soect ghy niet te scheyden / waer v ghewelt / eere / ende rijckdommen / daer is dat woort Gods teghen / daerom veruolcht ghijt / daer leget al mede daer neder.

Coorheere. Ja ghy en cont niet dan om die lieden wt te rechten / als dat herte vol is / so gaet die mont ouer. Luce int .vi.[300]

Schoenmaker. V is ghelijck Christus seyt. Lu. int .vij. ca. ghelijck den kinderen die aen die merct sitten / ende roepen / wi hebben v ghepepen / ende ghy en hebt niet ghedanst / wy hebben v gheclaecht / ende ghy en hebt niet gheweent.[301] Alsoo oock ghy / seytmen v van dat woort Gods troostelick / soo spot ghi daer mede / segghet men v neerstelick / soo verthoorent ghy.

Coorheere. Al songde ghy ghelijck een Leewerck / so en maeckt ghy my niet anders.

Schoenmaker. V herte is verhert gelijc die Coninck Pharao. Exodi van het .vij. capit. tot int xv. die noch wonder / noch plaghen aen en nam / ende meende die kinderen van Jsrael souden tichghelen branden / dat hi met sinen volcke vieren mochte. (D4ᵛ)

Coorheere. Weet vrij / het is eens gheraden.

---

[299] 1 Cor 1.24–25 *Denen aber die beruffen sind / beide Jüden vnd Griechen / predigen wir Christum / göttliche Krafft vnd göttliche Weisheit. Denn die göttliche Torheit ist weiser denn die Menschen sind / vnd die göttliche Schwacheit ist stercker denn die Menschen sind.* (L45).

[300] Lc 6.45 *Denn wes das hertz vol ist / des gehet der Mund vber.* (L45). The phrase 'wes das Herz voll ist, geht der Mund über' is given by Luther in his 'Sendbrief vom Dolmetschen' (1530) as an example of idiomatic German translation, instead of the Latin phrase 'ex abundantia cordis os loquitur' (literally: Out of the abundance of heart the mouth speaks), which is preserved in KJV, see the discussion in Jones 2022.

[301] Lc 7.32 *Sie sind gleich den Kindern / die auff dem Marckte sitzen / vnd ruffen gegen ander / vnd sprechen / Wir haben euch gepfiffen / vnd jr habt nicht getantzet. Wir haben euch geklaget / vnd jr habt nicht geweinet.* (L45).

## 'Shomaker & Parson' (1548) English Edition   159

(c2r) thy doctrine and lawes with Gods word, which is the power of God. 1. Corinthi*ans*. 1.[302]

Parson. All thys helpeth you neuer a whytte.[303]

Shomaker. Ye bringe not Gods worde / ye seke not the honour of God, but your owne power honour, and Ryches, against whyche the worde of God speaketh, a*n*d therfore do ye persecute it.

Parson. Yea, thou pratest nothing elles, but to here a manne, when the harte is full, then (C4r) ronneth the mouthe ouer. Luke. 6.[304]

Shomaker. I maye well lyken you / lyke as Christ lykeneth the chylderen syttyng in the markett place / criyng one to an other and saying. We haue pyped vnto you and ye haue not daunsed. We haue mourned to you & ye haue not wepte.[305] Euen so is it with you, If a man speake vnto you confortablye of the worde of God, then do ye deryde it. If a man do tell it you earnestlye / then are ye angry.

parson. Although thow dyddest synge lyke a Larke / thowe shalt not make me otherwyse then I am.

Shomaker. Youre harte is waxen harde and stony as kyng Pharao, Exodi. Rede from t*h*e .7. Chapter to the. 15. who neither regarded no wonder nor places. etc.[306]

Parson. Thou haddest almost hit the prycke.

---

[302] *1. Corinthians. 1.* 1 Cor 1.24–25 speaks about Christ as God's word being stronger than secular wisdom for those who are called.

[303] = 'not at all'.

[304] No marginalia. Lc 6.45 *for of the abundance of the heart his mouth speaketh* (KJV).

[305] *Luke. 7.* Lc 7.32 *They are like unto children sitting in the marketplace, and calling one to another, and saying, We have piped unto you, and ye have not danced; we have mourned to you, and ye have not wept.* (KJV).

[306] The report of the exodus from Egypt talks repeated about the 'hardening' of Pharaoh's heart, e.g. Ex 7.3 *Aber ich wil Pharao hertz verherten / das ich meiner Zeichen vnd Wunder viel thu in Egyptenland.* (L45) *Sed ego indurabo cor ejus, et multiplicabo signa et ostenta mea in terra Ægypti* (VLC).

## 160 'Schoenmaker & Coorhere' (c. 1545) Dutch Edition

Schoenmaker. Ja my duncket wel / v is gelijc die valsche ambachs man Luc. int .xvi. spreect hy / Wat sal ick doen / die Heere sal dat ambacht van my nemen / ic en mach niet grauen / ende ick schame my te bidden /[307] recht dat selue vreest ghy gheestelicke ooc / daer en helpt noch straffen / noch vermanen aen v.

Coorheere. Weet ghy niet Christus spreet Joan. int .xvi. Niemant en coemt tot my / ten sy dat hem die Vader trecke /[308] siet brengt roosen / wy weten wie den anderen bekeert.

Schoenmaker. Och Heere die woorden hoore ic geerne / het staet Joan .xv. Sonder my en cont ghy niet doen /[309] ende noch meer / ghy en hebt my niet vercoren / maer ick hebbe v vercoren /[310] daerom en leget aen ons niet / God moet ons bekeeren / dat wensche ic v allen van gronde mijns herten.

Coorheere. Wanneer luytmen te choore Kochin / lanct my den choorrock hier / wel aen lieue meester / gaet in vreden / het sal licht noch al goet werden.

Schoenmaker. Oft God wilt / wel aen / alle vrede sy (D5ʳ) met v

---

[307] Lc 16.3 *Der Haushalter sprach bey sich selbs / Was sol ich thun? mein Herr nimpt das Ampt von mir / Graben mag ich nicht / So scheme ich mich zu betteln.* (L45).

[308] Jo 6.44 *Es kan niemand zu mir komen / es sey denn / das jn ziehe der Vater.* (L45).

[309] Jo 15.5 *JCh bin der Weinstock / Jr seid die Reben / Wer in mir bleibet / vnd ich in jm / der bringet viel frucht / Denn on mich künd jr nichts thun.* (L45).

[310] Jo 15.16 *JR habt mich nicht erwelet / Sondern ich habe euch erwelet /.* (L45).

## 'Shomaker & Parson' (1548) English Edition 161

Shomaker. Me thynketh that thou arte lyke the false offycer Luk*e*. 6.[311] What shall I do? the lorde wyll take the offyce from me, I can not dygge, and I am ashamed[312] to begge.[313] Euen that same feare ye spyrituall menne (C4v) also no exhortacion nor admonishing can helpe.

parson. No man commeth to me vnlesse my father drawe him,[314] wyll you then conuert a man?

Shomaker. Oh syr I loue to heare the same wordes with all my harte. It is written Iob[315] 15. without me canst thou do nothing /ʃ[316] and further thou haste not chosen me, but I haue chose the,[317] therfore lyeth it not in our power, but it is God which must conuert vs. Which I do wysshe you all from the botome of my harte.

Parson. When do they ryng in the church? Katherin giue me my sirplys and tippet.[318]

Katherin.[319] Well beloued master / go in pease, I hope all thinges shalbe well.

shomaker. With the helpe of God, now peace be with you,

---

[311] Typographical mistake of '6' instead of '16'. No marginal chapter reference.

[312] Misprinted 'a shamed'.

[313] Lc 16(!).3 *Then the steward said within himself, What shall I do? for my lord taketh away from me the stewardship: I cannot dig; to beg I am ashamed.* (KJV).

[314] Jo 6.44 *No man can come to me, except the Father which hath sent me draw him.* (KJV). Chapter reference and the following proverb in G/D 'Time brings roses' left out.

[315] Typographical mistake for John, spelled *Joā* in the Dutch edition.

[316] No marginal reference, possibly because of the typographical mistake of Job instead of John. Jo (!) 15.5 *I am the vine, ye are the branches: He that abideth in me, and I in him, the same bringeth forth much fruit: for without me ye can do nothing.* (KJV).

[317] Jo (!) 15.16 *Ye have not chosen me, but I have chosen you.* (KJV). Mix-up of singular and plural here since with the wrong book title given this reference could not be verified.

[318] The surplice is the priest's linen vestment and the tippet is his scarf. Both were official clerical costume in the English Church, before and after the Reformation. G/D speak of the 'Chorrock', a cope or large garment worn over the cassock.

[319] In G/D this is part of the canon's speech and the 'lieber Meister' (dear master) refers to the shoemaker of which the priest is taking his leave.

162 *'Schoenmaker & Coorhere' (c. 1545) Dutch Edition*

(c2v) lieue heere / hout my niet voor ondanckelick / ende vergheuet my.

Coorheere. God vergheue ons onse sonden.

Schoenmaker. Amen.

Coorheere. Siet nv aen lieue Kochin / hoe spreken die leeken soo gheheel fraylick teghen ons ghewijden / ic meyne die duyuel sy in die Schoenmaker ghenayt / hy heeft my int harnas gheiacht / ende en ware ick niet soo wel gheleert / hy hadde my op den Esel gheset. Daerom en wil ic hem niet meer te arbeyden gheuen / maer den Hans Zobel / dat is een goet simpel manneken / ende en maect niet veele woorden met der heyligher schrift / ende Luytersche ketterie / ghelijck den leeken oock niet en betaemt noch oock met haren siel soeckers te disputeren / want Salomon seyt / Wie een simpel wandelinghe voert / die voert een goede wandelinghe / ende wandelt wel.[320] Ey die sprake soude ick den dullen Schoenmaker gheseyt hebben / soo waer hy by auentueren daer op stom gheweest.

Kochin. O Heere / ic hadde ommers sorghe na dien / dat ghi hem met die schrift niet en (D5ᵛ) const verwinnen / dat ghy hem met dye pantoffelen op sinen cop sout gheslaghen hebben.

---

[320] Possibly Prv 16.19 *Es ist besser nidriges gemüts sein mit den Elenden / Denn Raub austeilen mit den Hoffertigen.* (L45). It might be part of Sachs's strategy to show up the canon in that he is using a vague proverb, attributing it to Solomon as author of the Book of Proverbs, rather than quoting properly, including giving a precise chapter number, as the cobbler does for his Biblical references.

# 'Shomaker & Parson' (1548) English Edition  163

(c2v) beloued syr take no displeasure wyth me, but pardon me if I haue offended you.

Parson. God pardon and forgyue vs all our synnes.

shomaker. Amen.

(C5r) Parson. Beholde how quicke these lay men are in tellyng of their tale to vs which are anoynted. I thynke that the deuel of hell be patched and clouted in the sho*makers*[321] Skynne, he hath so stricken me vpon my brest plate / that if I had not bene so depely learned, he shuld haue made me a*n* asse, therfor he shall make no more shoes for me / but Hans zobell[322] shall be my shomaker, for he is a very symple man, and one that dothe not much reason of the scrypture / nor of the Lutheryans heresy, which apperteyneth not to the laye people, nether becommeth it them to dyspute with their soulekepers,[323] for Salomon sayth whosoeuer[324] walketh symply, walketh well.[325] Ah, the same saying ought I to haue layde to that dulheaded shomaker, peraduenture, he shuld haue had nothyng to say thervpon / but haue bene starke dome.

Katherin Ah master, I feared greatly (when I sawe you coud not ouercome hym wyth scripture) that you shuld haue strycken hi*m* vpon his pate with the slyppers.

---

[321] Abbreviated 'sho.' in the original, perhaps preserving Scoloker's manuscript copy-text.

[322] Christian names or surnames are very inconsistently capitalised in Tudor print.

[323] An English neologism from the Dutch.

[324] Printed 'who soeuer'.

[325] Possibly Prv 16.19 *Better it is to be of an humble spirit with the lowly, than to divide the spoil with the proud.* (KJV). But probably more a general reference to proverbial wisdom.

164 *'Schoenmaker & Coorhere' (c. 1545) Dutch Edition*

Coorheere. Jck sorchde meer van der ghemeynten oploop / anders
soude ick hem die pantoffelen int aensicht gheslaghen hebben /
Cristus noch Paulus en haddens hem in drie daghen niet
afghewist / hoe wel hy alle zijn betrouwen op hem sette.

Kochin. My gheeft groot wonder hoe die leeken soo gheschickt
worden.

Coorheere. Wilt ghi weten wat dat doet / men en gheest om die
gheestelicken niet meer / voortijden heeft die heylighe Vader die
Paus ende Bisschoppen / sulcken als Luther ende andere meer / die
op haer maniere preeckten / dat preeken verboden / na die
gheestelicke rechten / ende bedwonghen huer te wederroepen /
ghelijck met Joannes Hus te Constans gheschiede / wanneermen
nv die Euangelische Prekaren swijghen dede / so sout al goet
werden / maer wannermen die doet

*'Shomaker & Parson' (1548) English Edition* 165

Parson. If I had not feared that an oproare myght haue rysen among the comens / I (C5v) shuld verely haue layd the slippers in his face, so that neyther Paule no nor Christ hym selfe shuld haue swepte it from him in thre daies, for all that he trusteth so muche in them.

Katheryn. I maruell greatly how it commeth that the lay people are so learned.

Parson. If thou wilt know it, I shall tell it the. The cause is that the spiritualty is no more regarded. Here aforetimes[326] did oure holy father the pope of Rome wyth his bysshops forbydde such heretikes as Luther is, according to the spirituall lawe and compelled them to recant, lyke Ioan hus was serued at constance. If men dyd now compell these preachers of the Gospell to holde theyr Peace, then shulde it be as good as euer it was, and then shulde the spiritualty be honoured, but when we go aboute to cause them to

---

[326] = 'in previous times' (printed 'afore times').

166 '*Schoenmaker & Coorhere*' (*c. 1545*) *Dutch Edition*

(c3r) swijghen / soo comen si ende willen met den Paus ende Bisschoppen disputeeren / welcke onbehoorlic is by der weerelt / dat een met den alderheylichsten wilt disputeren / die (D6ʳ) niet weert en is met zijnder heylicheyt te spreken / maer het sal wel beter worden / alen willen die prekaers niet swijghen men salse wel doen swijghen / hoe wel sy sinte Paulus schrift voort halen / ende al hadden sy zijn sweert noch daer toe / soo moeten si nederligghen / als die heylighe Vader die Paus wilt / dan soo moeten die leeken oock swijghen / ende dan so sullen wy tot onser weerden weder comen.

Kochin. Het waert voorwaer Heere goet / want een yeghelijck veracht v / ghelijck ooc nv die Schoenmaker dede.

Coorheere. Hier voortijts soudemen eenen alsulcken inden ban vercondicht hebben / maer nu moeten wy van die leeken hooren / ende leeren / ghelijck die Phariseen van Christo / lieue Kochin roept onsen Calefactor die leest vele in die Bibel / ende by auentueren hy sal die schriftuere bat berechten dan ick / hy moet my van nieuwicheyt sommighe spraken soecken.

## 'Shomaker & Parson' (1548) English Edition   167

(c3r) holde their peace, then wyl they inmediatly dyspute with the pope and Bysshops, whiche is a thing that neuer was hearde in the worlde before, that such vyle[327] parsonnes shulde dyspute with the moost holyest father / whiche are not worthy to speke to his holines, but it shall shortly take an ende. Although these preachers wyll not holde their pea-(C6r)ce, they shall be compelled to holde theyre peace, for all that they lay Saynct Paulles wryting before them / and though they had Paules swerde also, yet muste they lye doune and not so much as ones kycke, when it pleaseth ones the Holye Father of Rome, then must the laye people holde theyr peace also, and then shall we come to oure former worthynes and prystyne[328] honour.

Katheryn. Verily Syr It were very good, for every man dispiseth and mocketh with you lyke the shomaker did euen now.

parson. Hertofore shulde such one haue bene excommunicate, but nowe muste we both heare and learne of the laye People / lyke the pharisees did of Chryst, good katherin I pray the call Iohan our coke,[329] he vseth much to rede in the Byble, perchaunce he shall declare the scrypture better then I / he must seke me some sentences out of the scripture.

---

[327] = 'lowborn/vulgar'.

[328] = 'pristine/untarnished'.

[329] In the English, the Parson summons his (male) cook, not the 'Calefactor', an errand-boy for heating the house. The contrast between lowly Gospeller servant and lofty Catholic cleric is thus not emphasised in the English as in the German and Dutch.

168 *'Schoenmaker & Coorhere' (c. 1545) Dutch Edition*

Kochin. Henrice / Henrice / coemt hier by mijn Heere.

Calefactor. Weerdighe Heere / wat wilt ghy? (D6ᵛ)

Coorheere. Onse Schoenmaker heeft my langhe ghequelt e*nde* vele wt die Bibel bewesen / ghelijck die Luytersche maniere is / ghy moet my sommighe Capittelen soecken oft hy ghelijck gheseyt heeft / op dat ick hem inder schrif vanghen mochte.

Calefactor. Ghy soudet met rechts selue weten / ghy hebt langhe die ghewijde helpe*n* examineren.

Coorheere. Daer ghebruycktme*n* meer scholierse leere / wat die mensche*n* hebbe*n* gheschreue*n* e*nde* ghemaect / ende seer weynich dat geestelick recht / welcke die heylighe vaders in dat Consilium hebben besloten.

Calefactor. Het en leyt daer niet aen / aen dat gene dat die vaders int Consilium hebben besloten / ende die menschen die na in comen zijn gheschreuen hebbe*n* / als die selue Wet e*nde* leere e*nde* gheschrift wt dat woort ende gheest Gods / niet en is / want dye Propheten ende Apostelen ende Euangelisten zijn oock menschen gheweest.

Coorheere. Ja / soo hebben sy oock moghen dwalen / maer die Lutherianen en willen dat (D7ʳ) niet gheloouen.

Calefactor. Neen / want Petrus spreeckt .ij. Petri int eerste: Het en is noch noyt ghee*n* Prophetie wt menschelicken wille wt ghebrracht / maer die heylighe*n* me*n*sche*n* Gods die hebben ghesproken / ghedreuen wesende vanden Gheest Gods /[330] ende recht daer na verco*n*dicht Petrus / Die valsche Propheten die vele verderffelicke seckte*n*

---

[330] 2 Pt 1.20 *Vnd das solt jr fur das erste wissen / Das keine Weissagung in der Schrifft geschicht aus eigener auslegung.* (L45).

## 'Shomaker & Parson' (1548) English Edition  169

Katheryn. Iohan Iohan / come to my master.

Iohan.[331] Honorable syr what is your pleasure?

Parson. (C6v) Our shomaker hath vexed me very long and hath shewed me muche out of the byble, lyke the maner of the Lutherians is / ye muste seke me oute some Chapter that I maye knowe yf he haue sayde ryghte or no, that I myght conuicte hym by scripture.

The coke. Ye ought with ryght to knowe it your selfe, for you haue longe holpen[332] to examine the anointed.

*Parson.* To that we vse but the doctrine of scoles / and that which hath bene written and made by men and very lyttel the spirytual lawe, which the holy fathers haue concluded in the councelles.

The coke. It maketh no matter of that which the auncient fathers haue concluded in the concell and what men (whiche are comme in afterward) haue written, when the same lawe doctrine and writtyng is not out of the woorde and spirite of God. For the Prophetes. Apostles and Euangelystes were men also.

Parson. Ergo they myght also erre, but the Lutheryans wyll not beleue it. (C7r)

The coke. No, for Peter sayth. 2. Petri in the fyrst Chapter. That no prophet in the scrypture hath any pryuate interpretacion. For the scrypture came neuer by wyll of man, but holye men of God spake as they were moued by the holy gost.[333] The false prophetes, which bryng many euell sectes

---

[331] The cook is here named John – apparently the same as the Parson and perhaps the Shoemaker too (who is called both John and Hans at the start). Having several characters called John was not unusual – John Heywood's *Johan Johan* (c.1525) contains a husband called John John and a priest called John, out of a cast of three! Anne Barton points out in *The Names of Comedy* (Oxford, 1990) that this was realistic at a time when almost half of all Englishmen were christened John.

[332] = 'helped'. Early English past participle of 'to help', reflecting the strong verb pattern, still in German 'geholfen' (and preserved in the 'Magnificat' in the Book of Common Prayers: 'hath holpen his servant Israel').

[333] *2. Petri. 1.* 2 Pt 1.20 *Knowing this first, that no prophecy of the scripture is of any private interpretation.* (KJV).

# 170 'Schoenmaker & Coorhere' (c. 1545) Dutch Edition

(c3v) umbrenghen / ende dat beduyt recht uwen gheestelicken staet / oorden / reghel *ende* allen menschen vonden / buyten den woorden Gods / daer mede ghi nv ter tijt om gaet

Coorheere Ja / het en is op ons niet ghesproken / maer op die ouders ende voorgangers.

Calefactor. O ghy sotten ende traech van herten / om te gheloouen / al dat die Propheten ghesproken hebben. Luce int .xxiiij.[334]

Kochin. Heere / heet v den haen craeyen / van my en lijds ghys niet.

Coorheere. O ghy luysiger truwant / wilt ghy my oock rechtueerdighen ende leren / ghy zijt oock vanden Luterschen boeuen een / pijnt v nv ter stont wt den huyse / ende en (D7ᵛ) coemt niet meer in mijn huys / ghy onbeschaemde beeste.

Calefactor. Aha / het doet v noch wee / dat v die Schoenmaker v ronde bonette bescaemt heeft / laet v dat niet verwonderen / want int oude Testament heeft God die herders zijn woort laten vercondighen / alsoo nv tertijt moeten (v Phariseen) die Schoenmakers leeren / Ja / het sullen v die steenen an die ooren roepen / Adieu / ick scheyde met wetenheyt.

---

[334] Luke 24.25 *VND er sprach zu jnen / O jr Thoren vnd treges hertzen / zu gleuben alle dem / das die Propheten geredt haben* (L45)

## 'Shomaker & Parson' (1548) English Edition 171

(c3v) in that signifieth euen your spirituall estate, order, rule, and all the inuencyons of men (without anye worde of God) where with you daly go aboute.

Parson. That is not spoken of vs, but of oure auncyent olde predecessours and foregoers.

The coke. O ye foles and slouth in harte to beleue all that the prophetes haue spoken.[335]

Katheryn. Harke Master, doth the cocke bydde you Crowe? ye wolde not suffer me to tell it you.

Parson. O thou lowsy vyllayn,[336] wilt thou now teach me? thou arte also one of Luthers knaues, get the out of the dores, and come no more into my house, thou vnshamefast[337] beast I councell it the for best.

*The coke*[338] (C7v) Ha ha ha / I perceaue it greueth you yet / that the shomaker hath stopt so well your mouth, lett it not be so greate wonder vnto you, for God suffred (in the olde Testament) sheapardes to declare hys worde, even so now must ye pharezees, and shauelynges[339] be taught of shomakers and cobblers / yea the very stones shall call it in to your eares: fare ye well syr domine.

---

[335] *Luke. 24.* Luke 24.25 *VND er sprach zu jnen / O jr Thoren vnd treges hertzen / zu gleuben alle dem / das die Propheten geredt haben* (L45) *then he said unto them, O fools, and slow of heart to believe all that the prophets have spoken:* (KJV).

[336] = 'commoner/unfree tenant' (Anglo-French 'villein'), and thus 'knave/fool'.

[337] = 'shameless'.

[338] The edition mistakenly has 'Shomaker.'.

[339] = 'tonsured clergy'.

## 172 'Schoenmaker & Coorhere' (c. 1545) Dutch Edition

Kochin. O gheschiet recht / my verwondert dat ghy met die groue beeste spreken mocht si en verschoonen noch v / noch v heylige wijtsel.

Coorheere. Jck wil my nv wel voor hem wachten / ghy verbannen kint / vreeset vier / wel aen / ick wil te choor gaen / ende gaet ghy op die merckt / ende coept ons een meerle voghel oft twee / hier sal noch eten die Cappellaen van mijnen ghenadighen Heere / met sommighe Heeren / ende wy sullen een Bancket houden / draghet die Bibel wt der stouen wech / ende besiet of dye dobbelsteenen al int verkerbert zijn / ende dat wy een schoon Caerte oft twee hebben. (D8$^r$)

Kochin. Het sal zijn. Heere sult ghy terstont na den ommeganck weder comen?

Coorheere. Ja ick / siet toe dat dat eeten bereyt si.

Kochin Ja Heere / in dien dattet my broeder Claues niet en belette.[340]

A M E N.

Gheschiet tot Nurenborch / int iaer ons Heeren

.M. CCCCC. XXJJ.[341]

---

[340] The last line by the cook, literally 'provided brother Nicholas does not stop me from it', has been added to the text. The meaning is unclear, perhaps a local reference. The E version only translated the first part of the sentence, obviously also not getting the meaning of this addition. In G it ends instead with a quotation from Paul's letter to the Philippians, Phil 3.19 *ir bauch ir gott*, their belly is their god.

[341] 'Happened in Nuremberg, AD 1522', i.e. the dialogue is presented as a factual report. The wrong date, 1522 instead of 1524, is probably a typographical mistake.

## 'Shomaker & Parson' (1548) English Edition   173

Katheryn. I maruayle that you can take the payne to speake to such Rude beasts, they neyther regarde you nor yet your holy oyntment.

Parson. I shall kepe me from him well inough, thow wycked and excommunycate knaue take hede of thy fyre / nowe I wyll go to the Church, and go you to the Market and buye vs a dosen of good quayles / for the chapleyn of my most reuerende Lorde the bysshoppe shall dyne here wyth more other gentlemen, we wyll kepe a banket[342], now Carye the bybble out of the parlour, and loke if the dyse are in the tables / and prouide vs of a fayre payre of cardes or two.

Katherin. It shalbe done, Syr, wyll ye come ho(C8r)me anone after the procession be done?

Parson. Yea, loke the meate[343] be ready.

Katheryn. yea forsothe Syr

Amen.

---

[342] = 'banquet'.
[343] 'meat' instead of the neutral 'food' in G/D.

# Facsimile

Taylor Institution Library, ARCH.8°.G.1523(8), cover

Taylor Institution Library, ARCH.8°.G.1524(26), a1r

176  *Facsimile*

Taylor Institution Library, ARCH.8°.G.1524(26), a1v

Bonus dies Köchin. Köchin. Semper quies
Seyt wylkum mayster hanns. Schüster.
Got danck euch/wa ist der herr? Köchin. Er ist
im Sumerhauß/Jch wil im rüffen/her:/her: d
Schüchmacher ist da. Kho:her:. A/Beneueneritis mayster hans. Schüst. Deo gratias. Kho:. Was bringt yr
mir die pantoffel? Schüst. Ja/ich gedacht/yr wert schon
in die kirchen gangen. Cho:. Mayn/ich bin hynde im sum
merhauß geweßt/vnd haß ab gedroschen. Schü. Wie höd
ir gedroschen? Cho:. Ja/ich hab mein horas gebeet / vnnd
hon alemit meiner nachtigal zü essen geben/ Schüst. Her:
was hond ir für eyn nachtigall/Singet sy noch. Cho:.
O nain/es ist zü spatt im jare. Schü. Jch waiß ein schüch
macher Der hat ein nachtigal / die hatt erst angefanngenn
zü singen. Cho:. Ey der teuffel hol den schüster/mit sampt
seiner Nachtigal/wie hat er den aller hayligisten vater den
Bapst/die hailige vetter/vn vns wirdige herren außgehol-
hipt/wie ein holhipbüb. Schüst. Ey/her: fart schonn/Er
hat doch nur ewern gozdienst/leer/gebot vn eynkomen/de
gmainen man/angezaygt/vn nur schlecht oben vberhyn/ist
dan solches ewer wesen/holhüpel werck. Cho:. Was get es
aber solchs vnser wesen den tollen schüster ane? Schüst. Es
steet Exodi am xxiij. So du deines feyndes Esel vnder dem
last sihest ligen/nit laß in/sonder hilff im / Soll dan eyn ge-
täuffter chust/seinem bruder nit helffen/so er in sech ligen im
der beschwert seiner gewyssen? Cho:. Er solt aber die gaist
lichen vnnd geweychten nit dareyn gemengt han (der Esel
kopff) die wissen vor wol/was sünd ist. Schüst. Seynd sy
aber sündigen/So spricht Ezechiel xxxiij. Syhest du deynen
bruder sündigen/so straff in/oder ich wil sein blüt von deine
henden fodern/der halß soll vn müß ein geteuffter seine sün
digen Brüder straffen er sey geweicht oder nit. Cho:. Seyt
ir Euagelisch/Schüst. Ja/ Cho:. Habt ir nit gelesen ym
A ij

Euangelio Mathei am vij.richtet nit so werdt ir nit gericht
Aber ir Lutherischen nempt solche sprüch nit zühertzē/süche
in auch nit nach/weñ sy sein wider euch. Schüster straffen
vnd richtten ist zwayerlay/wir vndersteen vnns mit zürichtē
(welches allayn got zügehört/wie Paul°sagt zün Römern
am viij.Nyemant sol einem andern seinen knecht richtē ⁊c.)
Sonder ermanen vnd straffen/ wie got durch den prophetten Esaiam am lviij.spricht/Schrey/hö: nit auff/Erhöch
dein stym wie ein busan zůuerkündē meinem volck sein missethat ⁊c. Chor. Es steet auch Exodi.xxij.du solt den obern
nit schmehen in deinē volck. Schü. Wer ist deñ der oberst
im volck/ist nit der Kayser/vnd nachmals Fürsten Grauen
mit sampt der Ritterschafft/vñ weltlicher oberhand?Chor.
Nayn/der Bapst ist eyn vicari° Cristi/darnach die cardinel
bischoffe/mit sampt dem gantzē gaistlichen stand/vo dē steet
in gaistlichen rechten.C.Solite.de maioritate et obedientia
Sy bedeutten die son/vnd der weltlich gewalt bedeut dē mon
Deßhalb ist der bapst vil mechtiger dañ ō Kaiser/welch er jm
sein füß küssen müß.Schüst. Ist der bapst ein solcher gewelt
tiger herr/so ist der gewißlich kain Stathalter Christi / wañ
Christus spricht Joañ.am.xviij.Mein reych ist nit von diser
welt/vnd Joañ.vj.Floch cristus da man in zům künig ma
chen wolt/Auch sprach cristus zů seinen junger / Luce.xx ij.
Die weltlichen küng herschen/vnd die gewaltigen haißt mā
gnedige herren/ir aber nit also/der gröst vnder euch sol seyn
wie der jüngst/vnd der fürnemest wie der diener/ Deßhalb ō
bapst vñ ir gaistlichen/ seyt nur dyener der christenlichen ge-
main/wa ir anderst auß got seyt/ōhalb mag man euch wol
straffen.Chor.Ey der Bapst vnd die seinen/ sein nit schuldig
gottes gepotten gehorsam zůsein/wie inn gaistlichen rechten
steet.C.Solite de maioritate et obedientia/auß dem schleusst
sich/das der bapst kain sünder ist/sonder der allerhayligist/
derhalb ist er vnstraffbar.Schüst.Es spricht Joañ.j.cano

nica.f.Wer fagt/er fey on fünd/d ist ein lugner/deshalb ist
der bapst ein sünder oder lugner/vñ nicht der allerhailigest
sonder züstraffen. Chor. Ey lieber/vnd wenn der Bapst
so böß wer/das er vnzälich menschenn mit grossem hauffen
zum teuffel füret/dörst in doch nyemant straffen/dz stet geschriben in vnserm rechten/dif.vl.si pa pa/wie gefelt euch dz
Shüst. Ey so stett im Euangelio Mathei.xviij.So deyn
Bruder sündiget wider dich/so gee hin vnd straff in zwyschen
dir vnd im/höit er dich/so hastu sein seel gewunnē/Eussert
si h der bapst dañ solchs haillamen wercks? Chor. Ist dañ
sollichs bruderlich gestrafft/Also am tag außzüschreyenn?
Schüst. Ey es volge weytter im text/wa dich dein brüd nit
höit/so nym noch ein oder zwen zü dir/höit er dich noch nitt
so sags der gemain/höit er die gemain auch nit/so laß in gee
wie ain hayden/wie da her dominē? Chor. Ey lieber wz ists
dañ nutz/wenn ir vns gleich lanng auß schreyt s wie hollüp-
per/wir kern vns doch nichts daran/wir halten vns des De
cretals. Schüst. Es spricht cristus Mathei.x.Wa man
euch nit höit/so schüttlet den staub von ewern füssen zü eyner
zeugknus/das in das reich gottes nahent ist gewesen/dē vo
Sodoma vnd Gomora wirt es treglicher sein am jüngsten
gericht/dann sollichem volck/wie wirt es euch dañ geen so ir
kain straff wolt annemen. Chor. Nu gib ich dz nach wo es
gelert/verstendige leüt thätē/aber den layen zimpt es nicht
Schüster. straffet doch ein Esel den prophetten Balaam/
Numeri.xxij.Warumb solt dañ nicht eynē layen zymen ein
gaistlichen züstraffen. Chor. Eynem schüster zympt mitt
leder vnnd schwertz vmb zügeen/nicht mitt der hailigen ge-
schrifft.schüster. Mit welcher hailiger geschrifft wolt irs bey
bringen/einem getaufften cristen nit in der schrifft zü forsch-
en/lesen/schreyben s dann Cristus sagt Johannes.v.durch
sücht die gschrifft/die gibt zeugknus vonn mir/so spricht der
Psalmist.j.Selig ist der man der sich tag vmnd nacht ye bett

A iij

ingesetz des herren / So schreybt Petrus in der ersten Epistel
am ii. Seynd alle zeyt vrbittig zuuerantwurtung yederman
der grund fodert der hoffnung die in euch ist / So leert Paulus die Ephesier am vi. Fechten wider den anlauff des teuffels / mit dem wort gotes / wolches er eyn schwert nent / Herr
wie wurd wir beston / so wir nichts yn der geschrifft westen?
Chor. Wie die gens am wetter. Schust. Ir spot wol die
juden wissen ir gesetz vnd propheten frey auß wendig / sollen
dan wir cristen nit auch wissen das Euangelium jesu christi
wolches ist die krafft gottes / allen die selig sollen werde wye
Paul'. i. Corint. i. Chor. Ja yr solts wissen / wie aber? wye
euch Cristus haißt Mathei xxiii. Auff Moses stul hand sich
gesetzt die schufftgelertten / vnd phariseyer / alles nun was sy
euch sagen / das thut / das bedeut die täglichen predig / handt
yr layen nit genüg daran? Schust. Ey es steet am selbenn
ort Mathei am xxiii. Sy binden schwere vnträgliche purdn
vnd legens dem menschen auf den hals / solche purden bedeüten on zweyffel vnd gewiß ewre menschlich gebot / damit ir vns
Layen dringt vn zwingt vn macht vns böse gewissen / Warumb solt wir euch dann volgenn? Chor. Wiewolt yr das
mit gschrifft beweysen. Schust. Cristus spricht im gemelten
capitel / Wee euch gleyßner vnd heuchler / Die ir das himelreych zuschließt vor den menschen / yr geet nit hin eyn / vn bye
hyneyn geen wellen / laßt ir nit hynein. Chor. Ey sollichs
hat cristus zu den priestern der Juden gesagt / Vmb vnns
priester ist es vil ein ander ding. Schust. Ey herr yr hond/
euch erst der phariseer angenomen / die auff dem stull Mosi
sitzen rc. Sam sey es von euch priestern vnnd münich geredt.
wie dann war ist / Also auch ist das von euch geredt / Wann
ewere werck gebn gezeugknus / dan ir freßt der witwe heüser
wie der teot weitter sagt. Herr ir habt euch verstigen. Chor.
Py pu pa / wie seind ir Lutherischen so naßweiß / yr hört das
graß wachssenn / wenn eyner eyn spruch oder zwenn wayßt/

auß dem Euangelio/so vexiert ir yederman mit. Schů. Ey
hertzürnet nit/ich meins gůt. Chor. Jch zürne nit/aber ich
můß euchs ye sagen/es gehört den layen nit zů/mit ô schůfft
vmbzegon. Schůst. Spricht doch cristus Mathei am vij.
Hůt euch vor den falschen propheten/vñ Paulus zůn Phi-
lipeñ. am iij. Secht auff die hund/so vnns dañ die schrift nit
zimpt zů wissen/wie sollen wir solche erkeñen. Chor. Solichs
gehört den bischoffenn zů/wie Paulus zů Thitto.j. Er soll
scharpf straffen die verfürer. schůst. Na sy thůns aber nit
sonder das wider spil/wie am tag ist. Chor. Da laß mann
sy vmb sorgen. Schůst. Nain vns nit also/welle sy nit/so
gepůrt vns selb darnach schaw enn/wann kainer württ des
anndern purde tragen. Chor. Ey lieber sagt was ir wôlt/
es gehört den layen nit zů/mit schrifft vmb zůgon/wie Paulus sagt.j. Cor.int.vij. Eyn yedlicher wie in der herz berůffen
hat/so wandel er/hôrt irs nun ir hand vor schrifft begertt
Schůst. ja Paulus redt vom eusserlichen stand vnd hand-
lung/von knechten vnd freyen/wie am selben ort vñ capittel
klar stet/Aber hie ist das wort gottes noch yederman vnuer
bottenn zů handlen. Chor. Ey hôrt ir nit Jr můst vor
durch die hailig weich berůfft sein/vnnd darnach vonn der
oberkait erwôlt werden darzů/sunst zimpt es euch nicht mit
der hailigen schrifft vmb zůgon. Schůster. Christ⁹ spricht
Luce an dem x. Die ernd ist groß/aber ô arbayter ist wenig
bit den herren der ernd/das er arbaiter schick in sein ernnd
Derhalb můß der berůff nit eusserlich sonder ynnerlich von
gott sein/eusserlich aber sind alle prediger berůffen ô falschñ
gleich so wol/als die gerechten. Khor. Ach es ist narrenn
werck mit eurem sagen. Schůster. Euch ist wie den jungern
Luce an dem ix. Die verdroß das ein ander auch teuffel auß
tryb in dem namen Christi/Christus aber sprach weret ynn
nicht/dann wer nit wider euch ist/der ist mit euch/Derhalß
wa ir recht cristen weret/soltt ir euch vonn hertzen frewenn

das man auch layen fünd so die feindtschafft diser welt auff
sich laden/vmb des wort gottes willen. Chor. Was geet
euch aber nôt an? Schüst. Da hond wir in der täuff dem
teufel vnd seinem reich wyder sagt/Derhalb sein wir pflich-
tig wider in/vnd sein reich züfechten/mitt dem wort Gottes
vnnd auch also darob zü wagen seinen leiß/eer vnnd güt.
Chor. Schawet ir leyen darfür wie ir weib vnd kynnd neret. Schüst. Christus verpeuts Mathey.am.vj.sprechend
sorget nit was ir essen vnnd trincken noch annthün wöllet/
vmb sollliche ding sorgen die heyden/sücht von erst das reych
gottes vnd sein gerechtigkeit/dyse ding werden euch alles zü
fallen. Vnd Petrus.j.cano.iiij.werfft alle eure sorg auf den
herren/dañ er sorgt für euch. Auch christus Mathei.iiij. Der
mensch lebt nicht allein vom brot sonder von einem yeglichñ
wort das durch den mund gottes geet. Chor. Lasst euch
daran benügen vñ bacht nit. Schüst. Arbeitñ sol wir/wie
Adam geporen ist. Gene.iij.vnd Job am v. Der mennsch ist
geporn zü arbeite/wie der vogel züm flug. Wir aber solltêns
sorgen/sond got vertrauen. Derhalb müg wir wol dem wort
gotes anhangen/welchs ist der beste teil. Lu.x. Chor. Wa
wolts ir layen gelernt haben: Kan eur mancher kain büchsta-
ben. Schüst. Christus spricht Joannis am vj.sy werden
all von got geleert. Chor. Es müß kunst auch da seyn/wa
für weren die hohen schül Schüst. Auff welcher hohe schül
ist. Joañes gestanden: der so hoch geschribñ hat (im anfang
wz das wort/vñ dz wort was bey got. Joan.j)war doch nü
ein fischer/wie Marci.j.steet. Chor. Lieber diser herr den
heiligen geist/wie Actu. am.ij. Schüst. steet doch Johelis
ij. Vnd es soll geschehen in den lesten tagen/spricht got/Ich
wil außgiessen von meinê geist/auff alles fleisch.zc. Wie weñ
es von vns gesagt wer. Chor. Nein/es ist von dê aposteln
gesagtt/wie Petrus anzeucht/ Actuu m.ij. Darun bpackt
euch mit dem geist. schüst. Christus sprycht Johannis.vij.

Taylor Institution Library, ARCH.8°.G.1524(26), a4v

wer an mich glaubt(wie die geschrifft sagt)von des leib wer/
den fliessen flüß des lebendigen wassers/das aber(spricht der
Euangelist)redt er võ dem heiligen geist/welichen entpfahñ
solten die an in glauben. Chor. Wie ich mayn jr styncke
nach Mantuano dem ketzer/mit dem hailigen geist. Schü.
Spricht doch Paulus.j.Corint.iij.Wysset jr nicht das jr der
tempel gottes seyr/vnd der geyst gottes in eüch wonet? vnd
Gallat.iiij.Weyl jr dann kinder seynd/hatt Gott gesanndt
den geist in eüre hertzen der schreyt Abba lieber vatter.Vnd
Tito.iij.Nach seyner barmhertzigkait macht er vnns selig/
durch das bad der wider gepurt/ vnd verneürung des haili/
gen gaists/welchen er außgossen hat reichlich in vns. Vnnd
zůn Römern.viij.So nun der geist des/der Jesum võ tod tñ
auferweckt hat/in eüch wonet. Chor. Jch empfind keins
heiligen geist in mir/ich vñ jr seyn nit darzů geadelt. schüst.
Warumb heißt jr dañ die gaistlichen/ So jr den geyst Got/
tes nit hond? jr sol thaissen die geistlosen. Chor. Es seinnd
ander leüt/weder ich vnd jr die den geist gotes habẽ. schü.
Jr dürfft nit vmb sehen nach infeln/oder nach roten piretũ
got ist kain anseher der person/Actuũ.x.Es stet Esa/lxvj.
Der geist gottes wirt rüen auf ein zerknischten hertzen.
Chor. Zeigt mir ein. schüst. Es spricht mit runden wor/
ten Paulus zůn Römern.viij.Wer Christus geist nitt hatt/
der ist nit sein. Chor. O des armen geists/den jr Lutherisch
en hand/ich glaub er sey kolschwartz.Lieber was thůt doch
eür heiliger geist bey eüch/ich glaub er schlafft tag vnd nachtt
man spirt in yenyendert. schüst. Christus spricht Math.
vij.Jr solt eür heiltumb nie den hunden geben /noch dye per/
lein für die schweyn werffen/anff das die selbigen nytt mytt
füssen zertreten. Chor. Lieber schempt jr eüch nitt sollyche
grobe wort vor mir aufzůziehen. Schüst. Ey lyeber Hern
zürnt nit/es ist die heilig schrifft Chor. Ja/ja/ja/jr Luthe/
rischen/saget vil vom wort gots/vnd werdt doch nur ye känn/
B

## 184  *Facsimile*

ſter. Chꝛiſtus ſpꝛicht Johannis am viertzehenden/ich bin
der weg/die warhait vnnd das lebenn/Er ſpꝛicht aber nyt/
ich bin die gewonhait/Derhalb müß wir der warhait anhan
gen/wellichedas woꝛt gottes vnnd Gott ſelbſt/das bleybet
ewig Matbey.rriiij. Aber gewonhayt kumpet vonn mennſchen her/wellych alllugner ſein.Pſalm.cᵱv.Darumb iſt gewonhait vergencklich. Choꝛherꝛ. Lieber ſagtt mir noch
eins wie das jr Lutheriſchen nimmer beicht/das iſt noch vil
ketzeriſcher. Schüſter. Da iſt es von gott auch nit gepo
ten/auch nicht gemeldt weder im alten nochnewen Teſta-
ment. Choꝛherꝛ. Spꝛach doch Chꝛiſtus.Luce.rvij.geet
bin vnd zaigt euch den prieſtern.ꝛc. Schü. Heißt dañ erzey
gen beichtt/das iſt mir ſeltzam Teutſch jr müßt mirß höher
mit geſchꝛifft beweyſen/Solt ſo ein groß nöttyg vnnd hayl-
ſam ding vmb die oꝛen beicht ſein/wie jr dauon ſagt/ſo müß
ers von not wegen klerer in der ſchꝛifft uerfaßt ſein. Choꝛ.
Ey wölt jr dañ gar nichs thün/dann was von Got gepottn
vnd in der gſchꝛifft verfaßt iſt:das iſt eyn ellenndeſach.
Schüſter Jch kann daſſelbig nit erfüllen/wie Actuum.rv.
Was ſoll ich dann erſt meer auff mich laden. Choꝛ Ey es
haben aber ſolche ding die hailigen väter in den Conciljs ge
oꝛdnet vñ beſtetigt. Schü. Von wem hond ſy den gwalt
Choꝛ. Chꝛiſtus ſpꝛicht Johannis.rvj. Jch hab euch noch
vil zü ſagen/Aber jr kündts yetznit tragen/wañ aber yhener
der geiſt der warhait komen wirtt/der wirt euch in alle warhait leyten/Höꝛt/hie ſeind die Concilia von Criſto eingeſetzt
Schü. Ey chꝛiſtus ſpꝛicht daruoꝛ Johannis.rv.Der trö-
ſter der hailigñ gaiſt/welchē mein vater ſend vñ wirt in meinē
namen/der ſellbyg wyrtt euch alles leeren/ vnnd euch er yn-
nern/alles des/das ich euch geſagt hab.Höꝛt herꝛ/er ſpꝛycht
nit/er werd euch new ding leeren/welches ich euch nit geſagt
hab/ſonder des das ich euch geſagt hab/wirt er euch erynn-
dern/erkleren/auff dz jrs recht verſtet wie ichs gemaint hab

Taylor Institution Library, ARCH.8°.G.1524(26), b1v

Also maindt ers auch hernach/da er spricht. Er würdt euch
in alle warheit leyten. Chor. So halt jr von keinem Conci
lio? Schüst Ja/von dem das die Apostel zü Jerusalem hiel
ten. Chor. Haben dann die Appostel auch ein conciliü ge
halten? schüst. Ja/hond jr ein Bibel. Chor. Ja/Köchin
bring das groß alt büch herauß. Köchin. Herr ists das?
Chor. Ey nein/das ist das Decretal/maculier myrs nit.
Köch. Herr ists das. Chor. Jakör den staub her aß/das
dich der rit wasch/wol an maister hanns wa sters. Schüst
Sücht Actuum apostolorum. xv. Chor. Sücht selb/Jch
bin nit vil darinn vmbgangen/ich weyß wol nützers zülesen.
Schüst. Secht da herr. Chor Köchyn merck Actuum am
xv. Jch wil darnach von wunders wegen lesen/wz die alten
gesellen güts gemacht habe. Schü. Ja lest/jr werdt sindn
das man die bürdt des alten gesetz/den Cristen nit auflaben
sol/ich geschweig dz man yetzund vil neüer gepot vnd sünnd
erdencken/vnd die christen mit beschwert/darü sein wir euch
nit schuldig zühören. Chor. Sprycht doch christus Luce.x.
Wer euch hört/der hört mich/wer euch veracht/der veracht
mich/ist das nit klar genüg. Schü. Ja wann jr das Euan
gelion/vnnd das wort gottes lauter sage/so soll wir euch hö
ren wie Cristum selbs/Wa jr aber eur eigen fünd vnnd güt
geduncken sagt/sol man euch gar nicht hören/wann Christus
sagt Math.xv.vergeblich dienen sy mir/dieweil sy leren sol
che leer/die menschü gepot seind/vñ weiter/ein yede pflätzüg
die got mein himlischer vatter nit pflantzet hat/wirt auß ge
reüt. Chor. Seind dann die concilia auch mennschen leer?
Schüst. Wann man im grund darvon reden will/so haben
die Concilia merdlicher schaden zwen inn der Christenhayt
thon. Chor. Welche zaigt an. Schüst. Zum erste die ge
bot der anzal vnd maß ist/wie jr wyßt/vnd dznoch bösser ist
schier alle mit dem Bañ besteet/vnd doch der meyst rail in der
schüfft nit gegrünt/Solche eure gepot hatt man dann hoch

B iij

# 186 *Facsimile*

ſter. Chriſtus ſpricht Johannis am viertzehenden/ich bin
der weg/die warhait vnnd das leben̄/ Er ſpricht aber nyt/
ich bin die gewonhait/Derhalb müß wir der warhait anhan
gen/welliche das wo꞉t gottes vnnd Gott ſelbiſt/das bleybt
ewig Mathey.xviiij. Aber gewonhayt kumptt vonn menn
ſchen her/welly ch all lugner ſein. Pſalm.cxv.Darumb iſt ge
wonhait vergencklich. Cho꞉herr. Lieber ſagt mir noch
eins wie das ir Lutheriſchen nimmer beicht/ das iſt noch vil
ketzeriſcher. Schüſter. Da iſt es von gott auch nit gepo
ten/auch nicht gemeldt weder im alten noch newen Teſta
ment. Cho꞉herr. Sp꞉ach doch Chriſtus.Luce.xvij.geet
hin vnd zaigt euch den prieſtern.꞉c. Schü. Heißt dañ erzey
gen beicht/das iſt mir ſeltzam Teutſch ir müßet mirß höher
mit geſchüfft beweyſen/Solt ſo ein groß nöttyg vnnd hayl
ſam ding vmb die o꞉en beicht ſein/wie ir dauon ſagt/ſo müß
es von not wegen klerer in der ſchrifft verfaßt ſein. Cho꞉.
Ey wölt ir dañ gar nichs thün/dann was von Got gepottn̄
vnd in der gſchrifft verfaßt iſt:das iſt eyn ellennde ſach.
Schüſter Ich kann daſſelbig nit erfüllen/wie Actuum.xv.
Was ſoll ich dann erſt meer auff mich laden. Cho꞉ Ey es
haben aber ſolche ding die hailigen väter in den Conciliis ge
o꞉dnet vñ beſtetigt. Schü. Von wem hond ſy den gwalt
Cho꞉. Chriſtus ſpricht Johannis.xvj. Ich hab euch noch
vil zü ſagen/Aber ir kündts yetznit tragen/wañ aber ÿ hener
der geiſt der warhait komen wirtt/der wirt euch in alle war
hait leyten/Hö꞉t hie ſeind die Concilia von Criſto eingeſetzt
Schü. Ey chriſtus ſpricht daruo꞉ Johannis.xv.Der trö
ſter der hailigñ gaiſt/welch̄ mein vater ſendñ wirt in mein̄
namen/der ſellbyg wyrt euch alles leeren/ vnnd euch er yn
nern/alles des/das ich euch geſagt hab.Hö꞉t her꞉/er ſp꞉ycht
nit/er werd euch new ding leeren/welches ich euch nit geſagt
haß/ſonder des das ich euch geſagt hab/wirt er euch erynn
dern/erkleren/auff dz ir ꞉s recht verſtet wie ichs gemaint hab

Taylor Institution Library, ARCH.8°.G.1524(26), b2v

Also maindt ers auch hernach/da er spricht. Er würdt euch
in alle warheit leyten. Chor. So halt jr von keinem Conci
lio? Schüst Ja/von dem das die Apostel zů Jerusalē hiel
ten. Chor. Haben dann die Appostel auch ein conciliū ge
halten? schüst. Ja/hond jr ein Bibel. Chor. Ja/Köchin
bring das groß alt bůch herauß. Köchin. Herr ists das?
Chor. Ey nein/das ist das Decretal/maculier myrs nit.
Köch. Herr ists das. Chor. Ja kör den staub heraß/das
dich der rit wasch/wolan maister hanns wasters. Schüst
Sůcht Actuum apostolorum.ꝟ. Chor. Sůcht selb/Jch
bin nit vil darinn vmbgangen/ich weyß wol nützers zů lesen.
Schüst. Secht da herr. Chor. Köchyn merck Actuum am
ꝟ. Jch wil darnach von wunders wegen lesen/wz die alten
gesellen gůts gemacht habe. Schů. Ja lest/jr werdt findn̄
das man die bürdt des alten gesetz/den Cristen nit aufladen
sol/ich geschweig dz man yetzund vil neüer gepot vnd fünnd
erdencken/vnd die christen mit beschwert/darū sein wir euch
nit schuldig zů hören. Chor. Sprycht doch christus Luce.ꝟ.
Wer euch hört/der hört mich/wer euch veracht/der veracht
mich/ist das nit klar genůg. Schů. Ja wañ jr das Euan
gelion/vnnd das wort gottes lauter sage/so soll wir euch hö
ren wie Cristum selbs/Wa jr aber eur eigen fünde vnnd gůt
geduncken sagt/sol man euch gar nicht hören/wañ Christus
sagt Math.ꝟ.vergeblich dienen sy mir /dieweil sy leren sol
che leer/die menschn̄ gepot seind/vn̄ weiter/ein yede pflātzūg
die got mein himlischer vatter nit pflantzet hat/wirt auß ge
reüt. Chor. Seind dann die concilia auch mennschen leer?
Schüst. Wann man im grund darvon reden will/so haben
die Concilia mercklicher schaden zwen inn der Christenhayt
thon. Chor. Welche zaigt an. Schüst. Zům erste die ge
bot der anzal vnd maß ist/wie jr wyst/vnd dz noch böser ist
schier alle mit dem Bañ besteet/vnd doch der meyst tail in der
schüsse nit gegrünt/Solche eüre gepot hatt man dann hoch
B iij

äuffgeblafen/vnd der menfchen gewiſſen darmit verſtrycktt
vnd verwickelt/dz ſy den waren gottes gepotñ gleich geacht
ſeind geweßt/vnd in fürgezogñ/dadurch die gepot gots ver
echtlich bey den mennſchen gemacht/Solche leut hat Paul⁹
verkündiget mit jren gepoten.i.Timotheon.iiij.das inn den
letſten zeyten werden etlich vom glauben abtredten/vnd an
hangen den irrigen geyſtern/vnd lern der teufel/durch die ſo
in gleyßnerey lugenreder ſeind/vnd brantmal in ire,angewiſ-
ſen haben/vnd verbieten eelich zü werden/vnd zü meyden die
ſpeyß die got geſchaffen hat zü nemen myt danckſagung den
glaußigen/vnd denen die die warhait erkant haben. Rot.
Wa iſt das geſchehen/mit welchem gepot? ſchüſt. Flayſch
eſſen am freytag hat man für gröſſer ſind geacht/deñ eebre-
chen/vnnd ſo ein pfaff ein recht eeweyb het gehabt/hat man
für gröſſer ſind gehalten / dañ ſo er ein hüren oder zwü het.
Rot. Wol verſton ſpricht der walch/was iſt dañ der ann
der ſchad. ſchüſt. Zum andern hat mã vil neuer gozdienſt
angericht/vnd güte werck genendt/Darmit dann am aller-
meyſten/münich/nunnen vnd pfaffen vmbgond/vñ iſt doch
(wañ man auffs höchſt daruon wil! reden) eyttel euſſerlych
laruenwerck/daruon got nichts gehayſſen hat /vnnd haben
dardurch(vnnd wir ſampt inen)die recht chriſtlychen güten
werck verlaſſen/die vnns got beuolhen hatt. Rhot. Wz
ſeind dañ recht chriſtliche güte werck. ſchüſt. chryſtus leret
vns Math.vij.alles das ir welt/das euch die menſchen tün
das thüt auch in/das iſt das gantz geſetz vnd propheten/vnd
Math.xxv.leeret er vns den hungrigen ſpeyſen/den durſty
gen drencken/den armen herbrigen/den nackenden klaiden/
den krancken beymſüchen/den gefangnen tröſten. Rhot.
Seind das allein chriſtliche gütte werck eines gantz chriſtlychen lebens. ſchüſt. Ja ein recht chriſtglaubiger/welches
widerumb geporen iſt auß dem waſſer vñ geyſt/wie Joã.iij.
dienet got allein im geiſt vnd in der warhait/vñ ſeinem nech

ſten mit den wercken der ließ/das iſt die ſumma einen chꝛiſtlꝵ
chen weſen/Aber diſe werck geen gar in der ſtillzů/da bencꝁt
man weder ſchilt/helm noch wappen an/ſo meinen daß die
werck hailigen/ſolche chꝛiſten thůn gar nicht mer/ſo ſy mit
irem larfen werck niñer vnmögend. Koꝛ. Maynd ir dann
vnſer ſingen vnd leſen gelt nichs. ſchůſt. Chꝛyſtus wyrtt
ye ſunſt nichs fodern von vns dann die werck der barmhertz
ygꝁeit im letſten vꝛtayl. Math.xxv. Da werdt ir Münnych
vnnd pfaffen beſten/wie die Kinctlerin/die ließ die oꝛen am
pꝛanger. Koꝛher. Ir habts wol dꝛoffen/geedt zům offen vnnd wermbt euch/leeret euch Luther ſollich dant theding. ſchůſter. Meyn. Koꝛher. Lyeber was halde
ir von dem Luther. Schůſter. Ich halde inn für einen
Chꝛyſtlichen leerer (welchen ich acht) Seydt der Appoſtel
zeyt nye geweßte iſt. choꝛher. Lyeber was nutz hatt er/
doch geſchafftet inn der chriſtennhait. ſchůſter. Da hatt
er eur menſchen gepot/ leer/ſund vnnd auffſatzung an tag
gepꝛacht/vnnd vns daruoꝛ gewarnet/Zům anndern hat er
vnns in die hailigen gſchꝛyfft geweyſet/darinn wir erkeñen
das wir alle vnder der ſünnd beſchloſſen vnnd ſünder ſeynd
Römern.v. Zům anndern/das Chꝛiſtus vnnſer einige erlö
ſung iſt wie zůn.i. Coꝛinth.i. vnnd diſe zway ſtuck treybt die
ſchꝛifft ſchyer durch vnnd durch/Darinn erleern wyr vnnſer einige hoffnnng/glauben vnd vertrawen in Chꝛyſto zů ſe
tzen/welchs dann iſt das recht görlich werck zů der ſeligꝁait
wie Chꝛiſtus ſpꝛicht Johannis am ſechſten. Koꝛ. darff
man kains wercks darzů/Spꝛichtt doch criſtus Mathei v
Laſt ewer liecht leuchten voꝛ den menſchen/das ſy eur güte
werck ſehen/vnd ewern vatter im himmel pꝛeyßenn ſchůſter
Paulus ſpꝛicht Roma .v. Wir haltens das der menñſch
gerechtuertigt werd allain durch den glasbē/on zů thůñg
der werck des geſetz/Vnd zů Römern am erſtenn / Der gerecht wirt ſeines gelauwßen lebenꝯ. Koꝛher. Spꝛicht

doch Jacobus.ij.Der glaub on die werck ist todt  Schůst.
Ein rechter götlicher glaub der feyret nit/Sonn der bryngt
steets gůtte frücht/dañ Christus spricht Matthey am. vij.
Ein gůtter boum kan kain bö8 frucht bringen/Aber solliche
gůte werck geschehen nicht den hymel zů verdienen/ welchen
vns Christus verdiendt hat/Auch nirr au8 forcht der helle
zů entpflyehen/vonn der vns Christus erlö8t hat/auch nit
vmb eer/wann alle eer soll man got geben.Mathey an dem
vierdten.Sonder au8 götlicher lieb/got zů eyner dancksa-
gung/vnd dem nechsten zů nutz/Wolan herr wie gefelt euch
nun des Luthers frucht. Chorherr.  Ist er dann so gerecht
Wye das im dann so wenyg geleerter/ vnnd mechtiger her
ren annhangen?Allayn der gro8 vnuerstänndyg hauff.
Schůster,  Christo hyeng weder Pilatus/Herodes/Cay-
phas noch Annas ann/ auch nirr die Phariseyer/Sonn der
widerstünden im/ allain das gemein volck hieng im an/Dar
umb erfrewet sich Jesus im gayst/Luce am zehenden/vnnd
sprach/Vatter ich sag dir danck/das du dise ding hast verborgen vor den weysen diser welt/vnd hast sy geoffennbart
den klainen.  Chor.  Ey lieber/der gemaynn hauff gybtt
auch des wenyger tayl dem Luther recht.  Schůster  Das
machen euer lumpen prediger/die schreyen es sey ketzerey vnd
das on all geschrifft.Christus hat aber den klainen hauffen
verkündt Mat.v.Get ein durch die engpfort/wañ die pfort
ist weyt/vnd der weg breyt der zů der verdamnus füret/ vnd
jr sünd vil die darauff wandeln/vnd Math.xxij.Vil seynde
berůfft/ aber wenig seind au8erwelt.  Chor.  Solylch wort
treibe im wirtzhau8 am marckt vnd überall/wie die narren/
vnnd gehört nit ann solliche ort.  Schůst.  Christus sprach
Math.v.Was ich euch ins or sag/das predigt auff den dech
ern.  Chorherr.  Wañ ich die warheit soll sagen/so baldt ich
den Luther für den grösten ketzer/der syder Arrius zeytn ist
gwe8t/vnd jr seyt sein nachfolger/an haut vñ har entweicht

als vil eur iſt/vnd nichts gůts iſt in euch/nichts gůts kumpts
von euch/wißt jr nun⁝den tittel gib ich dem Lutthervñ euch
zůſamen. Schůſt. Da habt jr ein mal eins erzadtten/wañ
niemandt iſt gůt dañ got/Math.xix.Wañ vnſer nattur iſt
gar in vnns verboße/wie Gene.viij.Des menſchen hertz iſt zů
boßhait genaiget von jugent auff/ welche man můß täglych
mit dem kreutz dempffen/das ſy den gaiſt nit fel/wañ ſy ladt
jr dück nit/ ob ſchon der gaiſt durch den glauben gerechtfert⁝
tiget iſt/wañ es ſteet Prouerbio.xxiiij.Der gerechtt feldt im
tag ſyben mal/Deßhalb bitt wir all tag/ vergyb vnns vnſer
ſchuld.Mat.vj.Vnd Paulus zůn Römern am.vij.das gůt
das ich wil/thů ich nicht/ſonder das böß/das ich nit wil/ das
thů ich/vnd ſchreyt darnach.O ich ellender menſch/wer wirt
mich erlöſen von dem leyb des todts⁝Zaygt damit ann/das
wir ſünder ſein biß in todt/Seyt jr aber on ſüud⁝So werffet
den erſten ſtain auf vns/Joañ.viij. Chor. Jr ſeyt halt vn
nutz leüt/kündt vil geſpayß/ich hoff aber man ſoll euch bald
den laymen klopffen / es hilfft doch ſunſt nichts. Schůſter
Wie wols jr mit dem ſchwert daran⁝es ſtett euch gaiſtlichñ
nit zů. Chor. Warumb nit⁝Hat doch Criſtus Luce. xxij.
zway ſchwert eyngeſetzt/ dz gaiſtlich vñ dz weltlich. Schůſt.
Verbot doch chriſtus Petro Math.xvj.vnnd ſprach / Wer
mit dem ſchwert fycht/wirt am ſchwert verderben. Chor
Hilfft ſyeß nit/ſo můß aber ſawr helffen / wann dye ketzerey
hat groß vßer hand genommen/vnd iſt hoche zeyt dareyn zů
ſchlagen.Schůſt. O nein/ſonder volgt dem radt Gamalli-
eus.Actuũ.v. Jſt die leer auß den menſchen würt ſy on alle
ſchwert ſchleg fallen/iſt ſy aber von got ſo kündt irs nit döpf
fen/auff das ir nit ſehen werdt/als die wider gott ſtreytten
wöllen. Chor. Es wirt nit anders darauß. Schůſt. Wo
lan herr dein wil geſcheh Mathey an dem .vj.Der junger iſt
nit vber den mayſter.Johañ.xv . Habñ ſy mich veruolgt ſy
weren euch auch veruolgen/vnd Luce.vj. Selig ſeyt jr wañ
C

euch die menschen hassen/verwerffen vnd schelten von mey
nesnamen wegen. Chor. Es wirt maniger schweigen der
yetzund schreyt. Schü. Cristus Math.x. Wer mich beken
net vor den menschen/den will ich bekennen vor meinem hyme
lischen vater. Chor. Es wirt schweigens gelten oder hyn
der dem kopff hyngeen. Schüst. Cristus Math.x. Fürcht
die nicht/ die euch den leyb tödtenn/der seele künnen sy nicht
thon/O herr gott/hye wer gut sterben vo deynes namés we
gen. Chor. Es wer verdienter lon. Einen ketzer mag man
nach dreyen warnungen hynrichten. Schüst. Jr müst vns
vor zu ketzer machen/vnd beweysen auß der hayligen schufft
Chor. Das mügen wir gar leychtiklich thon. Schüst. Ey
so wiert got vnser plut vo eurn hendé den er sodern/dz ir vns
(die armen scheflein christi)so lanng handt verfüren lassen
vnd habt soul prediger diser leer/also lang mit disputierenn
vnangefochten gelassen. Chor. Es wirt bald/wir habenn
vnser spech(alle predig)gut auf sy. Schüst. Ja ist dz war
Jr erfüle den spruch Math.xxij. Vnd die phariseyer giengé
hyn vnd hyeltten radt/wie sy in verstrickten in seinen worté
vnnd sandren zu im ir dyener mitsampt des Herodes diener
Chor. Warumb nit man müß die ketzer also erschleychen
wann sy seynd lüstig/das man sy darnach kolb. Schüster
O gott dise prediger wolten vns all gern zu Cristo füré nye
mand außgenomen. So wolt ir sy/mitsampt vns/gern zum
hencker füren/Jr wolt geren das fewr von himel auff vnns
fellen. Luce ix. Hört cristu der spricht. Wißt ir nit wölliches
gaistes kinder ir seynd? Des menschenn sun ist nicht kommen
der menschen seelen zuuerderbé/sonder zuerhalté.ij. Cor.xiij
Mir hat der herr gewalt geben nit zuuerderben sunder zu
besserung. Chor. Ey wir wöllenn auch also. Schüster.
Ey feüir vn schwert reympt sy aber nit darzu sonder dz wort
gotes zu Hebreern.iiij. Wölches durchdringender ist dan ein
zwyschneydent schwert Derhalb seyt ir auß gott/so y sechn

Taylor Institution Library, ARCH.8°.G.1524(26), c1v

ewre leer vñ wesen/mit dem wort gottes/wölches ist die krafft
gottes j.Corint.j. Cho:. Ja es hilfft aber nichts. Schüst
Ja ir braucht sein nit/wan gottes eere sücht yr nit zůschützñ
Sunder ewern gewalt/eere/vnd reychtumb/darwider ist dz
wort gottes darumb veruolgt jrs/da leytz als mit eynander
Cho:. Ja ir kündt nichtz dañ die leutt außrychtten / wenns
hertz vol ist so geet der mund vber Luce.vj Schüster. Euch
ist wie cristus sagt/Luce vij.vergleicht den kynnder/dye am
marckt sitzen/rüffen/wir hand euch pfyffen/vñ ir hand nit
tantzt/wir hand euch klagt vnd yr hand nit gewaynt / Also
auch jr/sagt man euch das wort gottes tröstlich. so verspot
yrs/sagt man euch ernstlich so zürnt yr. Cho:. Wenn yr
sungt als eyn zeyßlin so macht ir mich nit annders. Schüst
Euer hertz ist verhert wie dem küng Pharaoni.Ego. vom
vij.biß inß xv.capittel.Der weder wunnder noch plag ann
nam/vnd maynet ye die kind von Ysrael solten zyegel preñ
das er mit seynem volck feyrn möcht/Also auch yr halt vns
weyl yr vns halten mügt. Cho:. Wett frytz/Es ist eins er
radtñ. Schüst. Ja/Es dunckt mich wol / euch sey wie dem
falschen amptman Luce.xvj.Sprechent/was soll ich thon/
meyn hert nympt das ampt von mir/Jch mag nit graßen/
vnnd schem mich zůbeerlen/Eben das selbig fürcht yr gayst
lichen auch/darumm hilfft weder straffen noch ermanen ann
euch. Cho:. Ey wißt ir nicht Cristus spricht. Johannes vj.
Nyemant kumpt zů mir/der vatter zyech in dañ/zeyt bringt
rosen wer wayße welcher den andern bekert. Schů. O hert
die wort hör ich gern/es steet Johan.xv. On mich kündt yr
nichts thon/vnd weytter/ir hand mich nit erwöllet/ich han
euch erwöllet/darumß ligt an vns nicht got müß vns bekerē
das wünsch ich euch allen von grund meines hertzen. Cho:.
Man leütet in Kho:/Kechin lang den Korrock her/wol an
lieber may ster zyecht hin im frides wirt leicht noch als gůt/
Schüst. Ob gott will/wol an alde/der fryd sey mit euch lie-

C ij

194 *Facsimile*

ßer herr hand mir nichts verübel/vnd verzeycht mir. Chor
Verzeych vns gott vnfer fünd. Schüfter. Amen.
Chor. Secht nur an liebe köchin/wie redē die layen fo gar
freflich gegen vns geweychtten/Jch mayn der teuffel fey in
dem fchüfter verreet/er hat mich inn harnafch gejagt/Vnd
wer ich nit fo wol geleert/er het mich auff den efel gefetzt/da
rumb wil ich im nicht mer zů arßaytū geßen/fond dem hans
3obel/der ift eyn gůtz einfeltigs mendlin/macht nit vil wort
mit der hailigen gfchrifft/vñ Lutherifchen ketzerey/wie dañ
den layen nit zymlich ift/ noch gepürt mit jren feelfo:gern zů
difputiern/wañ es fagt Salomon/VVölcher eyn eynfeltig
wandel fürt/der wandelt wol/Ey difen fpruch folt ich dem
dollē fchüfter fürgeworffen han/fo wer er vileicht darob er-
ftumbt. Köchin. O her: / ich hett ymmer forg nach dem yr
in mit der fchrifft nit vberwinden kündt/jr wurd in mitt den
panttoffel fchlahen. Chor. Jch hab nur vonn der gemayn
eyn auffrůwr beforgt/funft wolt ich im die panttoffel in fein
antlitz gefchmeißt haben/im het Criftus od Paul° in dreyen
tagen nit abgewifcht/wiewol er all fein vertrauwen auff fy
fetzt. Köchin. Mich nimpt groß wunder/wie die layen fo
gefchickt werden. Chor. Wilt wiffen wz macht? Mā gyße
vmb die gaiftlikait nichts mer/vorzeitten het der haylig vat
ter der Bapft/vnnd die Bifchoff(folchen als Luther vnnd
ander mer/die auff fein geygen predigen) das predig ampte
auffgehebt nach laut des gaiftlichen rechten/Vnd zů wyder
rüffen benöttiget/wie mit dem Johañes huß zů Cofketzge-
fchehen ift/Wenn man nur die Euangelifchen prediger kūd
fchweygen machen/fo wurts alles gůtts/Aber weñ man fy
haift fchweigen/fo kommen fy vnd wöllen mit dem bapft vñ
bifchoffen difputiern/wellichs vnerhärt bey der welt/das ey
ner mit dem allerhayligiften will difputiern/der nitt genůg-
fam vnd wirdig ift mit feiner hailigkait zůredē/Aber es wyl
beffer werden/weñ die prediger nit wellē/fo müffen fy fchwei

Taylor Institution Library, ARCH.8°.G.1524(26), c2v

gen wie wol ſy ſant Paulus ſchꝛift fürʒyechen/ Vñ weñ ſy
ſein ſchwertdarʒů hetten/ſo můſten ſybarnyð ligen/weñs
der hailig vater der Bapſt chon will /dañ ſo můſte dyelayē
auch ſchweigen/vnnd wir wurdenʒů vnſern n irden wider⸗
umßkoṁen. Kechin. Es wer für warheꝛt gůt/wañ yeder⸗
man veracht euch/wie dañ yeʒund auch der Schůſter chon
hat. Choꝛ. Voꝛʒeytten het wir ein ſollichen inn Bañ ver⸗
kündt/Aber yeʒund müſſen wir von den layen höꝛen vñ ler⸗
nen/wie die Phariſeyer vð Criſtn. Liebekechin růff vnſerm
Calefactoꝛ/der lißt vil in der Bybel/vñ villeicht der ſchꝛifft
baß bericht iſt dañ ich/Er můß mir von wunders wegen ett⸗
lich ſpꝛüch ſůchen. Kechin. Heinrice/Heinrice. gee auff
her ʒům herꝛn. Calefactoꝛ. Wirdiger herꝛ was wölte
iꝛ. Choꝛheꝛꝛ. Vnſer ſchůſter hat mich lang veꝛiert / vñ vil
auß der Bybel angeʒaigt/wie dann der Lutheriſche bꝛauch
iſt/du můſt im etlich Capitel nach ſůchen/ob er gleich hab ʒů
geſagt/auff das ich in in der ſchꝛifft fahen möcht. Calefact
Jr ſolt es billich ſelbſt wiſſen/yr hand lang die geweychte eꝛ
aṁiern helffen. Choꝛ. Ja daſelbs bꝛaucht man nur ſchůl⸗
leriſche leer/was die menſchen haben geſchꝛiben vñ gemacht
vnd gar wenig das gaiſtlich recht/wölchs die hailigē vetter
in den Conciliis Beſchloſſen haben. Calefactoꝛ. Es leg an
dem nicht das die vetter in Conciliis beſchloſſen/vñ die men⸗
ſchen ſo nach in koṁen ſein geſchꝛiben vñ gehalten haben
wo die ſelben geſeʒ/leer vñ ſchrifft auß dem woꝛt vñ gaiſt go⸗
tes werē/wann die pꝛopheten/Apoſtel vnd Euangeliſten
ſeind auch menſchen geweßt. Choꝛ. Ey/ ſo haben ſy auch
yꝛꝛen müigen/Aber die Lutheriſchen wellen das nit glaubñ
Calefactoꝛ. Nayn/Wañ Petrus ſpꝛicht.ij. Pet.j.Es iſt
noch nye kain weiſſagung auß menſchlichem wyllen herfür
bꝛacht/ſonder die hailigen menſchen gottes hand geredt/ge
triben/von dem hailigen gaiſt/ Vnd eben darnach vkündt
Petrus/die falſchen Pꝛophetten/die vil verderblicher ſecktñ

C iij

ein werden füren/Bedeut ewrn gaiſtlichen ſtandt/Oder ein
Regel vnd alle menſchū fünd (auſſerhalß dem wort gotes)
darmit ir yetz vmbgeet.Rho:. Ja es iſt aber auff vnns nit
geredt/ſonder auff die alten vñ lengſt vergangē.Cale. O yr
thoren vnd tregs hertzen zūglaußen/alle dem/das ye Prophettenn geredt haben.Luce.xpiiij.Rechin. Herr haißt euch
den hanen mer kreen/von mir lydt yrs nit. Rho:. O du
lauſiger Bachant/wilt du mich auch rechtuertigen vñ leeren
Biſt auch der Lutheriſchenn bößwychter einer / Troll dich
nur bald auß dem hauß/vnd kum nit wyder du rnuerſcham-
tes thyer. Calefa. Es thūt euch and/das euch der ſchuſter
das rodtpyriet geſchmächt hatt / Laßt euch nit wunndern/
wann im alten geſetz/hat gott die hyrtten ſeyn wort laſſenn
ökünden/alſo auch yetz mũſſen (euch phariſeer) die ſchuſter
leeren/Ja es werden euch noch die ſtayn in die oren ſchreyen
Albe ich ſchaid mit wiſſenn. Rechin. Euch geſchycht recht
mich wundert das it mit den groben filtzen reden mũgt.Sy
ſchonen weder ewer noch der hailigen weych.Rho:. Jch wil
mich nun woll vor in hũttenn/verprentß kũnd/fürchtſewer
Woll auch wil in Rho: / ſo gee an marckt/kauff eyn kram
met vogel oder zwelff/Es wirt nach eſſen meines gnedigen
herren Caplan/mit etlichen herren kōmen/vnd ein pangett
halten.Trag die Bibel auß der ſtuben hynauß/vnd ſich ob
die ſtayn vnd würffel allim bietſpyl ſeyn/vnd das wir eyn
fryſche kartten oder zwū haben.Rechin. Es ſoll ſeyn.Herr
werdt ir von ſtund an nach dem vmgang heymher gen:Ro:
Ja ſchaw das eſſen berayt ſey.

Paulus
Jrbauch ir got.

Finis

Taylor Institution Library, ARCH.8°.G.1524(26), c4r

Taylor Institution Library, ARCH.8°.G.1523(8), c4v

Milton Keynes UK
Ingram Content Group UK Ltd.
UKHW022128291124
451915UK00010B/581